Whatcha Gonna Do
with
Whatcha Got?

W. Robert Daum
with
Scott D. Christiansen

World rights reserved. This book or any portion thereof may not be copied or reproduced in any form or manner whatever, except as provided by law, without the written permission of the publisher, except by a reviewer who may quote brief passages in a review.

The author assumes full responsibility for the accuracy of all facts and quotations as cited in this book. The opinions expressed in this book are the author's personal views and interpretations, and do not necessarily reflect those of the publisher.

This book is provided with the understanding that the publisher is not engaged in giving spiritual, legal, medical, or other professional advice. If authoritative advice is needed, the reader should seek the counsel of a competent professional.

Copyright © 2024 W. Robert Daum

Copyright © 2024 TEACH Services, Inc.

ISBN-13: 978-1-4796-1650-3 (Paperback)

ISBN-13: 978-1-4796-1651-0 (ePub)

Library of Congress Control Number: 2024905111

Scripture quotations marked AKJV are taken from American King James Version. Placed into the public domain on November 8, 1999 by Peter Engelbrite.

Scripture quotations marked AMPC are taken from Amplified Bible, Classic Edition. Copyright © 1954, 1958, 1962, 1964, 1965, 1987 by The Lockman Foundation.

Scripture quotations marked CEV are taken from Contemporary English Version. Copyright © 1995 by American Bible Society.

Scripture quotations marked KJV are taken from King James Version. Public domain.

Scripture quotations marked MSG are taken from The Message. Copyright © 1993, 2002, 2018 by Eugene H. Peterson.

Scripture quotations marked NASB are taken from New American Standard Bible®, copyright © 1960, 1971, 1977, 1995, 2020 by The Lockman Foundation. All rights reserved.

Scripture quotations marked NASB1995 are taken from New American Standard Bible®, copyright © 1960, 1971, 1977, 1995 by The Lockman Foundation. All rights reserved.

Scripture quotations marked NET are taken from New English Translation. NET Bible® copyright © 1996-2017 by Biblical Studies Press, L.L.C. http://netbible.com. All rights reserved.

Scripture quotations marked NCV are taken from The Holy Bible, New Century Version®. Copyright © 2005 by Thomas Nelson, Inc.

Scripture quotations marked NKJV are taken from the New King James Version®. Copyright © 1982 by Thomas Nelson. Used by permission. All rights reserved.

Scripture quotations marked NLT are taken from *Holy Bible*, New Living Translation, copyright © 1996, 2004. 2015 by Tyndale House Foundation. Used by permission of Tyndale House Publishers, Inc., Carol Stream, Illinois 60188. All rights reserved.

Scripture quotations marked RSV are taken from Revised Standard Version of the Bible, copyright © 1946, 1952, and 1971 the Division of Christian Education of the National Council of the Churches of Christ in the United States of America. Used by permission. All rights reserved.

www.TEACHServices.com • (800) 367-1844

Praise for This Book

"Bob Daum has rendered an invaluable service to Adventist believers by translating the timeless principles of Christian stewardship into a simple, yet thorough, contemporary approach that everyone can understand.

There are several important threads interwoven through the fabric of *Whatcha Gonna Do with Whatcha Got?* The Great Controversy theme is brought home reminding us that every action relating to our human possessions leads to eternal consequences.

The author exudes humility in his approach, yet no one can negate his profound knowledge in financial management acquired through years of service, in both the private and not-for-profit sectors. This treasure trove of knowledge makes him uniquely qualified to produce a masterpiece that will inspire God's faithful stewards for generations to come."

~ **Elder Daniel Honore,**
Former Attorney, Theologian, and Conference President

"During a lifetime of service in the Planned Giving & Trust Services ministries in the Seventh-day Adventist Church, Pastor Daum has not only taught the spiritual principles of grateful living but assisted in the most practical ways God's faithful stewards in moving their investments from this temporary world to the Eternal Kingdom.

Reading and applying the principles of this book will change your life now and forever."

~ **Jeffrey K. Wilson,**
Assistant to the President for Planned Giving,
Adventist World Radio; Retired General Conference
Director of Planned Giving & Trust Services

"If you are searching for spiritual guidance in planning your estate; if you need assistance in understanding the tax benefits and requirements of charitable gifts; if you want practical information on how best to distribute your financial assets—the answers to these perplexing challenges are found in this book written by W. Robert Daum, a trusted advisor to thousands who have benefitted from his advice. He provides easy-to-understand guidance in an area that is too frequently made complicated by references to mysterious tax laws, laws of inheritance and complex probate procedures."

~ **Charles Eusey,** Attorney

Table of Contents

1—Introduction—An Overview of this Book 9

SECTION I—The Moral and Ethical Background of
   Christian Estate Planning 14

2—Stewardship and The Great Controversy
   Holistic Stewardship and the Great Controversy
   Chart: Chronology of Last Day Events 15

3—Our Personal Spiritual and Stewardship Journeys and
   God's Call to Ministry 32

4—Bible Stories Reveal How Stewardship Improves Your
   Relationship with Jesus 49

5—My Interview with Dean and Pam Nice 57

6—Family Support and Inheritance Plans: Important 69
   Lessons for Today's Relationships with God and Family

   Lesson #1: What Do I Owe My Family?

   Lesson #2: God's Socio-Economic Systems in Four Eras

       Era #1: The Old Testament Model

       Era #2: The New Testament Model

       Era #3: The Apostolic Christian Church;
         the Spirit of Sacrifice

       Era #4: The Time of the End—All Belongs to God;
         with the Spirit of Sacrifice

       Chart: Summary of Socio-Economic Systems of
       the Old Testament, Apostolic Era, and End-Time Church

7—Why Estate Planning Is Important in the Great Controversy 102

My Personal Story on the Topic of Will Planning

Why All This Effort Before Seeing a Lawyer?

Will-Plan Design—More Introductory Thoughts

SECTION II—Completing an Estate Plan with the Assistance 109
of a Seventh-day Adventist Denominational Organization's
Planned Giving & Trust Services Department

8—Availability of Professional Adventist Ministerial Assistance
in the Will Planning Process 110

Preparation for Time of Trouble — Expect Individual Instruction

9—A Slice of History: A Variety of Operating Models for
Planned Giving & Trust Services Departments at Seven
Denominational Organizations (as of 2003) 121

10—Authorized and Unauthorized Practice of Law, Issues of
Legal Safety for the Will-Plan Design, and Documents
If Contested in Court After the Trust-maker's Death 125

The Lord's Double-Barreled Blessing

11—My Experience as a Seventh-day Adventist Estate
Stewardship Minister, Planned Giving Consultant, and
Trust Officer 144

My Background

My New Personal Covenant with God in 1981

12—Donor Delight or Donor Chagrin? Stories of Assisting
People in My Ministry: The Great Controversy in Action
on the Front Lines of the Conflict 154

SECTION III—Designing an Estate Plan Based on
Sound Principles 193

13—Will My Will-Plan Be in the Potter's Hands? 194

14—Designer Principles of the Spiritual Dimension in
the Context of the Great Controversy in Action 202

Faith—Whatcha Do with Whatcha Got Is a Salvation Issue

Ownership—How Does Ownership Impact My Will-Plan Design?

Family—How Does Family Influence My Will-Plan Design?

Estate Stewardship—How Does Estate Stewardship Affect My Will-Plan Design?

Personal Application—How Do I Apply Design Principles to My Plan?

Legal Issues in the Will-Plan Design

Section IV — Designing an Estate Plan Apart from Denominational Assistance—Concepts and Vocabulary 236

15—What Is a Will? 237

Disadvantages of Dying Intestate

Significance of Order in Our Lives

Contents of a Will

Advantages of a Legally Valid Will-Plan

The Foundation of All Estate Plan Documents

Advantages of a Will-Only Plan

16—What Is a Revocable Living Trust? 255

What is the Vocabulary of Trust Ownership?

Revocable Living Trust (RLT) May Serve as a Will Substitute

Estate Tax Issues

Life Estate Gift of Property

17—How to Select and Work with a Lawyer 265

My History of Working with Lawyers

Gift Planning for the Ministry of God's Word —a Finished Work

Legal Representation

Overcoming Stranger Danger

18—**Conclusion**—Final Thoughts 280

Technical Notes

Emphasis of words or phrases is indicated by *italics*.

Explanatory notes are inserted in brackets [ ].

Quotation marks are added where appropriate.

Related Collateral Resources

Further Reading Opportunities on Will Planning:

WILLS & LEGACIES *Testimonies for the Church*, vol. 4, pp. 476–485

TO WEALTHY PARENTS *Testimonies for the Church*, vol. 3, pp. 116–130

SACREDNESS OF VOWS *Testimonies for the Church*, vol. 4, pp. 462–476

THE CAUSE IN VERMONT. *Testimonies for the Church*, vol. 2, pp. 631–677

TRANSFERRING EARTHLY TREASURE. *Testimonies for the Church*, vol. 2, pp. 678–686

Appendices 281

Appendices can be found online at www.mystewardship.estate (use the QR code here, or go to 1ref.us/rdwgd2).

Appendix 1—Missouri Supreme Court Decision on Unauthorized Practice of Law

Appendix 2—The Making of Ellen G. White's Will of 1912 —Issues and Considerations

Appendix 3—Ellen G. White's Final Will of 1912

Appendix 4—Valuable Gems of Counsel from the Pen of Ellen G. White on Wills

Appendix 5—Life Insurance and Seventh-day Adventists

Appendix 6—Vocabulary

Appendix 7—Advanced and Creative Plan Models with Crescendo's PowerPoint Slides

Appendix 8—Estate Design Information Organizer (EDIO)

Chapter 1

Introduction
An Overview of this Book

This book is about the following:

- Family support and inheritance planning—issues and options
    - with pertinent legal issues in the context of the great controversy
- Descriptions of pertinent legal documentation for end-of-life planning
    - with pertinent spiritual principles for prayerful consideration

I served as a trust-certified employee for Seventh-day Adventist Church organizations in the North American Division (NAD) from 1980 to 2016 in the following roles and functions:

- Planned giving consultant
- Trust officer
- Estate stewardship minister

My work in this specialized ministry has been saturated in prayer for my Savior's guiding light every baby step of the journey. Therefore, it is my joy to present this material to you as a memoir of my ministerial work life. All this work has been done with the hope of Jesus' soon second coming and the acknowledgement that He promised He will come again to take us to be with Him and has a place prepared for us (see John 14:1–3). We know without a doubt there will be large, spacious dwelling places for us. We also know there will not be any room for our self or pride of opinion. Therefore, I present this material in humility of spirit for His glory.

The Lord led me to work with dozens of donors and lawyers from Hawaii to Maine and Washington to Florida. We are discussing my professional experiences in assisting God's people with wills, estates, trusts, and other pertinent documents for comprehensive end-of-life planning. While driving to the first appointment with someone who had requested a visit, I would often pray, asking the Lord to tell me the three questions I should ask the individuals I would be visiting in that appointment; and He always gave me what I needed. It was thrilling!!!

I am using concepts and vocabulary in the settings of actual case studies. I have included pertinent Bible stories. All the stories serve as examples for us people of God to pray about the possible application to our own will-plan design and documentation.

> **Driving to the first appointment with someone who had requested a visit, I would often pray, asking the Lord to tell me the three questions I should ask the individuals I would be visiting in that appointment; and He always gave me what I needed. It was thrilling!!!**

Eight appendices are referenced in the text of this book, as listed on page 281, and may be found at the following internet address: mystewardship.estate.

The *GOAL* of this book is to encourage you in your personal journey with Jesus Christ to ignite or reignite your passion for His mission to seek and save the lost, as well as create or update a personal plan for the end of your life.

The *KEY THOUGHT* of this book is there are two things we know and one thing we don't know. We know Jesus is coming again; and His coming is imminent [near]. What we don't know is who among us will either live through the great time of trouble or be laid to rest in mercy. Therefore, it is of utmost importance for all of us to have a current, legally valid, will-plan in place (formally documented plan for the end of life).

The *CONTEXT* of this book is the great controversy (between Christ and Satan) in action (as it impacts our lives, values, priorities, mission, and goals).

The *THEME* of this book is the just (righteous) shall live by faith (see Rom. 1:17; Gal. 3:11; Heb. 10:38) and, by extension, *die* by faith (see Rev. 14:13; White, *The Gospel Herald*, December 1, 1901).

I hope you discover helpful concepts for the design of your own legacy inheritance plan, in a thicket of sensitive issues. I hope and pray you find helpful information here that will motivate you to honestly pray for the Lord to enable you to reignite your passion for His kingdom. We know the passion of God is focused on the mission of Christ to seek and save the lost. You, dear reader, are a unique person in the family of God. There is only one of you, and God has a definite plan that is uniquely for you (see Jer. 29:11). It is a plan that is designed by Him to remake you to be ready for eternal occupancy as a forever citizen of His kingdom, whether you are in plenty or poverty; and whether you are dead or alive when Jesus returns for His precious bride.

When attending a continuing education conference for those of us who were working in Trust Services—it was held at the Columbia Union Conference office building during the late 1980s—a presenter was a lawyer by trade. He was a vibrant, youngish Christian man. The title of his presentation was "Whatcha Gonna Do with Whatcha Got." It was an excellent talk on Christian estate stewardship of accumulated assets when we die. He shared that he had done very well with his investments in real estate and always returned tithe to the Lord. When the tithe on his income got to be $10,000 per month, he began to feel it was too much to be giving it away. He knew it was the right thing to do. So, that feeling alarmed him so much that he gave all of his holdings away to the Lord's work, and started over. And the Lord blessed him again.

I hope this book assists you in your desire to discover or enhance your understanding of God's unique plan for your life; also, to assist you to prayerfully understand His will for the design of your will-plan. God is looking all over the globe for His humble, penitent believers—those who make up His body—the pure and blameless church. Yes, He is full of hope that you will be counted as one with Jesus and your family circle will be unbroken at that time. And Jesus is eager to assist each of us to love Him and be there with Him.

Notice the word from one of God's priests of ages past: "The eyes of the LORD search the whole earth in order to strengthen those whose hearts are fully committed to him" (2 Chron. 16:9, NLT). The Lord is constantly working for our salvation and loves to do it.

As Pastor Ted Wilson, president of the General Conference, wrote, "As the stream of modern culture rushes headlong toward destruction, standing firm on the solid rock of Scripture will make it appear as though we are removing ourselves from society. But seeking God's approval must always be our top priority" (*Adventist World*, February 2019, p. 17).

This introduction is a brief summary of some of the issues addressed in this book: to educate you on technical methods of estate planning, the business decisions to be made in the typical inheritance-legacy plan, and the spiritual dimension of planning today for tomorrow. We have included a biblical perspective on marriage and family because those relationships will impact your decisions in designing your own will-plan.

This book includes how to deal with linkage issues of conflict of interest and undue influence by your prayerfully chosen legal advisor and spiritual minister/planned giving consultant. The goal here is to maximize a delightful outcome and the legal security of your plan's integrity and minimize the potential legal insecurity, in case your plan is ever challenged in a court of law by interested people.

This book is designed to educate you on the basics of will-planning and the advanced use of trusts. Also, the most advanced, creatively exciting models and technical methods used in the transfer of assets is explained; the models and methods work whether you are healthy or sick—dead or alive.

You will also find our inclusion of material to address these issues of competent advisors. For example, It takes a highly skilled specialist to do brain surgery, right? The same is true of getting your will-plan done on paper. I've been told the typical lawyer might have had a three-unit class in wills and trusts in law school. However, in my experience, I've seen the best and the worst, so please choose a lawyer who specializes in estate planning. Therefore, we have included information on the following:

1. **What to expect** of a church employee who serves as your planned giving consultant when he or she exercises an influence by sharing spiritual principles of legacy plan design. This ought to be mild enough to allow you to still hear God's voice with individual instructions for you. It also speaks to times when the employee presents to you a proposed legacy plan that might include a gift to God's work as part of the process of providing you with legacy plan design advisory services without manipulating you.

2. **The importance of saturating your planning process in prayer.** My relationships with numerous donors is strong evidence of the significance of prayer regarding the structural design of your legacy plan, including the role of faith. And I know informed prayer is the most important preparation.

3. **How to design** your Christ-centered, mission-driven legacy plan within the framework of the legal considerations for your plan's safety if either challenged in court or lost or destroyed by someone who doesn't like your plan.

4. **How to avoid** undue influence and unauthorized legal advice that may potentially compromise the legal security of your documents (legal security is planning to avoid a lawsuit in a court of law against your will-plan when you are no longer alive).

5. **How you might select and work with a lawyer** in getting your will-plan documents done. As part of that process, you may read my thoughts on how to both select a few lawyers to prayerfully consider as candidates to represent you and interview those candidates—examples of questions to ask and what to look for when you interview them.

I hope, dear reader, this little overview has given you a bit of an appetite for the rest of the material being presented. Pray your way through the material, seeking to know God's will for your plans to take care of the future now.

Contributions to this book have been made by Pastor Scott Christiansen, author of Planet In Distress: Environmental Deterioration and the Great Controversy, published in 2012 by the Review & Herald Publishing Association. Scott's book is so popular that he has been invited to give weekend presentations on the topic at Seventh-day Adventist churches in many states around the country. Scott co-authored Chapter 6 of this book; his contributions are identified as such by quotation marks. (Material with no quotation marks was written by me.) For example, Scott explains: "The purpose of this chapter is to provide a big picture review of the topic from Scripture and White's counsels, while in the process we look at selected socio-economic systems of the Old Testament, the New Testament, and the modern (end-time) era. In doing this, we may just find more harmony, more wisdom, and more depth than we had previously read into Ellen White's writings on this subject."

This book has been completed with the editorial assistance of Roger Prather, M.A. He has massaged my words to make it much more readable. Roger's work is great.

DISCLAIMER: It is not the purpose of this book to provide legal or financial advice to anyone. Everyone must choose his or her own lawyer and financial advisor to represent their interests without the assistance of all other interested parties in the matter of creating legally valid end-of-life plans and related documents. Therefore, before you enter into the project of creating your own personal/family plan for the distribution of your accumulated assets at the end of your life, you should select a lawyer to be your legal representative who has sufficient expertise in estate planning.

Section I

The Moral and Ethical Background of Christian Estate Planning

Values-based estate planning is rooted in personal and family values, priorities, mission, and the goals of the family and its head leader, which are all established by an intimate relationship with Jesus Christ in the context of the great controversy in action and holistic stewardship.

Chapter 2

Stewardship and the Great Controversy

The great controversy is the grand theme of the Holy Bible, from Genesis to Revelation. The source of all evil, deception, and violence is revealed in it, along with God's method of dealing with the rebellion against Him and His righteous government of people who love Him. The origin of the great controversy occurred in heaven, and the author of the rebellion, Lucifer, brought it to earth. God's plan for counteracting this rebellion is clearly revealed in the Bible.

Discovering and learning more about the great controversy has been meaningful to me. Prior to becoming a Seventh-day Adventist, I had always believed everything within the spiritual realm was somehow of God. That misconception ended when I became a member of the Seventh-day Adventist Church in 1974.

This chapter is about good and evil. It reveals some of the lessons I have learned in my personal journey with Jesus. I have experienced ongoing struggles between God as Lord of my life and the devil and his angels in their respective efforts to win my heart. Their goal is to cause me to surrender my loyalty to either good or evil. Each day, this is a choice we must all make. To tell this story, I will relate some of the work God has done in my life in order to increase my understanding of the gospel of Jesus Christ.

> We do not understand as we should the great conflict going on between invisible agencies, the controversy between loyal and disloyal angels. Over every man, good and evil angels strive. This is no make-believe conflict. It is not mimic battles in which we are engaged. We have to meet most powerful adversaries, and it rests with us to determine which shall win. (White, *Testimonies for the Church*, vol. 7, p. 213)

Evidently, Ellen G. White and her staff were not exempt from being Satan's special target. She shared a personal testimony about the great controversy in her life and labor:

> Then our past life was presented before me, and I was shown that Satan had sought in various ways to destroy our usefulness; that many times he had laid his plans to remove us from the work of God; he had come in different ways, and through different agencies, to accomplish his purposes; but through the ministration of holy angels, he had been defeated. I saw that in our journeying from place to place, he had frequently placed his evil angels in our path to cause accidents which would destroy our lives; but holy angels were sent upon the ground to deliver. (White, *Testimonies for the Church*, vol. 1, pp. 346, 347)
>
> The spirits of darkness will battle for the soul once under their dominion, but angels of God will contend for that soul with prevailing power. The Lord says, "Shall the prey be taken from the mighty, or the lawful captive delivered? … Thus saith the Lord, Even the captives of the mighty shall be taken away, and the prey of the terrible shall be delivered: for I will contend with him that contendeth with thee, and I will save thy children." (White, *The Desire of Ages*, pp. 258, 259)

I first gave my heart to Jesus at age eight. Since that time, I have considered the Bible to be God's handbook for our lives here on earth and in the hereafter. The Lord continues to use it to reveal my ever-deepening need to surrender to Him. The more I study the Bible, the more I realize my mind must be filled with it in order to meet the devil's testing and prodding of my own weaknesses. I have found that obedience to God is only possible when Christ is alive in my heart, mind, and spirit. And that is only possible when the storehouse of my mind is filled with the Scriptures. It also means I am ready to hand out God's wisdom at a moment's notice to those who are weary and in need of a new life in Christ, whether they are unbelievers or already claim the label of "Christian." I have often claimed Isaiah 50:4–6 as an applicable promise during my morning devotional time of Bible study and prayer).

Claiming to be a Christian when we do not have a real trust relationship with God, fostered by the Bible, brings up the conflict between presumption and faith. Ellen G. White provides insight into this difference: "Faith claims God's promises, and brings forth fruit in obedience. Presumption also claims the promises, but uses them as Satan did, to excuse transgression" (*Ibid.*, p. 126).

I have known friends who curse the devil for every trial and trauma that comes into their lives. What we need to understand that these friends did not is while neither God nor His Son order bad things to come upon us, they do keep watch over us and see the devil's plotting to accomplish our defeat. In this process, the Lord weighs and sifts to allow some difficulties to come upon us for our own good. The promise remains that "there is no temptation taken you but such as is common to man: but God is faithful, who will not suffer [allow] you to be tempted above that you are able; but will with the temptation also make a way to escape, that you may be able to bear it" (1 Cor. 10:13, AKJV).

We are counseled to "not lose courage when assailed by temptation. Often when placed in a trying situation we doubt that the Spirit of God has been leading us. But it was the Spirit's leading that brought Jesus into the wilderness to be tempted by Satan" (White, *The Desire of Ages*, p. 126; see also Mark 1:12, 13; Matt. 4:1, 2; Luke 4:1–4). Thus, "When God brings us into a trial, He has a purpose to accomplish for our good." On the theme of presumption versus faith, the counsel continues: "Jesus did not presume on God's promises by going unbidden into temptation, neither did He give up to despondency when temptation came upon Him. Nor should we."

Our refusal to give up to despondency when temptation comes upon us should be fueled by our appreciation for the wisdom and counsel we find in the Bible. As I have already noted, the great theme we find there is the great controversy. I have read the Bible from Genesis to Revelation many times, and this theme makes itself manifest each time. I've also witnessed it unfold in people's lives. I've watched it demonstrated through cause and effect, both in the Bible and society today.

> *I have considered the Bible to be God's handbook for our lives here on earth and in the hereafter. The Lord continues to use it to reveal my ever-deepening need to surrender to Him. The more I study the Bible, the more I realize my mind must be filled with it in order to meet the devil's testing and prodding of my own weaknesses.*

In each of these cases, I've noted the fullness of God's plan of salvation contrasted with Satan's plan of deception and confusion, driven along by lies, violence, and every other conceivable form of evil. This is, of course, the great controversy in a nutshell. It is Satan's rebellious system of coercion pitted against God's government of freedom and selfless love. This controversy—this war—involves both heaven's occupants and all of us here on earth. And in this war, as strange as it may seem, God is at a great *dis*advantage. This disadvantage arises from the fact that God will always honor our freedom of choice and leave room for our own unencumbered wills. Satan, on the other hand, stoops to much lower methods of persuasion through deception and trickery.

It is not my purpose here to give a full treatment to all of this material. Rather, I want to give you an overview using Scripture and highlights of my own journey with Jesus. The purpose of this overview is to lay the groundwork for the primary argument I'm making in this book: that how you disseminate your material wealth at the end of your life is a vital consideration within the context of the Great Controversy.

Reading and studying the Bible—feeding on and ingesting the life and teachings of Jesus—is the most exalted privilege of my life, and I hope you will discover it is yours as well. I have discovered the choice that is available to all of us in each of the sixty-six books of the Bible. That choice is to accept either our portion with God's offer of Christ as our personal Savior from sin, with all of that offer's simplicity, or Satan's self-centered way, with all of its enchanting emptiness.

Scripture describes the very beginning of this cosmic conflict coming to earth in Genesis 3. Many of us are all familiar with the story of how the devil's deceptive temptation of Eve led to her and Adam's fall (see verses 1–7). And we are also familiar with how that fall necessitated God's pronouncement of judgment on mankind (see verses 8–19). However, as it is with all of God's judgments, there was also His provision of mercy (see verses 20–24).

> The spirit in which you come to the investigation of the Scriptures will determine the character of the assistant at your side. Angels from the world of light will be with those who in humility of heart seek for divine guidance. But if the Bible is opened with irreverence, with a feeling of self-sufficiency, if the heart is filled with prejudice, Satan is beside you, and he will set the plain statements of God's word in a perverted light. (White, *Testimonies to Ministers and Gospel Workers*, p. 108)

The prophet Isaiah was given more details about the fall of Lucifer prior to becoming Satan, the tempter in Eden, when he was still an angel of heaven who occupied an exalted position:

> How are you fallen from heaven, O Lucifer, son of the morning! How are you cut down to the ground, which did weaken the nations! For you have said in your heart, 'I will ascend into heaven, I will exalt my throne above the stars of God: I will sit also on the mount of the congregation, in the sides of the north: I will ascend above the heights of the clouds; I will be like the Most High.' Yet you shall be brought down to hell, to the sides of the pit. (Isaiah 14:12–15, AKJV)

Additionally, we are given a description of the war that resulted from Lucifer's rebellion, as well as the war's outcome:

> Then war broke out in heaven; Michael and his angels went forth to battle with the dragon, and the dragon and his angels fought. But they were defeated, and there was no room found for them in heaven any longer. And the huge dragon was cast down and out — that age-old serpent, who is called the Devil and Satan, he who is the seducer (deceiver) of all humanity the world over; he was forced out and down to the earth, and his angels were flung out along with him. [See Genesis 3:1, 14, 15; Zechariah 3:1.] Then I heard a strong (loud) voice in heaven, saying, Now it has come — the salvation and the power and the kingdom (the dominion, the reign) of our God, and the power (the sovereignty, the authority) of His Christ (the Messiah); for the accuser of our brethren, he who keeps bringing before our God charges against them day and night, has been cast out! [See Job 1:9–11.] And they have overcome (conquered) him by means of the blood of the Lamb and by the utterance of their testimony, for they did not love and cling to life even when faced with death [holding their lives cheap till they had to die for their witnessing]. Therefore be glad (exult), O heavens and you that dwell in them! But woe to you, O earth and sea, for the devil has come down to you in fierce anger (fury), because he knows that he has [only] a short time [left]! [See Isaiah 44:23; 49:13.] (Revelation 12:7–12, AMPC)

It is a great blessing to learn the reality of Satan's temptations of Eve and Adam into violating God's law. One important point to recognize is that

Eve was deceived in making her decision to rebel against God and His law, while Adam knew what he was doing and failed to trust that God would replace Eve. There are, in fact, three specific tests that Adam failed. First, he failed to exercise faith in God (see Gen. 3:1). Second, he failed to overcome the desires of the flesh (see verses 2–7). And finally, he failed to put away his own pride and ambition (see verses 5, 6).

Interestingly, Satan presented these same three tests to Jesus during His temptation in the wilderness. Jesus was driven into the wilderness by the leading of the Holy Spirit, where He was tempted by the devil for forty days without any food (see Matt. 4:1, 2; Mark 1:12). Imagine going forty days without any food. There can be no doubt that Jesus was intensely hungry and physically weak, which gave Satan the perfect opportunity. Jesus, unlike Adam, passed all three tests. He gained victory over the desires of the flesh (see Matt. 4:3); He maintained His steadfast faith in God (see verses 5, 6); and He did not give in to pride or ambition (see verses 8, 9).

Returning to Ellen White's explanation of faith versus presumption, we can understand the contrast between Adam and Jesus. "Faith would have led our first parents to trust the love of God and to obey His commands. Presumption led them to transgress His law, believing that His great love would save them from the consequences of their sin" (White, *The Desire of Ages*, p. 126). That is to say Adam and Eve exercised presumption when they should have, like Jesus in the wilderness, relied on faith.

Satan's fall from God's grace was caused by his desire for self-exaltation. Indeed, if Satan had honestly wanted to be like God, he would have remained in his appointed place in heaven. This is so because the Spirit of the Most High is revealed in unselfish ministry. Lucifer desired God's power but not God's character (ref. White, *The Desire of Ages*, p. 435). A common question prompted by Lucifer's fall is, Why has God allowed him to live since he has caused so much trouble on earth for over 6,000 years?"

The answer to this ostensibly vexing question is really quite simple. If Satan had been blotted out of existence at the time of his rebellion, angels and people would have served God out of fear rather than out of love. Instead, Satan's rebellion was allowed to come into full view of his fellow angels and thus became a lesson to the whole universe in all the ages that followed. Satan's rebellion stands as a perpetual testimony to the nature and terrible results of sin. When God made the announcement that Lucifer and all the angels who sympathized with him must be expelled from heaven, Lucifer boldly avowed his contempt for the Creator's law (ref. White, *The Great Controversy*, pp. 498, 499).

It is the devil's contempt for God's law that led him to cause all the trouble that has followed throughout earth's history. One very specific period of trouble was what we now call the Dark Ages, which was accurately predicted by John: "And the dragon was wroth with the woman, and went to make war with the remnant of her seed, which keep the commandments of God, and have the testimony of Jesus Christ" (Rev. 12:17, AKJV). John went on to provide a definition for "the testimony of Jesus Christ" as "the spirit of prophecy" (Rev. 19:10, AKJV).

In the last days of earth's history, God's chosen people—His faithful remnant—will apply this prophetic call with peculiar force. In the closing scenes of the great day of atonement (what Seventh-day Adventists understand to be human history after 1844), the remnant church will be faced with great trials and distress. Those who obey the commandments of God and hold dearly to the faith of Jesus will feel the ire of the dragon. He and his followers will do all they can to eliminate the faithful—you and me—from the face of the earth. However, our Lord and Savior will give us the victory as long as He lives within our temple of clay. Like His own temptation in the wilderness, He will enable us to practice faith over presumption (see 1 Cor. 6:19; White, *Prophets and Kings*, p. 587).

It seems to some of us that we are living in the "last days" now. The society of people who live in the last days reveal the great controversy in spades. It is described as a warning and advice to God's people:

> But understand this, that in the last days will come (set in) perilous times of great stress and trouble [hard to deal with and hard to bear]. For people will be lovers of self and [utterly] self-centered, lovers of money and aroused by an inordinate [greedy] desire for wealth, proud and arrogant and contemptuous boasters. They will be abusive (blasphemous, scoffing), disobedient to parents, ungrateful, unholy and profane. [They will be] without natural [human] affection (callous and inhuman), relentless (admitting of no truce or appeasement); [they will be] slanderers (false accusers, troublemakers), intemperate and loose in morals and conduct, uncontrolled and fierce, haters of good. [They will be] treacherous [betrayers], rash, [and] inflated with self-conceit. [They will be] lovers of sensual pleasures and vain amusements more than and rather than lovers of God. For [although] they hold a form of piety (true religion), they deny and reject and are strangers to the power of it [their conduct belies the genuineness of their profession]. Avoid [all] such people [turn away from them]. (2 Timothy 3:1–5, AMPC)

What all this should tell us is we who are disciples of Christ are involved in a war of stupendous proportions. When we took on the name of "Christian," we enlisted as soldiers of the cross of Calvary—members of His holy cavalry. We are not cruise travelers, content to enjoy the good life and watch the world go by. Although it is in God's plan for us to enjoy the blessings of life, as long as we allow Him to lead us in our choices, we must acknowledge it is He who is our provider and protector.

I have found God is generous with His blessings when we show signs of obedience to Him. The devil's design, on the other hand, is to hold us back from the abundant life promised by Jesus (see John 10:10). However, Christ's gift of an abundant life means so much more than what we, in our fallen state and limited capacity, can imagine. Most importantly, it means freedom—freedom from slavery and servitude to the perishable things with which the devil tempts us.

God spoke to this aspect of the great controversy when He wrote the Ten Commandments. With His own finger, on a tablet of stone, He wrote:

> You shall not make to you any graven image, or any likeness of any thing that is in heaven above, or that is in the earth beneath, or that is in the water under the earth. You shall not bow down yourself to them, nor serve them: for I the LORD your God am a jealous God, visiting the iniquity of the fathers on the children to the third and fourth generation of them that hate me; and showing mercy to thousands of them that love me, and keep my commandments. (Exodus 20:4-6, AKJV)

Jesus continued this thought during His earthly ministry. In a confrontation with some of the religious leaders in Judea:

> I tell the things which I have seen and learned at My Father's side, and your actions also reflect what you have heard and learned from your father. They retorted, Abraham is our father. Jesus said, If you were [truly] Abraham's children, then you would do the works of Abraham [follow his example, do as Abraham did]. But now [instead] you are wanting and seeking to kill Me, a Man Who has told you the truth which I have heard from God. This is not the way Abraham acted. You are doing the works of your [own] father." When the religious leaders continued to protest and claim, not Abraham this time, but God as their father, Jesus replied: "You are of your father, the devil, and it is your will to practice the lusts and gratify the desires [which are characteristic] of your father. (John 8:38–45, AMPC)

As combatants in the great controversy, an important question each of us should ask ourselves is whether or not our behavior is consistent with the side we claim to have chosen. Are we bowing down before earthly idols? Are we submitting to our lusts? Are we eager to gratify our sinful desires? We cannot escape temptations. We also cannot escape the fact that we do not even know our own hearts (see Jer. 17:9). However, God does know our hearts and intends for us, during difficulty, to discover our true heart conditions and, consequently, our need of Him. His desire for us is that we hunger and thirst for righteousness all the time (see Matt. 5:3, 6).

The result of such hungering and thirsting is that we will become effective actors on the side of good in the great controversy. We all have our intended roles to play. We ultimately learn what those roles ought to be from the testimony of Scripture. John emphasized Jesus' words:

> Seal not the sayings of the prophecy of this book: for the time is at hand. He that is unjust, let him be unjust still: and he which is filthy, let him be filthy still: and he that is righteous, let him be righteous still: and he that is holy, let him be holy still. And, behold, I come quickly; and my reward is with me, to give every man according as his work shall be. (Revelation 22:10–12, AKJV)

What exactly should our work be in the great controversy? No matter how big or small we think our role is in God's work, it amounts to a project of reclamation. Our job is to help Christ reclaim everyone and everything that is His. Rather than focusing on the trouble that is just around the corner, we should, as Pastor John Bradshaw, director of It Is Written, says, "focus on the coming of Christ rather than the coming crisis."

We are encouraged because Jesus has already won the victory on our behalf. Though we face difficult choices in life, we can rest assured that "he is like a refiner's fire, and like fullers' soap: And he shall sit as a refiner and purifier of silver: an he shall purify the sons of Levi, and purge them as gold and silver, that they may offer to the Lord and offering in righteousness" (Mal. 3:2b–4, AKJV).

This verse reminds me of a story about a woman who was confused by the comparison of God to a refiner of silver or gold. To try to find out why, she made an appointment with a silversmith to watch him at work. On the appointed day, she watched as the silversmith thrust the raw silver into the very heart of the fire. He explained that he had to sit and watch the silver carefully as all of the impurities were burned away. Still curious, she asked the silversmith how he knew when the silver was finished and purified. He answered, "When I see my image in it."

God desires that we be reflections of His image to those around us who need to see it. When He asks us to do difficult things or things that we might otherwise not want to do, it is often to bring us closer to being a bearer of His image, that others might come to know Him. He desires this because:

> All men have been bought with [an] infinite price. By pouring the whole treasury of heaven into this world, by giving us in Christ all heaven, God has purchased the will, the affections, the mind, the soul, of every human being. Whether believers or unbelievers, all men are the Lord's property. All are called to do service for Him, and for the manner in which they have met this claim, all will be required to render an account at the great judgment day. (White, *Christ's Object Lessons*, p. 326)

That means we do not own anything we think we own, including ourselves. It also means that, having claimed to take a side in the great controversy, we are responsible for putting everything we have, including ourselves, to work in the war between Christ and Satan. That naturally includes the material wealth we earn and accumulate, but not always in the ways we think we understand.

Holistic Stewardship and the Great Controversy

Does stewardship relate to the great controversy? The core meaning of the word "stewardship" is all about *relationship* with our personal Savior and Lord, Jesus Christ, and our response to the relationship in a spirit of mutual trust and grateful loyalty. When the testimony of both the Bible and the Spirit of Prophecy are taken together, it is undeniable that our faithful, holistic stewardship declares our standing as being with either Christ or Satan. That distinction—which side in this great cosmic war we choose—is determinative of how our individual roles are played out. On whose side are we?

When I use the term "holistic stewardship," I am talking about being a true disciple of Christ in all aspects of our lives. That includes all the roles and functions in which we engage at work, home, church, and in our communities. To be a Christian is to be Christlike, with caring transparency in our relationships with people, the church, and its leaders.

One place in Scripture to which we can turn for lessons in this regard is the end of the Old Testament. God declares his love for His people (see Mal. 1:2, 3). This is in spite of the fact that He said He would no longer accept their offerings. This refusal to have any regard for their offerings was on account of their disgusting, backslidden condition (see verses 6–14). God tells the people He has placed them under a curse on account of their serious spiritual problems (see 2:1, 2). There are three specific spiritual problems described here that run rampant in our community today.

The first problem in Malachi's time is the religious leaders at the close of history will have become morally bankrupt. They will turn away from God. Instead of guarding truth, they will actively participate in the spreading of error. Because of this, Ellen White warns us as God's people to not forget the past.

"The love of pleasure [will be] disguised by a 'form of godliness!'" She also said such religion will permit people to observe the rites of worship while devoting themselves to selfish, sensual gratification. This form of religion in the last days will be "as pleasing to the multitudes now as in the days of Israel." Some of our religious leaders, who hold positions of authority in the church, will be like Aaron the priest and "yield to the desires of the unconsecrated, and thus encourage them in sin" (White, *Patriarchs and Prophets,* p. 317).

It is important to note that this is not an indictment of or accusation about the current leadership of the Seventh-day Adventist Church. Rather, it is a warning to be on guard for that day when leaders will abandon the truth and their responsibility to it.

The second spiritual problem in Malachi's time is the bringing of profane offerings. When offerings are given with the wrong motivations or in the absence of a true conversion experience, then they are profane and therefore unacceptable. God desires—and commands—us to give willingly out of an abundance of gratitude for what Christ has done for us (see 2 Cor. 9:7). Just as profane offerings brought to the temple in Malachi's day could not accomplish the work of remitting sin, so the financial offerings given today, when profaned, will not accomplish the work of spreading the gospel and hastening the return of Christ. This problem is linked to the first.

When religious leaders direct the church away from the true, everlasting gospel, the spiritual condition of the people is not one that lends itself to cheerful, effective giving.

Finally, Malachi's third diagnosis is that men have become treacherous in their treatment of the wives of their youth. They divorce easily, which goes against God's plan. God hates divorce because his desire is that a marriage will produce godly offspring. Throughout the Bible, the church (God's people) is spoken of analogically as a spouse. The New Testament explicitly referred to the church as the bride of Christ (see 2 Cor. 11:2).

In Malachi, God is accusing the people of abandoning their faith like a husband divorces his wife. In the New Testament, eschatological context, the end-time church will be tempted to exchange their faithful husband, Jesus, for an unfaithful one. Our relationship with Christ should be one that produces godly offspring, not just literally but spiritually. A church that is in a right relationship with Christ will produce godly spiritual offspring through evangelistic work. While we have the time, we must commit ourselves to this work, not just through our own labors but also through the financial and influential support of the work. Time is running out.

The people of the USA continue to enjoy the good life now because of its most-favored-nation status with heaven (see White, *The Signs of the Times,* July 4, 1899). The evidence is easy to identify because our farmers are producing high-quality food of sufficient quantities that we can afford to buy in abundance. However, this will not always be the case. The great controversy will end at the second coming of Christ, an event that is quickly approaching, as current world events indicate. Thus, before continuing, it is helpful to review the sequence of events that will lead up to Christ's return so we can understand and know what to expect.

Probation will be closed when all of God's children have received His seal and the rebels have received the mark of the beast so they may continue to buy and sell. The great time of trouble, as predicted in Daniel 12:1–3, will begin after the USA legislates and decides to enforce that everyone is required (under penalty of death) to observe Sunday as God's holy day of worship. Such legislation will be viewed by heaven as an act of national apostasy, which will be followed by national ruin.

The seven last plagues and the time of trouble are parallel events. Both begin at the close of probation, when Jesus leaves the sanctuary; and both end at the coming of Christ (see White, *The Great Controversy,* p. 614). God pours out the seven last plagues against wicked people (see Rev. 15:1, 7; 16:1; 14:9–11; Isa. 28:21; White, *The Great Controversy,* p. 627; James

L. Howard, Sr. *The Time of The End*, p. 382–385). National ruin will lead to the death penalty for the Sabbatarians who remain faithful to God. No righteous people will die after the death decree against the Sabbatarians. The time of trouble will serve as a "crucible of affliction" that is to bring out the Christlike characters, designed to lead the people of God to renounce Satan and his temptations (see White, *Our High Calling*, p. 321; refer to the *Chronology of Last Day Events* chart at the end of this chapter).

You might ask how that works for those who don't live through the time of trouble. We are informed that "the crucible of God" tests all of His people in His time and timing. I've noticed that to be the case in my work as a trust officer, especially when I've walked through the final chapter of life for a number of people in our "ministry of compassion and sorrow" (see White, *Testimonies for the Church*, vol. 4, p. 540). How we dispose of our wealth when we come to the end of our earthly lives matters in the struggle for Christ's truth. Your will, trust, or estate has a part to play in the great controversy. So, you get a better idea of this, read chapters 6–12 of this book, **which** offer a review of some of my personal and professional experiences, as well as examples of assisting people plan for the end of their lives by pledging gifts to the Lord's work.

You might ask how and when Satan will be dealt with at the end of the great controversy. Satan will be bound for 1,000 years when there are no people or nations left on earth for him to tempt and torment, then released for a little while (see Rev. 20:1–3). The righteous are resurrected (see verse 4—the first resurrection). And the rest of the dead aren't alive again until the end of the 1,000 years (see verse 5). Satan is then released to lead a rebellion against the holy city of God that has come down after the second resurrection of the dead (all of the wicked—see verses 7–9). It is during the millennium, between the first and second resurrections, that the judgment of the wicked takes place, conducted by Christ with His saints (see verses 4, 6; 1 Cor. 6:2; White, *The Great Controversy*, pp. 660, 661).

What about the actual end of Satan's life? The Bible is very clear about it. You can read about the way Jesus will end Satan's life:

> Let no one deceive or beguile you in any way, for that day will not come except the apostasy comes first [unless the predicted great falling away of those who have professed to be Christians has come], and the man of lawlessness (sin) is revealed, who is the son of doom (of perdition), [Dan. 7:25; 8:25; 1 Tim. 4:1].Who opposes and exalts himself so proudly and insolently against and over all that is called God or that is worshiped, [even to his actually] taking

his seat in the temple of God, proclaiming that he himself is God. [Ezek. 28:2; Dan. 11:36, 37.] Do you not recollect that when I was still with you, I told you these things? And now you know what is restraining him [from being revealed at this time]; it is so that he may be manifested (revealed) in his own [appointed] time. For the mystery of lawlessness (that hidden principle of rebellion against constituted authority) is already at work in the world, [but it is] restrained only until he who restrains is taken out of the way. *And then the lawless one (the antichrist) will be revealed and the Lord Jesus will slay him with the breath of His mouth and bring him to an end by His appearing at His coming.* [Isa. 11:4.] The coming [of the lawless one, the antichrist] is through the activity and working of Satan and will be attended by great power and with all sorts of [pretended] miracles and signs and delusive marvels—[all of them] lying wonders—And by unlimited seduction to evil and with all wicked deception for those who are perishing (going to perdition) because they did not welcome the Truth but refused to love it that they might be saved. Therefore, God sends upon them a misleading influence, a working of error and a strong delusion to make them believe what is false, In order that all may be judged and condemned who did not believe in [who refused to adhere to, trust in, and rely on] the Truth, but [instead] took pleasure in unrighteousness. (2 Thessalonians 2:3–12, AMPC, emphasis added)

Paul also told us how to live for God here and now in order to live with Him eternally (see 2:13–16; 3:1–15).

Sabbath-keepers will be blamed for the national ruin, which causes me to wonder how my immediate neighbors will relate to me at that time. There is no trial or trauma like what we will experience then. The testing and trials we experience today are like kindergarten compared to the university that will be the final events just before Christ's second coming. Here is our prophetic expectation:

> In accidents and calamities by sea and by land, in great conflagrations, in fierce tornadoes and terrific hailstorms, in tempests, floods, cyclones, tidal waves, and earthquakes, in every place and in a thousand forms, Satan is exercising his power. He sweeps away the ripening harvest, and famine and distress follow. He imparts to the air a deadly taint, and thousands perish by the pestilence. These visitations are to become more and more frequent and disastrous.

Destruction will be upon both man and beast. "The earth mourneth and fadeth away," 'the haughty people ... do languish. The earth also is defiled under the inhabitants thereof; because they have transgressed the laws, changed the ordinance, broken the everlasting covenant." Isaiah 24:4, 5.

And then the great deceiver will persuade men that those who serve God are causing these evils. The class that have provoked the displeasure of Heaven will charge all their troubles upon those whose obedience to God's commandments is a perpetual reproof to transgressors. It will be declared that men are offending God by the violation of the Sunday sabbath; that this sin has brought calamities which will not cease until Sunday observance shall be strictly enforced; and that those who present the claims of the fourth commandment, thus destroying reverence for Sunday, are troublers of the people, preventing their restoration to divine favor and temporal prosperity. Thus the accusation urged of old against the servant of God will be repeated and upon grounds equally well established: "And it came to pass, when Ahab saw Elijah, that Ahab said unto him, Art thou he that troubleth Israel? And he answered, I have not troubled Israel; but thou, and thy father's house, in that ye have forsaken the commandments of the Lord, and thou hast followed Baalim." 1 Kings 18:17, 18. As the wrath of the people shall be excited by false charges, they will pursue a course toward God's ambassadors very similar to that which apostate Israel pursued toward Elijah. (White, *The Great Controversy*, pp. 589, 590)

The way we see things depends on where we stand. In my view, this is the most exciting time to be alive for us Christians as compared to all of Earth's history because of how bad the world has become, with severe tensions abounding in social, economic, political, and military areas. When people lament about it in my hearing, I say something like, "Isn't it wonderful? When it gets bad enough, Jesus will come to end it and take us home to live with Him in His heaven!"

As you and I continue our journey with Jesus in this life and place, it might help to remember He is bigger and more powerful than are all of our concerns that try to compel us to be fearful and struggle with a troubled mind over some situation. All of us are very good situation artists. Perhaps that is why Paul could write an amazing promise to give us confidence and comfort in continuing to choose the Christian life:

> For no temptation (no trial regarded as enticing to sin), [no matter how it comes or where it leads] has overtaken you and laid hold on you that is not common to man [that is, no temptation or trial has come to you that is beyond human resistance and that is not adjusted and adapted and belonging to human experience, and such as man can bear]. But God is faithful [to His Word and to His compassionate nature], and He [can be trusted] not to let you be tempted and tried and assayed beyond your ability and strength of resistance and power to endure, but with the temptation He will [always] also provide the way out (the means of escape to a landing place), that you may be capable and strong and powerful to bear up under it patiently. (1 Corinthians 10:13, 14, AMPC)

Great is our praise to God for this powerful promise, for this is who Jesus is!

All the Protestant reformers of 500 years ago would have loved to see what we are viewing daily in the fulfillment of Bible prophecy. When world events get bad enough, then Jesus will come to claim His bride, the church. Read about the conditions in the church when the Midnight Cry goes forth, announcing the coming of Christ (see Matt. 25:1–13). The ten players in the parable are referred to as virgins because their theological beliefs are pure and consistent with the entire Bible. The oil for the lamps refers to the Holy Spirit (see White, *Christ's Object Lessons*, pp. 405–421).

Don't worry about being able to go through the time of trouble. The Lord always gives us what we need in every trial and trauma of life when it is needed, not before. We can trust Him, for He is trustworthy because of His unlimited love for us.

The following chart is the *Chronology of Last Day Events* to which we referred earlier in this chapter:

Stewardship and the Great Controversy ◆ 31

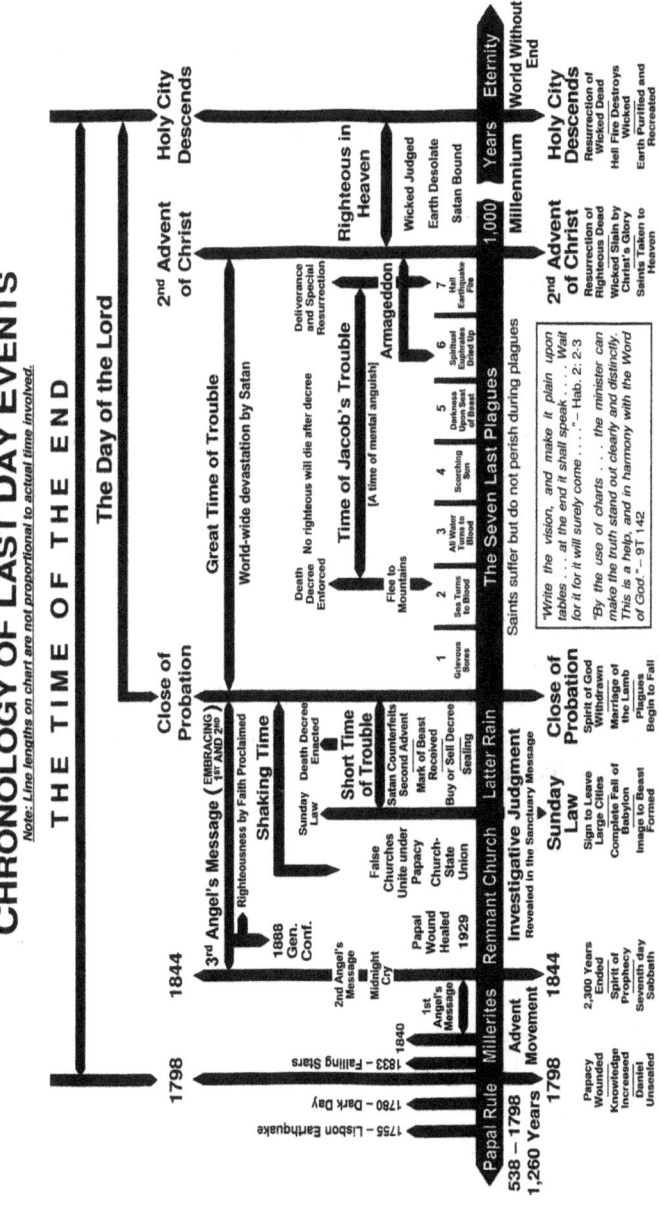

This chart is page 6 of the 624 page hardcover book, *The Time of the End* by retired Seventh-day Adventist Pastor, James L. Hayward, Sr., published by American Christian Ministries. You may find the book at an Adventist Book Center or online at www.AmericanChristianMinistries.org; 800-233-4450.

Chapter 3

Our Personal Spiritual and Stewardship Journeys and God's Call to Ministry

In this chapter, I want to give you an overview of the personal stewardship covenants that my wife, Mary Jo, and I have made with God and the effects these covenants have had on our personal finances and lives as Christians. I am not telling you these things to toot my own horn, so to speak. I will share some of the stories of stewardship successes and failures I have experienced or witnessed in my many years of working in this ministry.

Before I do that, I want you to know and understand that I have not spent my career recommending a course of action to which I was not willing to commit myself. Mary Jo and I made four Spirit-led covenants with God. We call them "spiritual covenants" because they are bathed in prayer and based on what we have learned from the Bible and the amplification of its teachings in the "testimony of Jesus" (Rev. 19:10). We made these covenants because of our understanding of the great controversy. We believed and still believe that Jesus is able and willing to protect us and provide for us. We have taken Him at His word: "Greater is He [Jesus Christ] that is in you than he [Satan] that is in the world" (1 John 4:4). We know our God is almighty, all powerful, and His essence is selfless love. We know He ministers to us according to our needs, and therefore, we have gladly entered into covenant with Him.

The first covenant we made with God was in regard to tithe. We again decided to take Him at His word and put Him first by returning to Him 10 percent of our gross income, plus offerings. What we discovered was 80 percent with God's blessing goes much farther than does 100 percent with God's curse (see Mal. 3:8).

Before becoming Seventh-day Adventists, we were Baptists. We were members of a congregation where the pastor suggested we should obey the Lord's commandment and tithe our gain. His suggestion was that we begin by giving 2 percent and increase our giving incrementally until we reached the 10 percent standard. Our understanding of this suggestion was that 10 percent was the ceiling—the ultimate goal—of giving to the church. When we became Seventh-day Adventists, we learned that 10 percent is the floor—the beginning point. It is where we start giving. Returning to Malachi, where God commands us to tithe, repeating what was established in the Pentateuch, we might ask why He has made this a requirement.

The Spirit of Prophecy offers some guidance in answering this question:

> Selfishness is the strongest and most general of human impulses, the struggle of the soul between sympathy and covetousness is an unequal contest; for while selfishness is the strongest passion, love and benevolence are too often the weakest, and as a rule the evil gains the victory. Therefore in our labors and gifts for God's cause, it is unsafe to be controlled by feeling or impulse. (White, *Counsels on Stewardship*, p. 25)

Tithing is a means by which God teaches us the value of selfless giving—selfless living. It has been said that "stewardship is the main ship of in-reach ministry." All other boats of ministry are carried by the main ship. Why is this so? Stewardship is not just about giving to God or paying back God. Rather, it is all about our relationship with Jesus—not just knowing *about* Jesus but actually *knowing* Him so intimately that He lives within us. When we know Him, we understand His words: "freely you have received, freely give" (Matt. 10:8b, AKJV).

Paul echoes this sentiment: "God loves a cheerful giver" (2 Cor. 9:7b, AKJV). Jesus did not begrudge the sacrifice He made for us on the cross. Likewise, in terms of tithes and offerings, "it were better not to give at all than to give grudgingly; for if we impart of our means when we have not the spirit to give freely, we mock God" (White, *Counsels on Stewardship*, p. 199). It is a mockery because giving with a grudge betrays the spirit in which God gave Himself to us. Thus, in our covenant of tithes and offerings, we committed to give freely and happily to the Lord's work, which is defined as the church's ministry as conducted by the conference—what Ellen White calls "the sisterhood of churches"—in our geographical region (*ibid.*, p. 102).

The second covenant we made with God was regarding the tuition for Christian education. As a result of prayer and our concern about the environment in the public schools, we decided to put our children all the way through the Seventh-day Adventist educational system—grade school through college—even if doing so required selling our home and using the gained equity. When we first enrolled our son in the eighth grade, we were not yet members of the Seventh-day Adventist Church. Touring the school prior to enrollment, we explained to the principal that our son was a Baptist and would remain a Baptist after he completed his schooling there. The principal told us he was fine with that. We joined the Seventh-day Adventist Church at the end of that school year. Twelve years later, both of our children had graduated from a Seventh-day Adventist college and married their spouses, precious Christians whom they met while attending. As it turned out, we did not have to sell our home to pay for it all, and they did not graduate with the burden of student loans. Amazing grace abounds!

> *I was an addict—a "credit-holic." I pleaded with God for His power to overcome my habits of buying stuff I did not need with money I did not have to keep up with people I did not know.*

The third financial covenant we made with God was to use prayer and cash in order to make all necessary purchases. We cut up our credit cards and agreed we would not buy anything on credit again—not even a tank of gas. We also agreed we would only make an exception to this rule if we received a definite, unmistakable indication from the Holy Spirit. When we made this covenant, I was an addict—a "credit-holic." I pleaded with God for His power to overcome my habits of buying stuff I did not need with money I did not have to keep up with people I did not know. Evidently, He effected a change in me because several years later, I was able to carry a credit card again and use it sparingly, and then only when we could pay it off at the end of the month. Sticking to this covenant, we were able to pay off a great amount of debt in two years and began replacing it with cash reserves to care for the unexpected expenses that always seemed to come along every month.

Sticking to this covenant was difficult for me at first, but it was a big relief for Mary Jo. I had operated with the philosophy of using OPM (other people's money) as much as possible. You may have heard this referred to in popular terminology as "leveraging." When I say I was a credit addict, I mean I was an intentionally serious credit addict. In the first several years of keeping this covenant, I had to continuously commit my addiction to the Lord.

I began working for a denominational organization in October 1974, just four months after joining the church in June. Doing so significantly reduced my income, by about half, and we started paying tithe and tuition, not just for our son but for our daughter also. The Lord and Mary Jo are what made this covenant work. She was a fully committed, full-time mother, homemaker, and helpmate. Our friends in the church, once they realized I had become a denominational employee, would ask her when and where she planned on finding work. Her answer was always, "We have not planned to approach it that way." And we never did, either. We have stuck to these covenants all the time since becoming members of the Adventist Church in 1974. However, these were only three of the four covenants.

The fourth and final financial covenant we made with God was to consecrate all we are and all we have. We had will and trust documents done that honor this covenant if our lives end before Jesus returns and we have not used up all our assets in personal ministry or support of Christ's mission to seek and save the lost. Through prayer, we literally transferred title and ownership of all we had, as well as all our relationships, to God. I remember kneeling in prayer before the Lord and talking out loud to Him. I read from a list of assets—along with hopes, ambitions, dreams, and relationships—and said, "Lord, from this moment on, all of this belongs to You and not to me."

Mary Jo and I have renewed this covenant of God's ownership from time to time over the years. We were inspired to do this by one of the first non-biblical books I read as a new Adventist, from which I have already quoted. We are told that when we honestly, genuinely place our "property on the altar and earnestly inquire of God for duty," He will lead us in how He wants us "to dispose of these things" (White, *Counsels on Stewardship*, pp. 59, 60). By doing this, we are freed from the burden that comes with tying our goals and ambitions to earthly, material accumulations and allow God's priorities to lead and rule.

A point of clarification about our will-plan: To say our will-plan honors this fourth covenant with God does not mean it omits our family. We both prayed about how much to leave to family while taking Ellen White's counsel (as included in this book) into account. Mary Jo came up with a number that was more than mine was. I thought about her number for a while and decided to ask her to accept my smaller number, but I prayed about that idea first, and the Lord told me to accept her number. And we are at peace.

Making these covenants required us to recognize that all we are and all we have belong to God, not to us, whether we are dead or alive—in poverty or plenty. That being the case, by conducting our affairs and business as if it belonged to us was to take on an unnatural responsibility. Pretending we own ourselves and our material gain creates unrest in our souls and distorts our values, priorities, and goals. Ultimately, it can ruin our relationships with God, His church, and other people. According to divorce lawyers, the cause of most divorces is conflict over the couple's personal finances.

Reflecting on these covenants and the need to consecrate everything to God reminds me of the proverbial story of the man who enjoyed eating a donut every day until, one day, he became fixated on the hole in the middle of the donut. The more he focused on the hole, the larger it seemed to get until he couldn't enjoy donuts anymore.

Of course, when Mary Jo and I first made these covenants with God, I was not working in the trust services and estate planning ministry. Prior to becoming a Seventh-day Adventist, I held a variety of jobs in the fields of sales and finance. From 1961 to 1970, I worked as both a field salesman, sales manager, and product manager out of an office in Los Angeles, California. In 1970, I decided to try business life on my own. I walked away from a good salary, bonus plan, company car, company credit card, retirement plan, and health insurance. I became a self-employed professional financial planner and investment broker with California licenses in real estate, securities, annuities, and life/disability insurance. I also became a registered investment advisor with the Securities and Exchange Commission.

When we became Adventists in 1974, I felt compelled to leave my business behind and find work with the church in whatever capacity God might lead me. We prayed about this decision for four months, waiting on an answer from the Lord. During a week-long family camping vacation in the High Sierra-Nevada Mountains, we talked it all over with one another and with God. The answer to our prayers finally came in October, when I went to work for Loma Linda Foods, where I remained employed until 1980—six years of service I truly enjoyed.

When it was time to move on from Loma Linda Foods, I again prayed that God would direct me to another church organization where I would be of service to His work. I fully surrendered and agreed to take any position in any place as long as it was in keeping with His will and timing. At that time, the parent organization of Loma Linda Foods was the General Conference of Seventh-day Adventists, and the motivation to find a new place in the church's work came during the time when the Sanitarium Health Food Company of Australia took over Loma Linda Foods' operations.

Although they were very kind to me by finding a place for me in the new company, I had become discouraged and upset with the new management.

I did not want to return to the business world from which I had come, so I again saturated my decision making in prayer. Again, for four months, I prayed. I listened many times to a sermon by my then pastor, Elder Morris Venden, on "How to Know God's Will in Your Life." I claimed the promise in Psalm 32:8–9.

That was on August 1, 1980. I remember clearly that in prayer, early that Friday morning, I said to the Lord, "Please make me willing to be made willing to listen—to know Your leading. Please give me a neutral will in the matter of my employment with Your church. Make a clean slate so You can write Your will on my heart and into my mind. And Lord, please make me willing to be made willing to stay at Loma Linda Foods with these managers being there until Jesus' second coming, if that is Your will for me and for Your work."

The Lord answered that prayer instantly for a neutral will. I jumped up off the floor with a spring in my step and went to the office in a spirit of good will and cheerfulness, full of praise to God. An hour later, at 9:00 that same Friday morning, a phone call came from Elder Stuart Jane, president of the Southern New England Conference in South Lancaster, Massachusetts. At that time, I lived and worked in La Sierra, Riverside, California. Elder Jane was inviting me to interview for an opening as the director of trust services and stewardship ministry for the states of Rhode Island, Connecticut, and Massachusetts. Talk about prompt answers to prayer! It still thrills my whole being as I write this. I know with certainty, in part because of this experience, that God will always do what He said He would do.

We had to wait three weeks before the interview could take place. That is how long it would be until all the necessary people could gather in South Lancaster to conduct the interview. During this intermission, Mary Jo and I went through the entire house. We cleaned, sorted, and organized all the things we would take if we had to move. When the call came that I had the job, our stuff was on a moving van the next week. We remained in Southern New England for five years.

In 1985, we became empty nesters. Also, after much prayer, we decided to accept a call to the New York Conference in Syracuse. Over the next two years, we seemed to be in one state of burnout or another. Trust Services and Stewardship were two separate departments, and both had been vacant for five years. That meant a lot of catching up while trying to meet the pent-up demand for help and services at the local church level. During this time, the General Conference also made a change by rolling the Stewardship Department into the Church Ministries Department. After a year, I again felt the need to prayerfully consider to where and what God was calling me. Some had mentioned to me the possibility of becoming a church pastor.

One morning, I prayed for God to direct me in these decisions. I again asked for a neutral will—that I would be willing to accept God's direction no matter what it was. I had been running two departments and dedicating forty hours per department per week. As I prayed, the Lord came very close to me and gave me the following train of thought: "It is trust services *ministry* that I've called you to. I've allowed you to do stewardship ministry for you to learn the stewardship and spiritual dimensions of a Christian's estate plan design." In other words, God made me realize what I was doing wasn't just all business and legal stuff. My professional history of financial planning and business management had led me to look on trust services as nothing more than a business run by the church. In that prayer session, the Lord corrected my mindset in a gentle and timely way. And *that* was all I needed to know.

From that day onward, decades later, I have focused on doing this one thing until I receive new instructions from the Lord. I committed to fulfilling my obligations to the New York Conference and resolved to renegotiate my job description at an upcoming constituency session. Instead, a year later, in 1987, a call came that asked us to move once again.

One evening in upstate New York, Mary Jo and I had the rare privilege of retiring to bed early. After we were sound asleep, the phone rang. It was an officer from the Ohio Conference inviting me to come and run their Trust Services Department. I told him we were not interested, for two reasons: One, we had not been in New York long enough to make such a move. Second, moving west was the wrong direction since our family was in the east. After I hung up the phone, we could not fall back asleep. After a couple hours of tossing and turning, I asked Mary Jo, "Are you awake?" She was, and we got out of bed and knelt down on our knees to pray to talk about the situation with God. We concluded that this was the Lord's call, so the next morning, I called them back and told them we were interested. The Lord sold our house, and we moved again. This time, it was to Mount Vernon, Ohio.

Every job assignment I have had has required a turnaround of one sort or another. After a couple years at the Ohio Conference, we had completely revamped the program for the Trust Services office. Then one morning, I was having my daily prayer and study time with the Lord. I had not asked for any specific guidance that day about the grand scheme of my life and work, but God reminded me of the fact that I had been called to ministry for Him at the age of 15 (1956). I had not thought about that calling since I was 18.

The scene flashed before my mind. I was plowing a field on the farm at 10:00 in the evening. The Lord had come near to me and let me know I'd been selected by Him to be His minister. This event with my Savior occurred in 1989. That morning, He reminded me of the call and placed the thought in my mind that that call—the specialized ministry I was now doing—was considered by heaven to be satisfied. What a thrill that was to know! Thrill of thrills! Praise God from whom all blessings flow! Therefore, it is easy for me to understand, live, and work in the perspective that God has called me to His Spirit-led, mission-driven estate and planned giving ministry of seeking transformational gifts from authentic donors who have a heart and mind to make spiritual transactions with heaven rather than business transactions with the church.

Since that time, my journey of ministering through trust services and estate planning has continued. We later moved to Berrien Springs, Michigan, where I worked for Andrews University. From there, it was on to Thousand Oaks, California, to serve and lead the work of planned giving and trust services for the Pacific Union Conference. Then, in 2001, we returned to Southern New England, where I took up the same position that had started the whole journey back in 1980.

Since then, the hardest decision of my whole life became the one to retire. Agonizing prayer was very meaningful to me during the process of making this decision. The Lord made it clear to me that it was possible to retire in order to avoid the grueling seventy-hour work weeks without quitting the work. Thus, I went on the church's retirement plan in early 2007 and began the experience (fourteen years at the time of writing) of working part-time for It Is Written Media Ministry while also working on small jobs for a few conferences from time to time.

I relate all of this experience to you, again, not to toot my own horn but to give you the sense I have: that planned giving through estates and trusts is a ministry and a vital part of continuing the church's mission to the world. How we handle our finances, along with every other material blessing God gives us, is part of the great controversy and our role within it. With this background in mind, I will share stories of specific examples of how this ministry has helped and changed individual Christians and their families in their devotion to the Lord and His mission on earth. There is an amazing story about a family that was documented in *Adventist Review* magazine in 1858. It is included in the "Faith" section of Chapter 14.

In conclusion, here are some additional lessons we learned about the great controversy as it has played out in our lives. Life experiences have worked together to make these lessons real to us. "The wise man saves for the future, but the foolish man spends whatever he gets" (Prov. 21:20, TLB). "It is required in stewards, that a man be found faithful" (1 Cor. 4:2). And when I spend more than I get without a repayment plan that is honest and in harmony with the realities of life and our family's economy, that is a big-time character problem.

The Ten Commandments weighed in on this for me. The spirit of wanting something for nothing is the same spirit as that of a thief. Therefore, the commandments that address lying, stealing, cheating, coveting, and idolatry convicted me of wrongdoing. We decided we could trust Jesus in all of this because He is the Almighty God who has demonstrated His loving care and ability and willingness to act on our behalf. He is much bigger than all our troubles, trials, and traumas could ever be. And He has demonstrated His ceaseless, selfless love so many times through the frequent evidence of His leading in our life choices.

We cannot separate our spirituality in Christ from our possessions of money and property. For example, in Matthew 6:19–34, we read about the impossibility of serving two masters (see verse 24), our hearts being where our treasures are (see verse 21), and the futility of worrying about tomorrow because each new day has its own trouble (see verse 34). It is very significant to me that Jesus did not command us not to serve two masters; He simply said it is not possible.

> *It is very significant to me that Jesus did not command us not to serve two masters; He simply said it is not possible.*

In all our lifestyle choices, we must decide that God is on His throne, and He promised to live on the thrones of our hearts and minds and thus give us His will, mind, heart, selfless love, faith, and power to make us conquerors and mighty witnesses. Angels and people now serve God out of love rather than out of fear because He didn't terminate the life of Lucifer immediately upon his rebellion. Therefore, we love the Lord as our precious Savior from sin to everlasting life and literally hate our life of self because it will always lead us to worship self and Satan rather than God.

For you and me, our income and other resources will be used to either honor God or *dis*honor Him by spending it on debilitating stuff—whether we are dead or alive—in poverty or plenty. In our home, we often say, "This was a tithe blessing" when finding a bargain. Every time we write a check for the Lord's work, it is a declaration of dependence.

As a stewardship ministry leader for the church since 1980, I've discovered that some people give their tithes like they pay the fire insurance premium on their home: to keep from burning in the judgment. Others pay it out of a sense of legalistic duty. Then in their minds, they say, 'Okay, that takes care of my stewardship obligation, so my leftover money will be used to do whatever pleases me.'

In the early history of the Seventh-day Adventist movement, when the founders were figuring out its doctrines and practices, financial stewardship was a topic with which they dealt over time. They decided to promote to the members a financial support system to which they referred as "Sister Betsy" (I've not found the reason for this name. It has been suggested that it could be because the sizable committee that made the recommendations consisted of all women). The plan consisted of returning the first tithe to support the ministry of the gospel pursuant to the Bible, plus a Second Tithe to be used as follows:

> To promote the assembling of the people for religious service, as well as to provide for the poor, a second tithe of all the increase was required. Concerning the first tithe, the Lord had declared, "I have given the children of Levi *all the tenth* in Israel." Numbers 18:21. But in regard to the second He commanded, "Thou shalt eat before the Lord thy God, in the place which He shall choose to place His name there, the tithe of thy corn, of thy wine, and of thine oil, and the firstlings of thy herds and of thy flocks; that thou mayest learn to fear the Lord thy God always." Deuteronomy 14:23, 29; 16:11–14. (White, *Patriarchs and Prophets*, p. 530)

They also encouraged what was called "systematic benevolence," which means we remove the tithe and offerings from our income first as it is received (read 2 Corinthians 8–9 and Deuteronomy 28 for great insights about our personal stewardship). Additionally, Paul admonished us to do the calculations to plan our giving during non-Sabbath time (see 1 Cor. 16:1–3).

It is interesting to note that our current definition of systematic benevolence is giving to the church of our time, talents, treasure, and temple. My whole life experience is filled with joy, peace, hope, and order when Mary Jo and I make voluntary gifts to God as acts of worship in the spirit of praise and thanksgiving with no strings attached (including restricted-purpose gifts of money and property), because Jesus gave of Himself voluntarily to buy our religious freedom. Jesus said, "I lay down My life … No one takes it from Me, but I lay it down of Myself"

(John 10:17b, 18a AKJV). "Systematic benevolence [giving] should *not* be made systematic compulsion. It is freewill offerings that are acceptable to God" (White, *Testimonies for the Church*, vol. 3, p. 396).

I can only give freely and cheerfully to the precious bride of Christ, the church, when I love Him and His precious bride with a loyal heart and grateful loyalty. I can only love Jesus fully when I trust Him in full surrender of all my heart's feelings, emotions, affections, and passions; all my mind's thoughts and imaginings; and all my will's choices—acknowledging Him as my Lord of all I am and have. I can only trust Jesus with all of life's outcomes when I learn to know Him by heart. I can only know Jesus enough to trust Him when I spend time alone with Him in self-revealing dialogue on a regular basis—feeding on Jesus—talking with and listening to Him in loving trust.

"Freely you have received, freely give" (Matt. 10:8b, AKJV). "It were better not to give at all than to give grudgingly; for if we impart of our means when we have not the spirit to give freely, we mock God" (White, *Counsels on Stewardship*, p. 199).

My family and I joined the Seventh-day Adventist Church at the campus of La Sierra University in Riverside, California, in June 1974; it was after seven months of careful Bible study with pastors. A couple months later, the senior pastor of that congregation, Elder Morris Venden, told the congregation one Sabbath morning, "Friends, you have been listening to me for three years, and I would like to give you the opportunity to talk back to the pastor. We will meet this afternoon for that purpose."

We were there for that meeting in the afternoon, along with about 200 others. One of our friends, Gwen, a life-long Adventist, said, "Pastor Venden, you are always talking about our need to have a devotional life with God. How do you do that? What do you read? Do you read the Bible from Genesis to Revelation? or do you read the Bible topically? or do you let the Bible fall open and expect that the Holy Spirit fingered the page for you?

Pastor Venden's answer came in the form of a formula for an intimate walk with God that was to change my whole life. Here is the formula. Pastor Venden is speaking:

> Clue #1: If you want to know Jesus, you have to read about Jesus. That means reading Matthew, Mark, Luke, and John in the Bible and reading the books *Steps to Christ, The Desire of Ages, Christ's Object Lessons,* and *Thoughts from the Mount of Blessing* by Ellen G. White and *Christ Our Righteousness* by A. G. Daniells.

Clue #2: After you have done your reading, prayerfully read it back to God, asking Him for an understanding of the spiritual lessons and how to apply them to your life.

biggest clue of all: After you have finished your praying—your praise, thanksgiving, and petitions—just remain silently knelt before God and wait for Him to speak back to you. You might have to wait a few minutes while your mind wanders out past the woodshed, but be patient, and He will communicate with you.

By this time, I was on the edge of my chair, silently praying, "Lord, this is what I've longed for and didn't know it was possible, but how am I going to do it?" I kept on praying about this for days, thinking of all the possible times when I might do it. I finally realized the best time was at the beginning of the day. However, I cried out, "Lord, You know that I'm a basket case about getting up in the morning. I just barely get up in time to get to the office ten minutes late."

Then a new thought came: 'You know how much bed rest you need at night. Just decide when you want to get up to study and pray; then back the clock up in your mind to the time you need to go to bed; and then do accordingly.' I had been going to bed after the 11:00 news went off at 11:30. After that calculation, I began going to bed at 9:30. That was a major change in the family dynamics!

Going to bed earlier, I'd naturally wake up early, look at the time, and think, 'It's way too early to get up.' And I'd go back to sleep and get up just in time to get to the office ten minutes late. After about a week of that pattern, I was reminded of my covenant with the Lord to get up earlier and spend time with Him in His Word; then I realized He was answering my prayer to wake me up early, so then I prayed for courage to get out from under the covers when He awakened me. He also answered that prayer and continues to do so to this day, to the thrill of my soul. His wake-up call each morning became an issue of mind over mattress.

I had to give up an alarm clock and depend on the Lord alone to wake me up each morning. I would buy a new clock to get a different ring but would not hear it after a week. I would put the clock in my dresser drawer on the other side of the bedroom, several feet from the bed. Then my wife would wake me and tell me it was ringing and I needed to shut it off so she could continue sleeping. I acknowledged to the Lord that I was a serious basket case in desperate need of His help. I just have to tell Him what time I need to wake up, and He takes care of it. Even when I was to get up at 4:00 a.m. to catch a plane, I knew to depend on my wonderful Lord alone, and He has not failed me since 1974.

I claim God's promise: "The Master, God, has given me a well-taught tongue, so I know how to encourage tired people. He wakes me up in the morning, wakes me up, opens my ears to listen as one ready to take orders. The Master, God, opened my ears, and I didn't go back to sleep, didn't pull the covers back over my head" (Isa. 50:4, 5, MSG).

I love to have a thoughtful hour at the Garden of Gethsemane (so to speak) in my devotional time. Peter, James, and John were invited to join Jesus in that place. Jesus had taken these three of His closest disciples with Him into one of His most severely trying situations—ever. He struggled in prayer with His Father God about the upcoming events that would end His life on earth with excruciating pain. Jesus would experience physical pain, but the more dreaded, extreme pain would be separation from His Father. He apparently thought He could depend on these three to support Him in prayer.

Jesus instructed the disciples, "Sit you here, while I go and pray yonder" (Matt. 26:36b, AKJV). He also told them, "My soul is exceeding sorrowful, even to death; tarry you here, and watch with me" (verse 38, AKJV). When Jesus came back to them between each of His three prayers, He found them sleeping. Of course, He aroused them, but they went back to sleep. One time, Jesus said to Peter, "What, could you not watch with me one hour? Watch and pray, that you enter not into temptation" (verses 40b, 41a, AKJV; see also Mark 14:32–42; Luke 22:40–46; White, *The Desire of Ages*, pp. 685–697).

I cherish these words of advice and practical help: "It would be well for us to spend a thoughtful hour each day in contemplation of the life of Christ. We should take it point by point, and let the imagination grasp each scene, especially the closing ones" (*Ibid.*, p. 83); "the thought of Calvary awakens living and sacred emotions in our hearts. Praise to God and the Lamb will be in our hearts and on our lips; for self-worship cannot flourish in the soul that keeps fresh in memory the scenes of Calvary. He who beholds the Savior's matchless love will be elevated in thought, purified in heart, transformed in character. He will go forth to be a light to the world" (*Ibid.*, p. 661).

One verse in the Bible that is most precious to me is, "And all of us, as with unveiled face, [because we] continued to behold [in the Word of God] as in a mirror the glory of the Lord, are constantly being transfigured into His very own image in ever increasing splendor and from one degree of glory to another; [for this comes] from the Lord [Who is] the Spirit" (2 Cor. 3:18, AMPC).

After a couple years of having early morning devotionals in my journey with Jesus, I realized it had gone from a joyful delight to a grueling drudgery—I had allowed it to become a legalistic ritual. I had become obsessed with what Jesus was doing in me to change me into a more exalted Christian. I was full of a self-gratulatory spirit, patting myself on the back for being such a wonderful Christian and always taking credit for my accomplishments. I became obnoxious, arrogant, and judgmental; I would dwell on the evil in everything and everyone. The Lord brought to my mind this Bible text: "Though I speak with the tongues of men and of angels, but have not charity [selfless love], I have become as sounding brass or a clanging cymbal" (1 Cor. 13:1, AKJV). I was horrified to realize I was working like the devil for the Lord.

In His mercy, the Lord didn't leave me there. He revealed to me that while I loved Jesus as my model and example in His life, ministry, teachings, and Him being my substitute, I had come to focus on Jesus as my model to the neglect of focusing on Him as my righteous substitute and sacrifice on the cross of Calvary. Therefore, I learned to go quickly to the foot of His cross, knowing the sacrifice of the divine Lamb of God was my only hope for an authentic spiritual life in Christ—with Jesus being my Savior from sin, the Lord of my life and labor, and my God of eternity, which begins here and now.

I also realized the importance of receiving the lessons of Jesus as my model, but regardless of what I study in the Bible, His Cross must be my dwelling place. I seek His gifts of an accurate sense of my need along with an authentic hunger and thirst for righteousness as Jesus described in His first and fourth beatitudes (see Matt. 5:3, 6).

I also seek to consecrate myself to God each morning by giving my life to Him. This involves me pleading with Him to breathe on me His Holy Spirit with the assigned task of removing my life of self and replacing it with the life of Christ. My understanding is that I'm saved from sin to everlasting life by Christ being alive within me. Therefore, I seek to give Him my mind and all of its thoughts and ambitions; my heart and all of its affections and passions; my will and all of its choices; and my values and priorities to be sanctified or set apart for His glory.

Jesus taught us that we might know all about Him without Him knowing us at the time of judgment. He can only know us if we have Him living within. When the Bible uses the word "know" in this context, it means intimacy. For example, Adam knew Eve, and she bore a son (see Gen. 4:1).

I've recently been blessed with extreme trials that have caused me to wonder if I'm converted or just conditioned. There is a Bible statement

I must have read dozens of times without noticing that it raised this question in a dialogue between Jesus and Peter. The conversation is recorded in Luke 22:31-34. Jesus told Peter Satan asked to be allowed to sift him as wheat, then said, "But I have prayed for you, that your faith fail not: and *when you are converted*, strengthen your brothers." (verse 32, AKJV, emphasis added).

It had never occurred to me that Peter could have been serving Jesus in His ministry for a few years without being converted. That was a solemn revelation to me. I could see this concept being applicable to my journey with Jesus. I'm encouraged ever more when looking to Jesus morning by morning to seek His fresh baptism of the Holy Spirit for the purpose of death to self—to be replaced by the life of Christ.

> *It had never occurred to me that Peter could have been serving Jesus in His ministry for a few years without being converted. That was a solemn revelation to me. I could see this concept being applicable to my journey with Jesus.*

I've always loved the meaningful help Jesus gave us: "And He said to all, If any person wills to come after Me, let him deny himself [disown himself, forget, lose sight of himself and his own interests, refuse and give up himself] and take up his cross daily and follow Me [cleave steadfastly to Me, conform wholly to My example in living and, if need be, in dying also]" (Luke 9:23, AMPC). "And He said to all, If any person wills to come after Me, let him deny himself [disown himself, forget, lose sight of himself and his own interests, refuse and give up himself] and take up his cross daily and follow Me [cleave steadfastly to Me, conform wholly to My example in living and, if need be, in dying also" (Luke 9:23, AMPC).

I often quoted this verse in my preaching but had not noticed the next verse, its linkage to verse 23, or its application to me until my experience during this episode of my life. I had the false idea that to deny self was to refuse some pleasure or something—maybe living a frugal lifestyle. Like Jeremiah 17:9 reveals, I didn't know my own heart was full of evil because my life of self was in charge—I sat on the throne of my own heart.

While I noticed the phrase "take up your cross daily," I would think of it as an instrument of death with no application to my experience. I didn't connect it to 1 Corinthians 15:31 or Galatians 2:16–20 until recently. Paul talked about dying daily and said, "*I am crucified with Christ*: nevertheless *I live; yet not I, but Christ lives in me*: and the life which I now live in the flesh *I live by the faith of the Son of God*, who loved me, and gave himself for me" (Gal. 2:20, AKJV, emphasis added)

For context, here is Luke 9:24: "For whoever would preserve his life [*of self] *and* save it will lose *and* destroy it, but whoever loses his life [*of self] for My sake, he will preserve *and* save it [from the penalty of eternal death]" (Luke 9:24, AMPC [* = supplied]).

I finally began to understand the meaning of the following statement of Jesus—one that had always puzzled me—suggesting I should hate my life. I now see and love its personal application: "Truly, truly, I say to you, Except a corn [kernel] of wheat fall into the ground and die, it stays alone: but if it die, it brings forth much fruit. *He that loves his life shall lose it; and he that hates his life in this world shall keep it to life eternal*" (John 12:24, 25, AKJV, emphasis added).

These two verses tell us self-serving equals self-destruction, while, if we choose Christ as our source of life, we shall be fully, joyfully alive, now and eternally. "The life spent on self is like the grain that is eaten. It disappears, but there is no increase. A man may gather all he can for self; he may live and think and plan for self; but his life passes away, and he has nothing. The law of self-serving is the law of self-destruction" (White, *The Desire of Ages*, p. 624).

Dear reader, the meaning of the above verses eventually became clear to me. To die to my willful *self* essentially means that I deny my *self's* right to live. This results in my hating the life of *self* (or self-will) that interposes, unbidden, between my soul and the living Christ who gives me a most joyful life full of cheerful hope as I look forward to everlasting fellowship with Him in person. It also gives me a spirit of grateful loyalty to Him and His precious bride—His body—the remnant church.

I began to understand and experience this truth, and my understanding continues to develop and grow. I also began to appreciate that "the lover of self is a transgressor of the law" (White, *Christ's Object Lessons*, p. 392). I embraced the awesome concept that the warfare against self is the most important, difficult battle ever fought by mortal humankind. The constant struggle is to submit to God in all things so He may renew us in holiness by the constant renunciation of self and dependence on Christ (see *Ibid.*, p. 159).

More and more significant to me are the words of Jesus. He declared He is the bread of life, and we must eat His body and drink His blood; if we're not feeding on Him (ingesting the Word), we have no eternal life in us. He also talked about the wonderful concept of Him dwelling in us, and we in Him. The passage is John 6:35–63—one of my three favorites. The other two are Ephesians 3:14–21, where I learned about the baptism of the Holy Spirit and His power that is available to me, and John 3:5–21, where I learned the gospel of Christ: being born again, the absence of condemnation, and the requirement of obedience to God.

I also have a deep love for Deuteronomy 28. The first 14 verses describe God's blessings when we diligently obey His law in a spirit of loving trust. "You shall lend … but you shall not borrow. And the Lord will make you the head and not the tail" (verses 12–13, NKJV). The rest of the chapter (fifty-four verses) describes His curses on the rebels who will not obey Him. "The alien who is among you shall rise higher and higher above you …. He shall lend to you, but you shall not lend to him; he shall be the head, and you shall be the tail" (verses 43–44, NKJV).

Additionally, I love the book of Malachi, which describes events that occurred about 430 years before Christ. What do you think of when this book is mentioned? Do you think of stewardship?

Imagine for a moment that you live in a warm climate someplace in the southern USA. You have made a home for yourself and your family in a small travel trailer that is permanently parked in an automotive junk yard. After the father of such a family came to faith in Jesus, he composed the song, "Thank You Lord for Your Blessings on Me." I love to see and hear the song writer's son and his wife, Jeff and Sheri Easter, sing it with Jeff at the piano. We have experienced it at Gaither concerts and now on YouTube (1ref.us/rdwg1).

Sometime after the father, James, came to faith in Christ, the family was able to relocate to more appropriate housing. The gospel message is always an uplifting message to the extent of our capacity to receive God's blessings (see Mal. 3:10).

Chapter 4

Bible Stories Reveal How Stewardship Improves Your Relationship with Jesus

Now that you have an understanding of how my involvement in the church and its stewardship ministry has affected my personal Christian walk, I want to provide you with some practical reflection on how it can affect you, too. I want to do that by first drawing from the Bible and the Spirit of Prophecy as authoritative sources of knowledge and principles that should guide us in how we conduct our affairs. We know, of course, the Lord came from heaven to save us from sin into everlasting life with Him. He became our substitute on the cross, as well as our example.

In His life and ministry, Jesus fulfilled the law to its fullest extent. In so doing, He sets the example and what the law means for us when we allow it to become our mirror—that into which we look for an understanding of how we really appear before God. Jesus tells us very plainly that if we love Him, we will keep His commandments (see John 14:15). This means loving Him with our whole hearts—more than anyone or anything (see Matt. 22:37 Deut. 6:5). Loving Him and trusting Him is our privilege; therefore, it is an honor to put our own accumulated resources at His disposal.

Perhaps the premiere Bible story about stewardship and how we should deal with accumulated resources and assets is found in Matthew 19. We find the story of a rich young man who approached Jesus and asked, "What good thing must I do to get eternal life?" Jesus first corrected him by pointing out that the only One who is good is God. This is an important point to notice. It is not our own actions that are, in and of themselves, good. Rather, when we combine our own efforts with God's purposes, it is He who brings about good results.

This is a significant lesson to remember when it comes to planning for how we dispose of our material wealth. Often, those who have accumulated wealth over the course of their lives become concerned with how it will be used by the church after ownership is transferred. Jesus' admonition to the young man holds a lesson here for us today. Persisting in doubts about how the church will utilize resources is not, ultimately, a concern over the wisdom of humanity but rather about the power of God to accomplish His purposes. Nevertheless, the lessons do not end here.

Jesus went on to tell the young man that to inherit eternal life, he should keep the commandments (see verse 17), to which the young man replied with a new question: "Which ones?" Jesus answers by listing the six commandments from the second tablet of the Decalogue: one's responsibilities to fellow humanity. When the young man told Jesus he has obeyed these commands, he inquired again, providing an important detail: "What do I still lack?"

In this one question, the rich young man revealed that he *knew* there was something holding him back—something that told him he had not fully committed to being a disciple. Jesus told him, "Sell your possessions and give to the poor, and you will have treasure in heaven. Then come, follow me" (verse 21). And "[w]hen the young man heard this, he went away sad, because he had great wealth" (verse 22). Jesus made the young man aware that he was not fulfilling the first tablet of the Decalogue: one's duties to God. The rich young man refused to part with his wealth, but why? He trusted in what his wealth could do for him more than what God could do for him and ultimately others *with* that wealth.

You can read the whole story for yourself, including other practical applications (see Matt. 19:16–30; Mark 10:17–31; Luke 18:18–30; White, *The Desire of Ages,* pp. 518–523; *Christ's Object Lessons,* pp. 390–404; *Counsels on Stewardship,* pp. 210, 232, 233). We are told specifically that the young man said, "No, I cannot give You all" to Jesus because "he loved the gifts of God more than he loved the Giver" (White, *The Desire of Ages,* p. 520). "He who uses his entrusted gifts as God designs becomes a coworker with the Saviour. He wins souls to Christ, because he is a representative of His character. … It may seem too great a sacrifice to give up all in order to follow Christ." (*Ibid,* p. 523). And this relates back to the opening point about God's ability to do good with us and what we have.

In the end, we do not own anything we possess. Everything comes from God and belongs to Him. When we covenant with God to return assets and resources to Him in order to advance the work of the church, we are neither giving God something He doesn't already have nor doing something for God He cannot do for Himself. On the contrary, we are simply recognizing the truth of things as they really are. Good stewardship is not about the power of our own resources to accomplish God's work. Instead, it's about the change God brings about in our own hearts when we obediently, humbly serve Him.

The Bible has several other stories dealing with accumulated assets that reflect on the condition of the possessor's heart. My favorite story in the Old Testament is the testimony of King David at the end of his life. It's my favorite because in the story, David essentially gave his last will and testament to the entire nation, publicly expressing his joy in giving back to God.

Over the course of his reign, David had collected resources in the public treasury dedicated to the building of the temple in Jerusalem. He told the assembled crowd that this public works project was fully funded by those resources in the treasury (see 1 Chron. 29:2). Even so, David made a public commitment to donate his own personal wealth to the project (see verses 3–5). In modern terms, David returned over $3 billion worth* of wealth to the cause of God's temple (see note below on value). It is instructive to consider David's actions in light of his prayer:

> From men by Your hand, O Lord, from men of *this* world [these poor moths of the night] whose portion in life is idle *and* vain. Their bellies are filled with Your hidden treasure [what You have stored up]; their children are satiated, and they leave the rest [of their] wealth to their babes. As for me, I will continue beholding Your face in righteousness (rightness, justice, and right standing with You); I shall be fully satisfied, when I awake [to find myself] beholding Your form [and having sweet communion with You]. (Psalm 17:14, 15, AMPC)

Not only this, but David ended his public declaration by encouraging his fellow Israelites to follow his example: "Now then, who will follow my example? Who is willing to give offerings to the Lord today?" (1 Chron. 29:5, NLT).

*Note on the value of King David's gifts: In the 1983 *New King James Open Bible* from the Thomas Nelson Publishers, the interspersed values at the end of verse 4 says the gold was worth $3.28 billion; the silver, $152,880 (see 1 Chron. 29:2–5; 1 Kings 9:28).

The fact is God knew David's heart. Ellen White writes that "In the days of ancient Israel the sacrifices brought to the high priest were cut open to the backbone to see if they were sound at heart. So, the sacrifices we bring today are laid open before the piercing eye of our great High Priest. He opens and inspects every sacrifice brought by the human race, that He may prove whether it is worthy of being presented to the Father" (White, *Letters and Manuscripts*, vol. 16, Ms. 42, June 2, 1901).

Like the rich young man, we cannot be solely concerned with fulfilling a requirement for eternal life, like checking off an item on a list. Instead, we must be focused on becoming like David, one who found joy in contributing to God's work by trusting Him to use those resources for good. David knew he would not live to see the temple built, but he trusted God by giving more than what he knew was needed to accomplish the task. David's bequest was an act of worship.

Jesus echoes these sentiments when He tells people to store their treasures in heaven rather than on earth. He reminds us that our hearts lie wherever our treasures are, reveals that the greatest factor is where we place our ultimate sense of value, and tells us we cannot serve both God and money (see Matt. 6:19–21). Interestingly, Jesus explicitly connects an unnecessary concern for money and material assets with paganism and unbelief (see verse 32).

In light of this, it is important to remember your last will and testament is your legacy, testimony, and heritage that you want to pass on. Would you—would any Christian—want that legacy and heritage to be one of unbelief? Or, like David, would we want to pass on the joy of giving to the Lord? And, as Paul also reminded us, Jesus suffered the torture of the cross with joy because of what He knew the Father would accomplish as a result of His sacrifice (see Heb. 12:1, 2). The Son of God gave His life with joy in faith. Like Him, "those who receive Christ by faith will receive also power to become the sons of God" (White, *Letters and Manuscripts*, vol. 20, Lt. 3, January 4, 1905). And like the Son of God, those who receive Him in faith will give joyfully to God's service.

The idea of giving joyfully brings up the issue of motives. The story of the widow's mite (see Mark 12:41–44) informs us that an attitude of sacrifice is part of how we give back to God. It was not the monetary value of the widow's offering that made it valuable; it was instead the sacrificial nature of the offering that counted. This was unlike the rich leaders, who tithed precise amounts publicly, with fanfare, and did so, not with an attitude of sacrifice, but, like the rich young man, to fulfill an obligation—to check off a box and receive their reward.

Like Cain and Abel, the widow and the rulers brought gifts with different motives in their hearts. Cain brought his offering to God "with murmuring and infidelity in his heart" that "expressed no penitence for sin." This made his obedience only partial. Outwardly, the sacrifices of Cain and Abel were equal, but internally, "the difference between the two was great" (White, *Patriarchs and Prophets,* p. 72). Cain's sacrifice was not truly an act of worship but one of begrudging compliance.

Compare such an attitude with that of the wise men who came from the east to worship Jesus when He was born. It would have been noteworthy in itself that men of power, learning, and renown prostrated themselves before a humble child in a small Judean village. With that said, in addition to this act of humility, they brought gifts as an act of worship. They gave not only their "highest mental and spiritual endowments" but also their "most precious earthly possessions" (White, *The Desire of Ages,* p. 65).

The motive of worship and sacrifice are of utmost importance. Consider, for example, the fact that even though Jesus knew the content of Judas' heart and that he was stealing from the treasury of the disciples, He never discouraged those who wanted to give gifts to help in their work. God does not turn away genuine sacrifice offered in worship and thanksgiving. Even more to the point, Jesus was so focused on the salvation of His thieving disciple that He neither exposed nor censured him (see *Ibid.*, p. 722). Even the priests who paid Judas for his betrayal recognized the value of motives when it came to what went into the work of God. When Judas attempted, out of guilt, to return their thirty pieces of silver, they refused to return the money to the temple treasury (see Matt. 27:3–7).

One of the saddest stories in the Bible regarding offerings to God and the motives behind them is that of Ananias and Sapphira (see Acts 5:1–11). This husband and wife had pledged to offer the proceeds from the sale of land to the work of the church. However, when the time came to deliver on their promise, both of them lied about the amount for which the land had sold and kept back the difference for themselves. Peter, having been informed prophetically by the Holy Spirit of their scheme, put them on the spot, so to speak. Both of them stuck to their contrived story and were struck down. As Peter told them, they had lied, not to the church, but to God.

This story teaches us not only about God's "hatred and contempt for all hypocrisy and deception" (White, *The Acts of the Apostles,* pp. 75, 76) but also that when we make a vow or covenant to put assets at God's disposal, "the one who vows has no longer any right to the consecrated portion" (White, *Conflict and Courage,* p. 330). This episode from Scripture illustrates, perhaps more than any other does, the relationship between the great controversy and the issue of end-of-life stewardship. Ananias and Sapphira had professed citizenship in the kingdom of God yet treasonously left their loyalty—their ultimate sense of value—behind in the kingdom of darkness.

Seeing the great controversy in action has been a common occurrence during my years in planned giving ministry. My ministerial relationships normally grew into a personal relationship because I considered each donor with whom I worked to be a member of my flock whom I carried on my heart, continuously praying for them. Therefore, it is always a bittersweet loss to me when the life of one of my donors ends: sweet because their life and death were consistent with the gospel of Christ; bitter because of my sense of losing a dear brother or sister in Christ.

However, in my work of estate stewardship ministry, another grievous loss for me is to hear dear friends declare that all they have and all they are belong to God, only see them draft a will-plan that makes a lie of such a testimony. It always reminds me of the text in James 1:5–8 about the double-minded man—an apex of struggle in the great controversy: "Of the double-minded man—he who seeks to follow his own will, while professing to do the will of God—it is written, 'Let not that man think that he shall receive anything of the Lord'" (White, *Patriarchs and Prophets*, p. 384).

The Spirit of Prophecy offers several points of insightful counsel that bear directly on the issue of end-of-life estate planning: "Would you make your property secure? Place it in the hand that bears the nail prints of the crucifixion. Retain all in your possession, and it will be to your eternal loss" (White, *Counsels on Stewardship*, p. 49). So often, when those who have been blessed with material resources in life approach their death, the spirit of greed seeps in. This is in direct opposition to the gospel since "the spirit of liberality is the spirit of heaven. The spirit of selfishness is the spirit of Satan" (*Ibid.*, p. 19).

The fact of the matter is God blesses us with wealth and material resources for the purpose of advancing the gospel and doing the work of the church—in this life and after we pass from this earth. We are counseled to "now, while alive, make diligent, faithful work, that after your death gifts and offerings may come into the treasury of the cause of God. By making this provision you express your interest in the work of God which must be sustained and the standard of truth lifted in new places" (White, *The Gospel Herald*, December 1, 1901).

It is worth pausing for a brief moment to consider a question that inevitably comes up at this juncture: What about one's children, grandchildren, and other family members? Do we not have an obligation to take care of and look after those who depend on us in life? Two points speak directly to this concern. The first comes directly from the mouth of Jesus: "Anyone who loves their father or mother more than me is not worthy of me; anyone who loves their son or daughter more than me is not worthy of me" (Matt. 10:37; see also Luke 14:26).

We are commanded to put God and the gospel first in all things. Just as Jesus promised that our physical needs would be met if we seek His kingdom first (see Matt. 6:33), can we not also rest assured that He will meet the needs of those we love? This counsel is consistent with the message: "Of all our income we should make the first appropriation to God" (White, *Testimonies for the Church,* vol. 4, p. 474). Just as we are to make God first in our working life, so, too, should we make God first in considering how we allocate our assets at death.

Jesus told a parable to illustrate this point (see Luke 12:13–21, NLT). When someone in a crowd yelled out, "Teacher, please tell my brother to divide our father's estate with me," Jesus answered him, "Friend, who made me a judge over you to decide such things as that?" He then went on to tell the parable of a rich farmer with overflowing barns full of harvested crops. Instead of giving away the surplus to the poor or hungry or in some other worshipful way, he built bigger barns to hold it all. Afterwards, the farmer comforted himself, saying, "You have enough stored away for years to come. Now take it easy! Eat, drink, and be merry!" However, God had different plans and warned the farmer, "You fool! You will die this very night. Then who will get it all?" In the farmer's greed, he had failed to put his wealth to work in causes that would have pleased God. It is a lesson to which we should pay attention in living the Christian life and planning our estates.

Finally, one last related point: We should consider whether or not leaving large amounts of wealth to our children and grandchildren actually helps them in their own Christian journeys. We are told that Jesus refused to "take up the dispute over a piece of land" because to do so "would have turned Him from His work," causing him to be "diverted from His mission" in the interest of "human greed" (White, *Christ's Object Lessons,* pp. 252–255). Thus, we should consider whether the burden of unearned wealth tends to discourage our dependents and loved ones from engaging their own vocations by which they, too, can advance the cause of Christ.

Jesus would not allow himself to be distracted by questions of greed and unearned wealth. Taking Him as our supreme example, neither should we put our children and grandchildren in a position to be so distracted. We see this example played out in the early apostolic church, when those who owned land and homes, upon being converted, sold them and gave the profits to the church and its work (see Acts 4:32–35).

This chapter covered a lot of ground, but I think you see it was important ground to cover. It started with the observation that returning gifts and offerings to the Lord is an act of worship that should be prompted by the right motives of sacrifice, repentance, and obedience. While we all recognize our responsibility to contribute to the work of the gospel in life through tithes and offerings, we tend to forget the same duty applies to how we dispose of our earnings when we leave this life behind.

> *Returning gifts and offerings to the Lord is an act of worship that should be prompted by the right motives of sacrifice, repentance, and obedience.*

Thus, gospel-focused estate planning is not only an act of worship but also a test of our obedience. In the Old Testament, there were four categories of offerings that encompassed forty-nine different kinds of specific offerings. In each case, they were given as an act of worship that encompassed things like gratitude, atonement, dedication, and goodwill towards God (see *Seventh-day Adventist Dictionary*, pp. 964–965, for a full list and breakdown of these offerings).

As we near the end of our lives, those of us who have been blessed with material gain and comfort should find joy, like David did, in giving it back to the One who gave it to us. Doing so not only provides a faithful example but also prevents us from burdening our descendants with unearned wealth that stands the chance of interfering with their own obligations to the gospel.

In the next chapter, I will give one more practical example in the form of an interview I once conducted with a couple looking to plan for retirement (yes, stewardship ministry isn't *just* what we do with our money after we die). The next chapter will also start to introduce some key terms and issues of which we need to be aware going forward.

Chapter 5

My Interview with Dean and Pam Nice

Before we get into the actual interview, I need to make you aware of several points that are important to understand going forward. These points will be illustrated in the interview:

(1) The accumulation of assets should begin early in life, but even if you haven't started, it is never too late to begin.

(2) Giving our children a Christian education is always possible if we are committed to do it by God's grace and commit it to Him in prayer.

(3) In making preparations for retirement, it is important that your home be paid off with no outstanding debt obligations.

(4) Retirement transition planning that includes models for contributing to God's work is a thrilling part of entering this state in life.

(5) There is a spiritual question involved in our assets related to the difference between owning property and controlling property.

(6) There are no hard or fast rules for retirement planning. As you'll see, it's even sometimes possible to retire early while still contributing to God's work.

Also, before going further, you will start to notice some technical terms being introduced. Don't let this deter you. You can refer to "Appendix 6—Vocabulary of Terms" online at mystewardship. estate.

And, over the course of a few chapters of this book, many of the technical terms will become clearer.

This interview was conducted on Tuesday, October 24, 2000, while I was working as the director of the Gift Planning & Trust Services Department of the Pacific Union Conference of Seventh-day Adventists in Westlake Village, California. Pam and Dean Nice (not their real names) were a most unusual couple with a high-impact testimony. I met with them at Pam's office in Southern California. As the depiction of this interview progresses, you will hopefully notice a certain passion that illustrates the importance of the points noted above.

Dean: (Introducing his wife, Pam Nice, to Pastor Bob Daum). She's now having a lot of fun here selling real estate. I have always been the type that liked to get involved as the principal [owner of property], so we ended up buying a little fixer-up house and got started that way. Then several years later, when we tapered off on that, she started selling real estate, helping people find a place for them to make a life.

Bob: Tell us about your children.

Dean: We have a daughter, and she's the older one, about 31, and then our son is about 30. Our daughter is married. Our son went through Walla Walla, just got married. So, we're kind of done with educating our children.

Bob: Would you feel comfortable sharing how you became a Seventh-day Adventist, each of you?

Dean: Well, I was born into the church. I was born right here in this town at the old sanitarium up on the hill. I was raised in the Adventist educational system—elementary school, the academy, and college. And my wife was born into the church, too, back in the south—South Carolina.

Bob: Pam, how did you get from South Carolina to way out west here?

Pam: Well, I had to come find a good Adventist husband! There aren't many in South Carolina. I grew up in a small little church—only about thirty members—where there are still only about thirty members. And my parents were the main people; they kind of built the church, and they've always been very giving to their church and think of that as a special place for them.

Dean: We found out later as we learned more about each other that both of our parents had helped establish small churches. My parents helped establish a little church in Cedar Springs, on the other side of Crestline [California], where the lake is now. That church moved and is now the Crestline Seventh-day Adventist Church; they helped to establish that church—purchased the property and that sort of thing—and helped to keep it going for a long time. And her parents have done about the same thing in South Carolina in about the same size church of just about twenty or thirty people.

Bob: Would you please share your story with us about your personal financial and retirement transition planning?

Dean: Yes ... we had accumulated a few properties, kind of by default, because we were really more into the fixing/renovating properties, but we ended up with a little rental business.

Bob: So, you would buy, and fix up, and sell? That was your primary plan?

Dean: Yeah, we kind of got into that, and then we ended up with a little rental business and thought 'Well, maybe that could be our retirement, because we would keep a few properties and live off that the rest of our lives.' So we kind of kept what we thought were the best ones, or maybe the best locations. After 25 years, we learned the better locations, where the values were kind of stable and the tenants were good. And at some point—we've always known that everything belonged to God—but at some point, we just verbalized it and said, "Okay, let's just admit openly that everything, these properties, are part of God's properties and we're just the managers." And even though we knew this all along and had known it all our lives, things kind of seemed to start happening at that point that were kind of amazing, even to us. At one point, we did just say in our minds, 'Now let's keep this as a primary thought, that we were the managers of what actually belongs to God.' And we were impressed to do things that were seemingly not what we would have picked. For instance, we sold properties that we said we'd never sell—this was back in 1989. And we kept other property that we thought we would sell ... and not knowing really why, because we had certain ideas in our mind as to kind of a master plan. We didn't realize it at the time, but as we looked back at the end of the year, we could see these things happening.

Pam: We realized we weren't in control at all. We were being led.

Dean: We felt guided to do something more with our properties than just have them for our retirement. There had to be something more for the properties than us managing them for retirement income for ourselves. We were asking ourselves, 'And then what?' And the end of this story is that these CRTs are the answer for us. That's jumping clear to the end, of course. But we realized that it was not necessary for anyone to do the long hours of heavy labor, especially the elderly; it was not necessary for them to do that. They could convert these into trusts and receive virtually the same amount of money, net money, and not have to do the labor. Labor is good, but we thought that if we could turn our talents into doing something more useful, possibly, in the line of the Maranatha-type projects, we would really like that.

__Bob__: So you're saying that you saw the Charitable Remainder Trusts (CRT) as an opportunity to be freed up from all the work of maintaining and managing the properties and dealing with the tenants so that you could do something more effective for the mission of Christ to seek and to save the lost. I grew up on a farm, and sometimes I hear people liken operating a business to running a dairy. You've always got to be there, like with a restaurant—you've always got to be there in the morning to open up and get things set up, and you've got to be there late at night to close up or whatever the hours are. With a dairy, you've got to milk those cows morning and night, seven days a week.

__Pam__: It's the same way with taking care of tenants.

__Dean__: We felt that we were on duty twenty-four-seven. And when we were gone—we would be hesitant to be gone for even a day or two because usually, that's when something would happen or they'd be trying to get hold of us. But we were hands-on type people, so if something did happen, like a plumbing situation emergency, we would try to have numbers where they would call, and basically, we did that ourselves. So, you can see where we felt dedicated to be there for the tenants.

And we didn't think about this at the time—remember, the CRT idea, we didn't think about how this worked until we actually had done one. So maybe we can give some other people a pre-idea of how this works, because once we figured out that we could get approximately the same amount of money from the trust in cash as we were getting from the rents without having to do any of the manual labor, then we realized that this was a benefit to the charity and to us and possibly to a Maranatha-type project, so all three people benefited. And the church, or the charity, can basically send out a regular cash payment over our joint lifetimes. And the instrument that worked for us was that CRT.

Also, we looked back and realized that times have changed. The rental business isn't what it used to be. The liability, the problems that arise, are amazing, and then there's the employees, the workmen's compensation, and everything you're supposed to have when you hire someone to get some work done on a project. So, by letting the charity handle that, they would either convert to cash or keep it, or whatever the case. That became somebody else's problem who was possibly more able ... a larger management company than we alone could do.

__Bob__: Let me ask you a question: Owning properties—being able to go down to the courthouse and find your deed there in the public record, that has your name on it as the owner—was there a time in your life when that was a particular thrill—when that was a particularly important thing to you that is maybe not as important now?

<u>Dean</u>: I think that's very well put. We used to think—and I'm kind of a do-it-yourselfer type, and that was part of the enjoyment and fun of the whole thing—a feeling of accomplishment. We're very quiet people. We're very to ourselves, as far as our belongings and things. But there was some satisfaction in the fact that these properties were in our name and had our name on them. We could look and see, even though it was very small—we're just a mom-and-pop type of operation, and don't forget that. We're very small, and we're barely able to make it with our retirement. But it's easier by gifting to the charity.

We also have realized that having our name on the properties could be a detriment. We're wide open for lawsuits, and we've never been sued, and we've never sued anybody. But that possibility exists because we're in a very high litigious business, being even just one little rental property, and you're in one of the highest litigious areas you can be in with tenants. The tenant/landlord laws have changed to really favor the tenant, or the little man, and that may be good in some ways. But if it appears, if you have your name on the property, that you're a wealthy person, that may not be. See, we have no other retirement, and being self-employed for twenty-five-plus years, we have to supply our own retirement, and that became an interesting question to us—How do we do this?—because we don't have any retirement fund or anything other than a couple of properties. So I think that we actually went through that phase, as you suggested, that it was tough for us to see our name off and another name go on, but now we just think that's the greatest thing because we want our name off.

<u>Pam</u>: I think, too, once we did one of the trusts, we didn't realize the blessings and everything that we got. It was like so much opened up for us.

<u>Bob</u>: What do you mean? Give some examples.

<u>Dean</u>: We actually felt relieved in some ways because we were getting a little nervous about all those landlords that were being sued, for maybe not having a porch light that worked and somebody slipped, or something that was innocent. But still, the courts would go after whoever they thought might have some money to pay for some of this. So, we would read about this, and thankfully, it never happened to us.

<u>Bob</u>: So, with the CRT, I hear you saying that you are enjoying the benefits of ownership without the liability of ownership.

<u>Dean</u>: It seems like it, indirectly we're still … the owner.

<u>Bob</u>: At least you have some control. Have you thought about the difference between ownership and control?

Dean: Uh-huh ... In the fact that your name is not on the title.

Bob: So, you're not the owner?

Dean: *And* you're not the one that's liable; *and* you're not the one having to do the physical work and labor, which we may have been able to do, but we see people that are very elderly who are still trying to maintain an apartment or a house, and they are becoming basically unable to do that.

Pam: The elderly people we see in that situation have always been in control themselves. And there is the trust factor, wondering if they do this charitable trust, are they really going to be taken care of for the both of the lives of the couple? They are so independent that they can't imagine that somebody could actually do that for them.

Bob: You're saying because of the unknown, they are living with some fears that they haven't yet heard enough information to offset.

Pam: Well, I think they have gotten information that's overwhelming to them, and they can't imagine that it could actually be the case, that somebody could actually do that for them.

Dean: It's a big step, and that was hard for me, harder for me than for my wife. If you can imagine these little houses being like our babies, brought along, we bought them in various states of disrepair and brought them along and nurtured them and spent our time on them, spending eight, ten, twelve hours a day bringing them along and getting them livable, and we had the satisfaction that people could live there.

Pam: There was "sweat equity"!

Dean: And then basically to turn that over to someone else, sort of like your kid's gone off to college, somebody else is all of a sudden in charge, and you're not. That was a very tough step for me.

Bob: Being your own trustee gives you control without the liability of ownership?

Dean: We thought that was the way to go, but then we realized that it's really nice when the charity can take it over completely, and you don't even have to manage the money. And that was another step. So finally, we've come full circle and said, "Okay, now we realize the real benefit of these trust departments." In our case, the CRT was the one that worked best for us, but there are other ones that can work similarly. But that's the one that still gives us an income for both of our lifetimes.

Bob: And because of your young age, you have the potential of the assets in the trust growing tax-free inside the trust and generating a greater income to you because of the growth.

Dean: One of the reasons that this all came about was because of the capital gains. We realized that we'd be giving a fourth of our money to the government, or a third. And this avoided all that so that basically we had 100 percent of our equity going to the charity. And therefore, that was the principal amount that was bringing us our retirement. There was room for error there and still be way ahead of selling it and paying capital gains. Even if things don't go perfect, it's still better than giving a fourth or a third of it up right at the beginning.

<u>Bob</u>: Okay, I hear you saying, Dean and Pam, that part of the motivation initially, perhaps, was the business consideration.

<u>Dean</u>: I think it was, and that all tied in because before this, we had given the properties to the Lord and were just trying to manage them from our viewpoint.

I thought, 'Okay, there's the answer.' When I first studied, I did sort of a self-taught study about CRTs and trusts, and I didn't know anything about them. We knew about real estate, but we had really no knowledge on trusts, and it's really amazing because they really are designed for real estate, I think, in a lot of ways. I literally took about five years and went to seminars and did kind of a self-study with books and reading. It took a while for it to sink in, it really did, I have to say that. But once I got the connection that this could work with a charity, and we could feel like we had done something that the Lord wanted us to do with the property, as well as making a wise business decision, then it all came together for us.

<u>Bob</u>: What has this done for your walk with the Lord, day by day?

<u>Pam</u>: I think it gave us a different perspective and probably realizing again that really everything we have comes from God. And when we look back, we just realize He has led us from the beginning. He really has control over the whole big picture; we didn't.

<u>Dean</u>: We've never really tried to put it into words before, but we would look back at the end of the year, and usually this was done in January. We'd look back and say, "What happened last year?" And then we'd realize that that was a neat thing that happened; we had no idea how neat that was at the time it happened, and what a good business decision that was, and a good management decision that we were led to, not by us, but somehow through the Lord's guidance, and we had no idea at the time.

And we can we look back over the whole period of time, twenty-five-plus years, and see that before we even asked for help, before we even thought about this, that we were being led then, too, really. And that was very inspirational to us, and it did help us to go on to the next level, I think. The next property was easier to do. We have three trusts now, and we have another two or three that we manage ourselves, and we'll probably convert those over. They're all gifted to charity, and we feel good about it, and we feel better about them all the time as time goes on.

They are really an amazing way to go as far as I am concerned. I don't think they're perfect—nothing is perfect—but I'm glad to see the church using them. They work, as a kind of a win-win situation.

Pam: I think it's intimidating for people. It was for us. For a long time, we thought that the only people that would ever do anything like that would be multimillionaires, not just simple people like us. I think we thought it was just set up for the rich and wealthy, but it actually can be more beneficial to someone with limited income and few assets, because it really can help your family and take care of them. They have all types of situations to set up, even for the next generation to help your grandchildren … and maybe to set up a trust fund for educational purposes … So I think the general public or church people just need to be educated that it's not just for the wealthy.

Bob: Excellent point. Now, you have made a full-time occupation for about twenty-five years, if I understand it right, in accumulating and managing and improving houses, and buying and selling. That's a lot of years to do that as a full-time thing. I've known people who are teachers, for example. They get the summer off, and you know the schedule isn't all that terrible during the school year. So, they have time that they can paint and fix up, and they can spend time getting acquainted with the local real estate market and discover those opportunities that are around, and then when they retire, they have a few houses that just are like the frosting on the cake of their retirement. But you've made this a full-time pursuit. Are you comfortable sharing, how many properties have you had in that time?

Dean: It's sort of a personal question, but we don't mind sharing it because it's not an exact amount anyway. We ended up, I would say after the kids were educated, with fewer than ten properties, but we would sell one and pay off another. At one point, we had apartment units, but we realized the flexibility of having the little houses, and it was easier for us to do the rehabilitation and renovating.

We see this happening around us to other owners so often, and we feel sorry and we feel sad because they've done so well. Like you said, they've accumulated a few extra little properties, and they've done well. They've rented them out; they've collected the rent; they've paid them off; they've come to the point where it's paid for or nearly so. And then they become a burden to them because it's a lot of work. We were headed towards the fact that we were going to just keep the rentals forever and live off the rent and die and somebody else would take them over. But that's really a tough way to go because the children have other jobs, and they're not really into taking over the family business.

Bob: I find that most people either want to benefit the Christian educational work of the Seventh-day Adventist Church, or they want to benefit the outreach evangelistic program of the church, or both. Sometimes people want to do both. But you know, those two areas, those are the biggies, aren't they, as far as the Seventh-day Adventist Church is concerned.

We have covered a lot of ground, and I really appreciate it so much. Let me ask you if you can give us just a little bit more of a feel for what took place at the time that you made this decision to turn the ownership over to God. You referred to it at the beginning.

Dean: You know, we think it kind of happened gradually, but there was probably one day when we just sat down and told ourselves this verbally, to each other, and prayed about it, and said, "Okay, here's where we're at now. What do we do?"

Bob: You said that in your prayer to the Lord?

Dean: We actually said that in our prayer to the Lord. I remember it. And we can't say that things just changed overnight. Like we said, we had to look back after things happened.

Bob: But you learned a lot of it by doing it.

Dean: We learned a lot by doing it. We made mistakes; it sounds like we didn't, but we made our share of mistakes. And we don't think about those because overall, that was maybe a learning experience, not a negative thing, in our minds. We don't think about that.

Pam: We can't waste energy on that.

Bob: Right. Well, thank you very much, both of you.

Dean: Let me just tell you one more thing. I just noticed, way back at the beginning—this is just sort of an interesting story—we used to tell our tenants when they'd want to know who the owner was, who to complain to—we had some apartment units, and we would tell them—we were the owners, but we didn't tell them that—that actually, there were several owners, and there wasn't any one single owner—that we were the managers, and that we would take their complaints and deal with them and get them to the right people. But we would never tell them who the owners were.

We would tell ourselves that there were actually *five* owners to the property, and those five owners were: the mortgage company (they were part-owner, even legally); the government (because they're going to get the taxes); the local government (which collects the property taxes and really tells you what you can do as far as zoning laws); and then we were partly owners, I would say my wife was part-owner, and she would say I was part-owner; and then the fifth person was God. He was the owner of all properties; everything belongs to God. So, we would tell people, if they would ask us, that there were about five owners, so we would literally disperse their thoughts of going to the owner and trying to cause a ruckus or have a complaint by using that method. And through the years, we realized that God is really the owner, and we're just the manager, even more prominently. But this was something we used to tell ourselves way back in the beginning when we first owned units twenty-five-plus years ago.

<u>Bob</u>: But I gather that the concept that God really owns all you have is reality for you now.

<u>Dean</u>: Yes, we didn't really think about this much. We went on just trying to raise our family and educating them, and just trying to put food on the table, and really had very little cash flow because we were the type to try to let this thing grow. We started from nothing. We had no help; we weren't given anything by any parents or rich uncles. We started with virtually zero when we got married. We didn't know how we were really going to make our first rent payment, that sort of thing—we actually rented for a little bit.

<u>Bob</u>: That's beautiful. Thank you—both of you—for sharing from your heart.

You see, dear reader, the possibilities for your life's goals and will-plan are only limited by legal constraints and subject to the leading and blessing of God.

One of my all-time favorite Christian songs that I love to read and sing is "I Cannot Tell Why":

> I cannot tell why He whom angels worship
> Should set His love upon the souls of men,
> Or why as Shepherd He should seek the wanderers,
> To bring them back, they know not how nor when.
> But this I know that He was born of Mary
> When Bethlehem's manger was His only home,
> And that He lived at Nazareth and labored;
> And so the Savior, Savior of the world, has come.
>
> I cannot tell how silently He suffered
> As with His peace He graced this place of tears,
> Nor how His heart upon the cross was broken,
> The crown of pain to three and thirty years.

But this I know He heals the broken hearted
And stays our sin and calms our lurking fear,
And lifts the burden from the heavy laden;
For still the Savior, Savior of the world, is here.

I cannot tell how He will win the nations,
How He will claim His earthly heritage,
How satisfy the needs and aspirations
Of east and west, of sinner and of sage.
But this I know all flesh shall see His glory,
And He shall reap the harvest He has sown,
And some glad day His sun will shine in splendor
When He the Savior, Savior of the world, is known.

I cannot tell how all the lands shall worship,
When at His bidding every storm is stilled,
Or who can say how great the jubilation
When all our hearts with love for Him are filled.
But this I know the skies shall sound His praises,
Ten thousand thousand human voices sing,
And earth to heaven, and heaven to earth will answer,
At last the Savior, Savior of the world, is King!

(Fullerton, W.Y. "I Cannot Tell Why." *Seventh-day Adventist Hymnal*, Review & Herald Publ. Assn., Hagerstown, MD, 1985, song 255.)

Would you now join me in prayer? Oh, my Father, with a humble heart that is full of praises to You for Your gift of Jesus, Your only Son—and for entrusting to these mortals His message and mission in this darkened place. Please shine the countenance of Jesus through my face today so that all who see me will long to know You more and love You more. I pray, Father, in the name of Jesus, asking for Your guiding light to give me clarity of thought on planning today to care for tomorrow, while I daily trust You for my financial and material security and seek enhanced spiritual fulfillment in Christ at all cost to self. Thank you, dear Lord. In Jesus' name, amen.

Dear reader, this comes to you with my prayer that you will take the journey of planning today for tomorrow—that your plan design will indeed be approved in the eyes of heaven.

> And the congregation of those who believed were of one heart and soul; and not one *of them* claimed that anything belonging to him was his own, but all things were common property to them.

And with great power the apostles were giving testimony to the resurrection of the Lord Jesus, and abundant grace was upon them all. For there was not a needy person among them, for all who were owners of land or houses would sell them and bring the proceeds of the sales and lay *them* at the apostles' feet, and they would be distributed to each to the extent that any had need. (Acts 4:32–35, NASB)

Chapter 6

Family Support and Inheritance Plans: Important Lessons for Today's Relationships with God and Family

As the author of this book, I have invited Pastor Scott Christiansen to be the co-author of this chapter, and have set his contributions in quotation marks. He writes, "This chapter provides a 'big picture' review of Heaven's perspective on family support and our inheritance planning—from Scripture and selected counsels of Ellen G. White. In this process, we look at pertinent socio-economic systems of the Old Testament; also, the New Testament and the end-time [modern] era. In doing this, we may just find more harmony, more wisdom, and more depth than we had previously read into Ellen White's writings on this subject."

I saw a bumper sticker on a huge motor home that read something like, "Driving my children's inheritance." There are definite cultural expectations today that say, "All I have belongs to my children; if no children, then to siblings, cousins, aunts, uncles, etc." This is not in harmony with God's design. Again, the great controversy is very active in the area of creating a will-and-trust plan for the distribution of my assets—as it relates to my family. That is probably the reason Ellen White instructed us to be reformers in the making of such plans (see White, *Testimonies for the Church*, vol. 4, pp. 482, 483). This naturally raises a particular question:

Lesson #1: What Do I Owe My Family?

What do I owe my children? The very first thing I owe to my children is to provide a home atmosphere that feels secure and safe to them. That begins by having a mom and dad who genuinely love and trust each other. In this connection, you might like to take a test on the quality of your relationship with your spouse, or with Christ if you're not married. I've included a test-form in this chapter and the personal experience my wife and I had with it. The next most important thing we owe to our children is to make a constant effort to convince them that they are loved, wanted, and needed in the home enterprise.

> *Mary Jo and I were both raised on farms, which gave us a real sense of being loved, wanted, and needed. Raising our children in the 1960s and 1970s, we determined to do all we could to help them know they were loved, wanted, and needed while raising them in town in Central California and in the suburbs of Los Angeles. And we are greatly blessed by the outcomes.*

In the early 1900s, the USA was a rural agrarian society in which only a small portion of the population lived in towns and cities. In that era—on average, according to the United States Department of Agriculture, a family could expect each child to add $4,000 to the net worth of the family enterprise by the age of eighteen. With that kind of economic impact on the household, it was natural and easy for children to feel needed and useful with a purpose in life.

Updated in recent years, the USDA numbers for a two-parent home are based on various household income levels. Here are three examples (the numbers are annual averages of household income and costs of raising a child to age seventeen in each of three income levels):

Household Income Level—Cost to Age Seventeen

$38,000—$169,000

$80,000—$235,000

$180,000—$390,000

Therefore, we can understand it is much easier to help a child know he or she is needed when the parents are being enriched financially by the child's participation in the family enterprise. It is much more challenging when the child is a costly drain rather than an economic contributor.

Mary Jo and I were both raised on farms, which gave us a real sense of being loved, wanted, and needed. Raising our children in the 1960s and 1970s, we determined to do all we could to help them know they were loved, wanted, and needed while raising them in town in Central California and in the suburbs of Los Angeles. And we are greatly blessed by the outcomes. No small part of the outcome for our children is that Mary Jo was a full-time mother, homemaker, and helpmate; I was a workaholic.

It would be a good thing if you asked yourself, 'Is there a word from the Lord on how to do this?' Yes—more on this later.

Scott Christiansen suggests, "The customs of the world have become the standard expectations of how money and possessions are distributed to family members after a death, which is contrary to Heaven's plan."

Family support is an important issue in planning today to take care of tomorrow, especially when there is a special need of support, such as an adult child who is mentally or physically disabled—unable to support oneself.

For example, I've known and worked with cases of such disabilities due to mental or physical limitations. A Special Needs Trust, also known as a Supplemental Needs Trust—to supplement but not jeopardize governmental support systems—may be created. Such a trust is normally funded according to provisions included in the will or trust distribution plan, to be implemented when death claims the parents or other loved ones who may devise such a plan.

There are other cases where a grown child's disabilities are of his or her own making—where alcohol or drug addictions (past or present) have left these loved ones with a significant disability. In cases such as this, the question always arises as to whether a support mechanism will help the person or lead to further abuses. In such cases, trusts that are managed by a third party working under very specific guidelines may adequately address the situation (more on trusts and other instruments later in this book).

This is one example of a Give-it-Twice Trust, in which the trust provides benefits to family while needed and then goes to the Lord's work upon the termination of the trust.

In many cases where I've served as a consultant, the children are doing better than the parents ever did and have no need of depending on their parents' estate. On the other side of that coin, in far too many cases, the children never quit depending on their parents' estate. I've observed firsthand the cases of parents helping their children by paying off their credit card debt time after time, to prevent them from going through personal bankruptcy, or sending them and their families an allowance of up to $300 each month—and that was in the 1970s!

However, water still runs downhill. In other words, we prefer to take the path of least resistance. Likewise, the spending habits that cause people to get deeply into debt with credit cards never are abated when they are rescued with no effort on their part. Thus, they repeat the same spending patterns over and over again. We found that most people have not learned to deny self enough to live within their income.

Mary Jo and I have conducted many family finance seminars that we called "Bible Principles for Personal Money Management in Chaotic Times." We've done them at churches and camp meetings. We usually made ourselves available for personal, confidential counseling at the homes of those who made a request. We've been amazed how often we found homes where the people felt they could get along just fine on their income if it was just $200 or $300 per month more than it is. In all of those cases, the people were not being faithful to the Lord. I always say 80 percent of our income (after 10 percent tithe and 10 percent offerings) goes much farther with God's blessings than 100 percent goes while living under His curse because we have stolen what is His; also, if we don't return God's tithe to Him, the devil will collect it in one way or another, such as with self-destroying habits or other forms of carelessness.

Inheritance Planning—What About Accumulated Assets? One man of significant affluence and influence in the church whom I know has helped each of his children with education and to get established in their own home and business. He said if his children cannot make it with the help he has given them, they would not be helped with whatever they might receive at his death—that all he has is going to God's work when that time comes.

<u>Author Scott Christiansen offers helpful insights for this context:</u>

"It's been said that Ellen White's counsel to God's church on the subject of financial management during the time of the end – particularly the design of our Last Will and Testament plan – is more restrictive than was the Old Testament system—at least as regards leaving assets to family at death.

"Perhaps it is exactly because of this perception that we do a relatively poor job of following the counsel we were given. Perhaps we perceive it as too out of step with the worldly culture in which we live. Or perhaps we think it too radical for a prudent person to follow. But–and this is a big "but"—is our perception of what was said reflective of the actual counsel we were given?

"Tradition says that our accumulated assets should pass to our families – to our spouse and children or to our brother and sisters and their children.

In fact, if you die without a will, there is a formula used in most states to determine the distribution of your goods to family members based on how close the family relations are to you. The expectation that a person will give their goods to their family is very strong. In fact, the customs of the world have become the standard in how money and possessions are distributed to family members after a death.

"But are the expectations of the world also the instructions of God. Perhaps you are asking, if God has a different plan, what are we to do about the disparity between what heirs expect and what God instructs? Won't this expectation result in them perceiving that we don't care for them? Perhaps you further ask, what benefits my children more, giving all to them, giving nothing to them or giving them something in-between? And, is there an estate design that honors the Lord and helps my kids?

"If you are asking any of the above questions, or anything like them, you are on the right track. Or at least, you are on the right track if you are taking these questions directly to the Lord believing He can and will give you individual instructions about this matter, and studying them out. "This whole question of what duty we owe to whom, and the degree to which we are in tension with expectations from society or family or God, is a very difficult question. Let's take the subject up by first looking at the tensions and expectations as reflected in the writings of Ellen White. In fact, let's ask a provocative question: On this subject, was she a bomb-throwing radical or a pragmatic conservative?

"Ellen White wrote quite a bit about our management of the resources God has entrusted to us. Some of the things she said ruffled a good number of feathers and got her branded as quite a radical, at least by some. For the most part, she unsettled (and still unsettles) some folks by saying, in a number of different ways, that all that we have belongs to the Lord (both before and after our death) and that we should not burden ourselves with wealth or excess possessions but instead should invest unreservedly in completing the Lord's work. She went so far as to say that we should inquire of the Lord if He wants us to sell our houses and other major possessions and that, when it comes to planning our estates, the Lord's work should come first—before family and friends.

"Members of the church have, by and large, not accepted her counsel on this subject, rejecting it as too large a departure from the norm prevailing in the world. This rejection seems to beg the question: Were her comments blatantly radical or were they quietly pragmatic? The answer is not obvious, probably because a person's answer very much depends on whether they have accepted the prevailing deception in our society – the deception that says that a person should accumulate as much wealth and possessions as they can and that our worth in society is measured in large part by our possessions. In this paradigm, giving up the pursuit of wealth and possessions makes no sense at all. After all, it would mean dropping out of a race everyone else is trying to win, and that would mean being wildly out of step with everyone else. Further, this deception says that we should give all we can to our children so they have the best chance of winning this same race. To a vain and selfish world focused on grasping as much as possible, Ellen White's counsel is beyond radical – it is crazed.

"Of course, things of God seem increasingly crazed to a world that is under the sway of Satan. For all of history, Satan has established false gods for each age. The false gods of our age seem to be mammonism and selfishness. If we worship (or even highly regard) the false gods of this age, then Ellen White's counsel will seem to us to be radical and unsound. People who lean toward these false gods will, in fact, resent the counsel being brought up. Some will use it as an excuse to exit the company of God's believers and this is a tragedy because we are told in the Spirit of Prophecy that in the last days our possessions will weigh us down and those that hold on to them will either perish with them or will fail to use them for the Lord while they can – a mistake they will achingly regret.

"If you accept that we truly can see the events of the last days unfolding and can see the fulfillment of prophecy taking place around us, then the task of escaping the deceptions and false gods of this age becomes a critical priority. We know that in these last days members of the church will move closer to the practices of the apostolic age, where we are sacrificing much and selling possessions in order to close the work of the Lord.

"When you step back from modern society for a moment and consider that our global culture is steeped in mammonism, and when you consider that those who are in God's church in these end-times will be wrenched away from this global religion, then the counsel we are given from the pen of inspiration takes on a whole different cast. Instead of seeming excessive or restrictive, Ellen White's counsel if anything seems conservative, urging us toward conservative and gradual reforms and changes in practice that move us progressively away from the world's practice of exalting money and possessions and toward the apostolic model of advancing the Gospel message, especially through the offering of our resources to God. In the end, Ellen White was not a radical on the subject of our relationship with our resources in the end days—she was a gentle pragmatist. So just how relatively gentle and conservative is this counsel from Sister White? Here is a core sampling: 'The Lord requires that those to whom He has lent talents of means make a right use of them, having the advancement of His cause prominent. Every other consideration should be inferior to this' (White, *Testimonies for the Church*, volume 2, p. 659)."

Scott continues with more valuable insights:

"*Back to the central question of what our obligation is to our family,* and how that fits in with our obligation to our Lord. Let's start with making sure we are using the right metric. If we use the right metric – if we measure the right thing – then it is far more likely that the actions we take based on that measurement will be right actions. Consider this as your metric: Will what you provide for your family lead them into a closer relationship with Christ?

"Take, for instance, the provisions you make for your children. Each child – whether still very young or an adult – is very different. Some children have mental or physical disabilities that require special care throughout life as discussed earlier in this chapter (both authors of this book have a family member in this situation).

"These special cases aside, let's look at the vast bulk of typical heirs – children who have reached adulthood and are making their way in the world. What is our duty toward such children? The answer, in its most succinct form, is that our duties cannot be expressed in dollars or goods. Our duties instead are to do everything we can throughout our entire lives and in our estate planning to point our children toward Christ. Here, then, is the critical metric: Does what we provide to our children in our estate planning move them closer to Christ? And, are we simultaneously fulfilling our obligations to our children and to God? Do we put God first or do our children become our idols?

"These are deep – and deeply personal – questions which parents can only truly resolve on their knees by persistently seeking the will of the Lord. And – good news! – when you come to know the will of the Lord, you will also come to know peace in regard to your estate planning. Such peace is well worth the effort you will expend on persistently seeking the will of the Lord.

"For whatever reason, it seems that most adult children who inherit some or most or all of their parent's estate break down into three groups. Let's take a look at each of the three groups and at one or two Spirit of Prophecy quotes that deal with each. Frequently there are cases where the adult children of a couple are making their way in the world and are financially more successful than the parents ever were. In this case, what counsel do we have on the duty of the parents to these children and to the Lord in preparing their estate?

"When it comes time to make your Last Will inheritance plan, it really is a giant struggle if you give it significant thought rather than simply adopting the world's default plan."

I greatly appreciate this significant contribution by Scott Christiansen. Now we'll continue with some of my experiences.

When I was a professional financial planner, I had clients who frequently allowed their adult children to continue depending on them for support. This can mean parents, time and again, step in to make credit card payments for one (or more) of their children or intervene with financial support to prevent the child from going through bankruptcy. What counsel do we have on the duty of the parents to their children in such cases?

In working with many family situations, and for whatever value you might find in it, my experiences suggest that the struggles to make decisions on how to distribute your accumulated assets may be made easier if you have more information. Information often drives a decision. For example, this decision may involve having you explore your personal aspects of the business and technical issues and options to be considered. Probably the most difficult struggle is the emotional-spiritual area. Accordingly, we are presenting material about the spiritual dimension of Christian estate planning for your prayerful consideration.

Here is special insight from the Spirit of Prophecy:

> If parents, while they live, would assist their children to help themselves, it would be better than to leave them a *large amount* at death. Children who are left to rely principally upon their own exertions make better men and women, and are better fitted for practical life than those children who have depended upon their father's estate. The children left to depend upon their own resources generally prize their abilities, improve their privileges, and cultivate and direct their faculties to accomplish a purpose in life. They frequently develop characters of industry, frugality, and moral worth, which lie at the foundation of success in the Christian life. Those children for whom parents do the most, frequently feel under the least obligation toward them.... Parents have shifted their stewardship upon their children. (White, *Testimonies for the Church*, vol. 3, pp. 122, 123, emphasis added)

The struggle to decide how to design your last will-plan often revolves around how much to leave to your children and how much to leave to the Lord's work. We all know a "large amount" is more dangerous than it is good for our children.

What is a large amount? I never try to define that for anyone. One told me $1 million is not too large for their children, while others have felt $100,000 is way too much, and some have said $10,000 is about right. It is a very personal, individual decision to be bathed in surrendered prayer for the very best outcome.

However, I question the wisdom and value of leaving enough to our children to make them independently wealthy because of the warning Jesus gave us: "Then said Jesus to His disciples, 'Truly I say to you, That a rich man shall hardly enter into the kingdom of heaven. And again I say to you, It is easier for a camel to go through the eye of a needle, than for a rich man to enter into the kingdom of God.'" (Matt. 23,24, AKJV; see also Mark 10:24, 25).

Two factors that help determine how you design your plan are:

1. If a member of your family has "special needs"
2. What you parents have already done to help your children in their quest to get established in a home and career.

Some have set up plans to fund projects of ministry with one of their children participating in the direction for each of the projects—matching a project with the interests and talents of each respective child.

By the end of life, most Christians are concerned about inheritance goals for their

> *I had clients who frequently allowed their adult children to continue depending on them for support. This can mean parents, time and again, step in to make credit card payments for one (or more) of their children or intervene with financial support to prevent the child from going through bankruptcy. What counsel do we have on the duty of the parents to their children in such cases?*

children when planning for an absence of parental influence, hoping and praying to be **able to make the following transfers:**

- Parents' values of love to God and for mankind
- Parents' love for eternity
- Parents' values of initiative, integrity, and industry
- Enough of the parents' money and possessions to send them a certain message of care and not enough to neutralize the above three values in them.
- Transfers to the Lord's work to honor the above values and magnify Him as the real owner of all we have—hastening the advent of eternity so we don't have to sleep so long awaiting His physical presence.

The Very Best Legacy Parents Can Leave to Their Children: "The very best legacy which parents can leave their children is a knowledge of useful labor and the example of a life characterized by disinterested benevolence" (White, *Testimonies for the Church*, vol. 3, p. 399). [Today, we view disinterested benevolence as "gifts being made to God as an act of worship in the spirit of thanksgiving and loving trust in Him with no strings attached"].

The Only Three Valuable Uses of Money: "By such a life they show the true value of money, that it is only to be appreciated for the good that it will accomplish in relieving their own wants and the necessities of others, and in advancing the cause of God." (*Ibid.*)

Scott Christiansen begins to conclude his thoughts in this area: "Finally, there are the children who have not out-earned their parents and who live modest, somewhat financially strained lives but who are stable and responsible. What counsel do we have on our duty in planning our estates with regard to such children? And finally, there is the question of what our duty is to our surviving spouse. This is a fairly straightforward question if you are still married to your spouse and you are both of one mind about doing the Lord's will. In such a case, the wills of both spouses will specify that the entire estate passes into the hands of the surviving spouse. However, in cases where there have been two or more marriages or where there has been one marriage but the spouse is far from being of the same mind in regard to doing the Lord's will, then the situation is far more complex and requires a prayerful consideration and deliberate will design. I've only known of one case in which one wished to follow God's will in this matter and the other spouse wanted to leave all to their children. The last I knew, they were exploring the concept of each one making their own separately different will even though their assets were held jointly. Sounds like a major mess.

"Just as frequently there are cases where adult children never stopped depending on their parents for support. This can mean that parents time and again step in to make credit card payments for one (or more) of their children, or intervene with financial support to prevent the child from going through bankruptcy. What counsel do we have on the duty of the parents to their children in such cases?

Fortunately, we have some guidance for situations such as this.

The Spirit of Prophecy offers financial help for families:

> **Balancing the Budget**—Many, very many, have not so educated themselves that they can keep their expenditures within the limit of their income. They do not learn to adapt themselves to circumstances, and they borrow and borrow again and again and become overwhelmed in debt, and consequently they become discouraged and disheartened.
>
> **Keep a Record of Expenditures**—Habits of self-indulgence or a want of tact and skill on the part of the wife and mother may be a constant drain upon the treasury; and yet that mother may think she is doing her best because she has never been taught to restrict her wants or the wants of her children and has never acquired skill and tact in household matters. Hence one family may require for its support twice the amount that would suffice for another family of the same size.
>
> All should learn how to keep accounts. Some neglect this work as nonessential, but this is wrong. All expenses should be accurately stated. (White, *The Adventist Home*, p. 374)

Scott Christiansen concludes his thoughts on this topic:

"What is our duty to our children? Well, when the counsel is taken all together, we find that our duty is overwhelmingly a spiritual one and that this duty is upon us each day of our lives, with our estate planning being only the capstone of our lifelong spiritual efforts. What we also find is that our duty to our Lord calls us to actions and commitments that are far, far away from the prevailing practice of designing a will that divides our assets among our closest relatives. In fact, doing so would in some

cases be spiritually harmful to the recipient of the accumulated assets." (emphasis added)

What is the bottom line? God calls us to be different from the rest of the world by honoring Him first and foremost and thereby be an example to our loved ones and the world. Again, is there word from the Lord on having a godly home? We have touched on it briefly. Here is a little bit more.

The first thing now is to give you a test on the quality of your marital relationship. My precious Savior gave me a beautiful woman to wed on June 9, 1959. Mary Jo (Moore) Daum has been a wonderful bride to me, with no hesitation at any time. Our oneness continues to get better with each passing day.

Here is a significant way to examine the second most important relationship in our life.

TEST—Rating the Quality of My Marital Relationship

I wish to rate the quality of my oneness with my spouse on a scale of 1 to 10, with 1 being "disaster" and 10 being "no room for improvement." If you are *not* married, then rate your relationship to Christ. Does your rating also relate to the precious bride of Christ, the church?

This is for your own personal information; and you are not being asked to share your scores with anyone else.

___Mental

___Mutual Loving Trust

___Mutual Grateful Loyalty

___Social

___Physical

___Parenting

___Spiritual

___Financial

___Responsibility/Accountability

___Integrity

___Industry

___Initiative

___Unconditional Commitment to Each Other—"Until Death Separates Us"

In my ministry of counseling people on their personal finances, I tell them, "If you are not one financially and spiritually, you cannot be one."

In 1981, Mary Jo and I attended an event where the Sabbath School class did this kind of relationship testing exercise. Since my philosophy is there is always room for improvement, that was a guide to my scoring the quality of my relationship with the bride of my youth. I scored 9 on every item except "Spiritual," where I scored 7.

A few months later, Mary Jo was with me when we drove some distance to a ministry appointment for my work. Always being openly transparent and totally honest with each other, we compared notes about this test. We discovered each of us had scored it the same on all items for the same reasons. We focused on the reason for our weak relationship in the spiritual realm of life; we agreed it was because I related to her as if I was the missionary being her savior while she was the heathen. This was extremely painful for me to accept as reality.

I was reminded of the Bible admonition to married men to "live considerately with [your wives], with an intelligent recognition [of the marriage relation], honoring the woman as [physically] the weaker, but [realizing that you] are joint heirs of the grace (God's unmerited favor) of life, in order that your prayers may not be hindered and cut off. [Otherwise you cannot pray effectively.]" (1 Peter 3:7, AMPC). I was blown away and made a commitment to stop thinking of my wife as spiritually inferior to me. This was the most helpful text that became my constant guide and stay to get me through the crisis.

I was especially motivated at first by both a great desire that my prayers to God not be hindered and a great love for my beloved life mate. As I constantly sought the Lord for His help, my motivation was more and more focused on my loving concern for Mary Jo and my mistreatment of her.

Again, is there word from the Lord on how to create a godly home for our families?

Let us prayerfully consider selected Bible passages that are pertinent to this discussion:

God said, the two shall become one: "*Some* Pharisees came to Jesus, testing Him and asking, 'Is it lawful *for a man* to divorce his wife for any reason at all?' And He answered and said, 'Have you not read that He who created *them* from the beginning MADE THEM MALE AND FEMALE, and said, "*FOR THIS REASON A MAN SHALL LEAVE HIS FATHER AND MOTHER AND BE JOINED TO HIS WIFE, AND THE TWO SHALL BECOME ONE FLESH*"? So, they are no longer two, but one flesh'" (Matt. 19:3-6, NASB, emphasis added).

"God created man in His own image, in the image of God He created him; male and female He created them" (Gen. 1:27, NASB).

"For this reason a man shall leave his father and his mother, and be joined to his wife; and they shall become one flesh" (Gen. 2:24, NASB).

Marital Oneness—Why One? "But did He not make *them* one, Having a remnant of the Spirit? And why one? He seeks godly offspring. Therefore take heed to your spirit, And let none deal treacherously with the wife of his youth" (Mal. 2:15, NKJV).

God Hates Divorce. "And did not God make [you and your wife] one [flesh]? Did not One make you and preserve your spirit alive? And why [did God make you two] one? Because He sought a godly offspring [from your union]. Therefore take heed to yourselves, and let no one deal treacherously and be faithless to the wife of his youth. For the Lord, the God of Israel, says: I hate divorce and marital separation and him who covers his garment [his wife] with violence. Therefore keep a watch upon your spirit [that it may be controlled by My Spirit], that you deal not treacherously and faithlessly [with your marriage mate]" (Mal. 2:15, 16, AMPC).

A Word to Husbands, Wives, Children, Servants (Employees): "Wives, be subject ("submit" in the KJV) to your husbands [subordinate and adapt yourselves to them], as is right *and* fitting *and* your proper duty in the Lord [personal aside: I understand the word "submit" really means to "voluntarily yield in love," and in our genuine sense of partnership, that has become a mutual habit for us]. Husbands, love your wives [be affectionate and sympathetic with them] and do not be harsh *or* bitter *or* resentful toward them. Children, obey your parents in everything, for this is pleasing to the Lord. Fathers, do not provoke *or* irritate *or* fret your children [do not be hard on them or harass them], lest they become discouraged *and* sullen *and* morose *and* feel inferior *and* frustrated. [Do not break their spirit.] Servants, obey in everything those who are your earthly masters, not only when their eyes are on you as pleasers of men, but in simplicity of purpose [with all your heart] because of your reverence for the Lord *and* as a sincere expression of your devotion to Him. Whatever may be your task, work at it heartily (from the soul), as [something done] for the Lord and not for men, Knowing [with all certainty] that it is from the Lord [and not from men] that you will receive the inheritance which is your [real] reward. [The One Whom] you are actually serving [is] the Lord Christ (the

Messiah). "For he who deals wrongfully will [reap the fruit of his folly and] be punished for his wrongdoing. And [with God] there is no partiality [no matter what a person's position may be, whether he is the slave or the master]" (Col. 3:18–25, AMPC).

"Husbands, love your wives, just as Christ also loved the church and gave Himself up for her, so that He might sanctify her, having cleansed her by the washing of water with the word, that He might present to Himself the church in all her glory, having no spot or wrinkle or any such thing; but that she would be holy and blameless. So husbands ought also to love their own wives as their own bodies. He who loves his own wife loves himself; for no one ever hated his own flesh, but nourishes and cherishes it, just as Christ also does the church, because we are members of His body. FOR THIS REASON, A MAN SHALL LEAVE HIS FATHER AND MOTHER AND SHALL BE JOINED TO HIS WIFE, AND THE TWO SHALL BECOME ONE FLESH" (Ephesians 5:25–31, NASB emphasis added).

> *I knew it was not my place to demand that my wife and children submit to me as the grand authority in a harsh spirit and tone. Rather, I felt I must initiate the quality and character of our relationship in which she would desire to "voluntarily yield in love."*

Marriage—Like Christ and the Church? "Wives, be subject to your own husbands, as to the Lord. For the husband is the head of the wife, as Christ also is the head of the church, He Himself being the Savior of the body. But as the church is subject to Christ, so also the wives ought to be to their husbands in everything" (Eph. 5:22–24, NASB1995).

"Fathers, do not provoke your children to anger, but bring them up in the discipline and instruction of the Lord. Slaves, be obedient to those who are your masters according to the flesh, with fear and trembling, in the sincerity of your heart, as to Christ; not by way of eye-service, as people-pleasers, but as slaves of Christ, doing the will of God from the heart. With goodwill render service, as to the Lord, and not to people, knowing that whatever good thing each one does, he will receive this back from the Lord, whether slave or free" (Eph. 6:4–8).

We noted earlier that God hates divorce. We also know it is impossible to separate personal finance from our personal faith relationship with Christ.

According to surveys of lawyers, the cause of most divorces is conflict over finances. Therefore, I have endeavored to minimize my strongly held opinions in our decisions about the management of our family finances.

I knew it was not my place to demand that my wife and children submit to me as the grand authority in a harsh spirit and tone. Rather, I felt I must initiate the quality and character of our relationship in which she would desire to "voluntarily yield in love."

My wife has always had an excellent analytical mind and an amazing skill to look ahead and anticipate future results of our decisions being made now. Her strong-minded determination about expressing those thoughts caused me to take offense until after I began to develop this set of understandings. She is methodical, and I'm impetuous—maybe like the apostle Peter. One day, I shared that with a brother in the church, and he said, "I pity your wife."

Obstacles to Oneness

In my long life of working with people in business and then in ministry, I've observed certain obstacles that often prevent husband and wife from becoming one:

- Personality clash—a combination of temperaments that are not compatible with each other or converted to Christ.
- Low level of commitment—50/50 vs. 100/100; God calls for unity, not equality.
- Deficit spending—conflicts over money are the primary cause of divorce in the vast majority of cases.
- Unshared expectations.
- Untamed tongue.
- Absence of a plan to make the difficult decisions in life—when there is a difference of strongly held opinions.

The overarching solution to any obstacle is to pray to God as our Father and the Lord of our lives in full surrender of ourselves to Him—always in the spirit of Christ when He prayed to the Father, telling Him the outcome He preferred and then saying, "Thy will be done" (see Matt. 26:36–42). Other components to this include:

- A daily new birth in Christ.
- A daily seeking of a fresh baptism of the Holy Spirit.

- Partaking of the divine nature of Christ, alive in the heart of each one.

The most important goal is to love Jesus and His second coming (see Heb. 9:28). A second goal is to constantly reveal the likeness of Christ's character and labor for the enlargement of His kingdom. This includes:

- A surrender heart, mind, and will to God, along with body, soul, and spirit.
- Prayer—individually and jointly.

Perspective A— "It requires more grace, more stern discipline of character, to work for God in the capacity of mechanic, merchant, lawyer, or farmer, carrying the precepts of Christianity into the ordinary business of life, than to labor as an acknowledged missionary in the open field. It requires a strong spiritual nerve to bring religion into the workshop and the business office, sanctifying the details of everyday life, and ordering every transaction according to the standard of God's word. But this is what the Lord requires" (White, *Counsels to Parents, Teachers, and Students*, p. 279).

Perspective B—While we are not doing a study on personality temperaments here, we need to touch on the subject a bit in the context of interpersonal relationships in the home circle. Indeed, it can be a great source of difficulty in all relationships with other people and the institutions to which we relate in the normal flow of life. There are many reasons that contribute to interpersonal difficulties. At least part of the solution may be an understanding of the **Dominant Spiritual Struggle** of each type of personality makeup. Dr. Gordon Botting suggests the following definitions of the Dominant Spiritual Struggle for each temperament type:

Powerful Choleric: Sovereignty of God—the need to learn to trust and depend on the Lord rather than being God in other people's lives.

Popular Sanguine: Practicing spiritual disciplines such as Bible study and prayer.

Peaceful Phlegmatic: Self-worth—the need to constantly be reminded that "I really am a gifted child of God."

Perfect Melancholy: Fairness of God—why does God permit suffering? "We are just bystanders in the Great Controversy between Christ and Satan."

The following Spirit of Prophecy paragraph has proven to be a most helpful, revolutionary insight to my benefit over and over again, both at home in my work:

> **Varied Temperaments Must Blend**—It is in the order of God that persons of varied temperament should associate together. When this is the case, each member of the household should sacredly regard the feelings and respect the rights of the others. By this means mutual consideration and forbearance will be cultivated, prejudices will be softened, and rough points of character smoothed. Harmony may be secured, and the blending of the varied temperaments may be a benefit to each. (White, *Adventist Home*, p. 427)

Scott Christiansen adds some contemporary insight, interspersed with more inspired counsel, which is also helpful and beneficial:

"As we look at the three periods – Old Testament, New Testament, and Last Days, you might find it helpful to keep in mind that the common thread running through each era is that all we are and all we have belong to Him absolutely—whether we are dead or alive, in poverty or plenty. "Of the three periods, this perspective is least obvious and least accepted in our current time, but it is no less true. In fact, in these last days, it is true now more than ever, since the "god" of this era that the Lord is forced to compete with for our allegiance is the god of money and possessions—mammonism. May those who read this have or develop born-again ears to hear, born-again eyes to see, and a born-again heart to understand.

"If you wish, you could now read our 'Comparative Grid: Summary of Socio-Economic Systems of the Old Testament, Apostolic Era, and End Time Church, which will give you a quick overview of the three eras we will look at. You may find it listed on the Table of Contents.

Looking first at the Old Testament system, we find that God's ownership – of everything – was explicitly and implicitly acknowledged both in private and publicly. Property was conveyed from God to tribes and families, and was to stay within those tribes and families through the Jubilee system and through restrictions on inter-tribal marriages. "Sales" of property were conducted only under detailed and restrictive conditions given by God. 'Sales' were in fact more like revocable time-limited leases. Through these conditions, God supplied each family with the resources necessary to generate a living, either through the production of food, feed, and fiber, or through the collection of rent.

"This system, ordained by God, limited economic interdependence and strengthened the family unit by making them primary producers who were largely self-sufficient. The disparity between this system and the socio-economic system of the current day is massive, and that is no small thing because the Old Testament socio-economic system, ordained by God, was the best that man has known, or at least the best since the Garden of Eden.

"Ellen White speaks to this in the following reference—'In God's plan for Israel every family had a home on the land, with sufficient ground for tilling. Thus were provided both the means and the incentive for a useful, industrious, and self-supporting life. And no devising of men has ever improved upon that plan. To the world's departure from it is owing, to a large degree, the poverty and wretchedness that exist today.' (*Ministry of Healing*, p.183)

"One of the deceptions of the current age of mammonism is that we have progressed since ancient days – that our ability to accumulate wealth and gain luxury has put us above the generations that went before us. But, if we measure the age and our lives by the degree to which God is central to all things, we find we live in profound impoverishment. "Ellen White has a good deal more to say about the Old Testament socio-economic system and if you are not familiar with this subject and her comments on it, we have included a generous set of Scriptural and Spirit of Prophecy quotes and references in regard to this system.

"Of course, with man becoming ever more distant from God and ever more rebellious, and with the intermingling and intermarriage between Israelites and heathen, the plan He gave in the Old Testament was discarded long before apostolic times. The fact is that the jubilee system does not function well in a more heterogenous (mixed) society where there is not universal recognition of the system; if one side of a transaction does not recognize the jubilee system, then it necessarily breaks down. Fortunately, we were given another economic system in the New Testament—the apostolic model.

"In the apostolic era, the members of the young church recognized the spiritual burden that accompanied greed or the pursuit of property and possessions. But more to the point, they recognized the overriding importance of spreading the gospel. The members of the church often sold their property to advance the cause of carrying the message to the world. The community also shared among the members and cared for the destitute among them.

"If you are not very familiar with the socio-economic model for the apostolic era or with Ellen White's comments on that era (or on greed); hopefully, this section will serve you well.

"We are told by Ellen White that the economic plan for God's church in the final days will be similar to that of the apostolic church. We are further told that we will return to a primitive godliness. We are told that there will be a significant urgency attached to seeking the will of the Lord and disposing of property and possessions so that they do not become a burden and snare to us:

> I saw that if any held on to their property, and did not inquire of the Lord as to their duty, He would not make duty known, and they would be permitted to keep their property, and in the time of trouble it would come up before them like a mountain to crush them, and they would try to dispose of it, but would not be able. I heard some mourn like this: "The cause was languishing, God's people were starving for the truth, and we made no effort to supply the lack; now our property is useless. O that we had let it go, and laid up treasure in heaven! (*Counsels on Stewardship*, p. 60)

"The bane and snare of this generation is the pursuit of wealth, which society as a whole has almost single-mindedly engaged in, and which many members of God's end-time church have also given their time and talents over to. In a way it is understandable. Indeed, *we are told that this fascination with the accumulation of wealth is the sterile remnant of a God-given drive to achieve a greater purpose:* "All this energy, this perseverance, this determination, this industry after earthly power, is the result of the perversion of his powers to a wrong object. Every faculty might have been cultivated to the highest possible elevation by exercise, for the heavenly, immortal life, and for the far more exceeding and eternal weight of glory. The customs and practices of the worldly man in his perseverance and his energies, and in availing himself of every opportunity to add to his store, should be a lesson to those who claim to be children of God, seeking for glory, honor, and immortality. The children of the world are wiser in their generation than the children of the light, and herein is seen their wisdom. Their object is for earthly gain, and to this end they direct all their energies. O that this zeal would characterize the toiler for heavenly riches!" —R. & H., March 1, 1887. (*Counsels on Stewardship*, pp. 148–149)

"It is to a primitive godliness and to the socio-economic model of the apostolic era to which those in God's end-time church will largely return. Let that sink in for a minute, because in any worldly context the thought is completely without logic. We, who live in a highly interdependent global complex society, who live in a society that values our ability to consume over our ability to produce, who live in a culture that celebrates vanity and greed, will largely return to a model that recognizes, celebrates, and affirms God's ownership of everything. Those who remain in God's end-time church in the final days will return to a model of sacrificing what we have and unburdening ourselves of possessions in order to advance God's cause. We will return to a model that trusts God for our daily sustenance instead of trusting in ourselves and our resources.

"In this more comprehensive light, consider these statements by Ellen White: 'The cause of God is to have your first consideration' (AH 397), and, the 'advancement of His cause' is to be made with our assets whether in plenty or in poverty, whether we are dead or alive. (See White, *Testimonies for the Church*, Vol. 2, p. 658).

"When you step back from modern society for a moment and consider that our global culture is steeped in mammonism, and when you consider that those who are in God's church in these end-times will be wrenched away from this global religion, then the counsel we are given from the pen of inspiration takes on a whole different cast. Instead of seeming excessive or restrictive, Ellen White's counsel if anything seems conservative, urging us toward conservative and gradual reforms and changes in practice that move us progressively away from the world's practice of exalting money and possessions and toward the apostolic model of advancing the Gospel message, especially through the offering of our resources to God. In the end, Ellen White was not a radical on the subject of our relationship with our resources in the end days—she was a gentle pragmatist. So just how relatively gentle and conservative is this counsel from Sister White?

"We who live in this end time have a great deal of change to go through. We also have great trials to go through. The wise will not leave all of the change until the end, so that we must go through change and trials simultaneously. We can and should change now. We can and should move toward an apostolic model now. Doing so requires that we grow progressively colder to the world, that we reject its measurements of worth, its values, its vanity.

"This process of growing away from the world is extremely difficult and—let's face it—unpopular as well. But it is exactly because *it is urgently needed that those who look to the Lord in a prayer-saturated process of deciding on the design of their will plan, should not shirk from giving careful and prayerful attention to Ellen White's statements on how we should treat our assets in these final days of Earth's history.*

"As you consider your own battle with mammonism in the process of planning for the disposition of your accumulated assets when you are absent from this life, you will want to face up to your awesome responsibility—considering that souls hang in the balance. Yes—the task of planning today to take care of tomorrow is a salvation issue, and at its core is a message that a dying world does not want to hear: That all we have belongs to God whether we are dead or alive, in plenty or poverty, and that we must increasingly lay it on the altar before Him.

"All of God's church must, in these end-times, be engaged in the process of growing colder to the world and growing closer to Him. And as with any growth process ordained of God, it starts and is sustained by our seeking Him. Meditate on the steps outlined below and see if you agree that they will bring you closer to Him and His designs for you while drawing you further from the world and its influences. Ask yourself, 'What is my preferred design for my personal plan for my absence from this life? How would I want my legacy to be transferred at such a time?'"

While meditating on how these concepts by my co-author could become part of a vibrant personal planned giving and estate (inheritance) planning process for you and your family, keep these ideas in mind:

1. Accept God's offer of the new birth and know He is your Savior from sin to everlasting life; submit to God and be at peace.

2. Accept the fact that He is your joy—that the joy of the Lord is your strength.

3. Accept and always acknowledge that He is your Sovereign Master—the Lord of your whole life here and now, in plenty or poverty, whether you live or die.

4. Acknowledge your great sense of need of His protection and provision.

5. Acknowledge that God is the owner of all you have and are.

6. Study spiritual principles from the Bible and the Spirit of Prophecy that govern your management of your assets and even extend to the design of your will, and pray for His individual instruction for your application of those principles to guide you in creating the design of your will plan.

7. Your job now is to make a covenant with God by sacrifice and learn to know Jesus enough to trust Him, love Him, and give Him your whole life in a relational spirit; and listen for His still, small voice with individual instruction in the use of the possessions He has entrusted to you.

8. Your next job is to lay claim to the Lord's promise in Psalm 32:8–9, coming to Him for instructions with a teachable spirit.

9. When you place everything you are and all you possess on His altar, He then will take the responsibility for it as you release that to Him.

10. You can trust Him to care for your best interests in His ongoing instructions to you.

11. When you obey His instructions in the sacred writings of the Bible and the Spirit of Prophecy, He takes responsibility for the outcomes and impacts.

12. You may trust Him with the impact your plans will have on people and His mission to seek and save the lost.

13. *The living God of heaven and earth is your protector and provider*; He is all-powerful and all-loving; nothing that concerns you is too big for Him to handle or too small for His notice.

14. All of your trials and traumas in life are designed to grow you in Jesus so you can come through them with good cheer, a greater hold on Him, and a life filled with His gifts of joy and hope while being peaceful and grateful in Christ.

15. Each member of your family must be allowed to enjoy the same privileges with which you have been blessed: to experience His transforming, sustaining grace and power for a life filled with victory and witnessing.

16. Your next job is to make a last will and testament plan that will honor your covenant with God in the event you have to lay down your life on earth before Jesus comes again and you still have unused resources.

17. Prayerfully consider the idea of looking to your favorite Seventh-day Adventist organization for assistance with your will-plan. Many Adventist conferences, ministries, and institutions are equipped to provide competent professional assistance for you. See chapters 8–11 of this book for more on this.

18. Planned gifts of money and possessions that are made to the church (by will, trust, or charitable annuity) as gifts to God in the spirit of praise and thanksgiving will be accepted by Him. It will then be used with efficiency and effectiveness under His direction to advance the mission of Christ to win the lost.

19. Such planned gifts that are *not* made in the spirit outlined here will be regarded by the Lord the same as those gifts that were "given" to Him by Adam and Eve's firstborn son, Cain, and Ananias and Sapphira.

20. Such planned gifts that are made in the spirit of Christ will be accepted by the Lord and used with efficiency and effectiveness.

Lesson #2: God's Socio-Economic Systems in Four Different Eras

Era #1: The Old Testament Model

This is our initial time period for this study. We begin by asking, *What does the Bible say about all of this?* For starters, it tells us God was intimately involved in supplying property to His chosen people. Indeed, He gave the land in the original apportionment by tribe, as recorded in the Bible. The Lord instructed Moses' successor to "Include all this territory as Israel's inheritance when you divide the land among the nine tribes and the half-tribe of Manasseh. Half the tribe of Manasseh and the tribes of Reuben and Gad had already received their inheritance on the east side of the Jordan, for Moses, the servant of the Lord, had previously assigned this land to them" (Josh. 13:7, 8, NLT).

The Bible specified the plan for the property to remain in the family. It is known as the "law of inheritance," which favored the firstborn son:

> Suppose a man has two wives, but he loves one and not the other, and both have given him sons. And suppose the firstborn son is the son of the wife he does not love. When the man divides the inheritance, he may not give the larger inheritance to his younger son, the son of the wife he loves. He must give the customary double portion to his oldest son, who represents the strength of his father's manhood and who owns the rights of the firstborn son, even though he is the son of the wife his father does not love. (Deuteronomy 21:15–17, NLT)

God's design for that time was a system and spirit of mutual support, as described by Moses, where God gave detailed instructions on the conditions and terms for any sale-and-purchase transaction of property among His people:

> When you make an agreement with a neighbor to buy or sell property, you must never take advantage of each other. When you buy land from your neighbor, the price of the land should be based on the number of years since the last jubilee. The seller will charge you only for the crop years left until the next Year of Jubilee. The more the years, the higher the price; the fewer the years, the lower the price. After all, the person

selling the land is actually selling you a certain number of harvests. Show your fear of God by not taking advantage of each other. I, the Lord, am your God. (Leviticus 25:14–17, NLT).

God's Permanent Ownership of the Property of His people

Leviticus 25 sets forth God's instructions about transactions of various kinds of property in great detail. Among those instructions, we find these highlights:

1. The Lord said, "The land must never be sold on a permanent basis because it really belongs to Me" (verse 23, NLT)
2. When misfortune compelled the sale of property, the Lord specified the terms for it to be returned to the original family and how the value was to be determined. All of that was different for a farmer's land compared to a house in a village (see verses 24–29)
3. The sanctuary priests never owned land but had a house in the village. And the pastureland the priest used for his livestock could never be sold under any circumstances (see verses 32–34)
4. The Lord introduced the Year of Jubilee, with His directive that property returns to the original family each fiftieth year (see verses 9, 10).

God's strategic design of the economic system for His people provided for every family to have a home and land to support the family. The number of acres was sufficient for them to till the land and produce their own food and fiber. It also gave the opportunity for children to both learn to work in a useful, industrious pursuit that would feed and clothe the family and experience the value of a self-supporting lifestyle. There were no such things as an eight-hour work day or forty-hour work week. It is widely recognized that mankind has not improved on that plan in modern times. And that is why there is so much poverty and wretchedness among God's children today, which must grieve Him to no end (see White, *Patriarchs and Prophets*, pp. 534, 535; *Welfare Ministry*, pp. 195, 196).

Amazingly, God's design was for the work of the Messiah and His redeeming Spirit to be promise-based, not law-based (see Gal. 3:15–18; Rom. 14:23). A question of inheritance was raised about property going to daughters when there was no surviving son (see Num. 27:1–4). And God said "Yes" to the women. The daughters were given the right of property ownership (see verses 5–11). However, the Lord specified the responsibility of women regarding who they could marry to prevent property from going from tribe to tribe. The daughters in the case under consideration at the time did as the Lord had commanded Moses (see 36:6–11).

Era #2: The New Testament Model

Regarding this version of God's socio-economic system for His people, perhaps the best place to begin is Christ's teaching on the law of inheritance. Someone called to Jesus from the crowd, asking Him to intercede on his behalf in his efforts to get his brother to divide their deceased father's estate with him.

> Jesus replied, "Friend, who made me a judge over you to decide such things as that?" Then he said, "Beware! Don't be greedy for what you don't have. Real life is not measured by how much we own." And he gave an illustration: "A rich man had a fertile farm that produced fine crops. In fact, his barns were full to overflowing. So, he said, 'I know! I'll tear down my barns and build bigger ones. Then I'll have room enough to store everything. And I'll sit back and say to myself, "My friend, you have enough stored away for years to come. Now take it easy! Eat, drink, and be merry!"' But God said to him, 'You fool! You will die this very night. Then who will get it all?' Yes, a person is a fool to store up earthly wealth but not have a rich relationship with God." (Luke 12:14–21, NLT 1996)

Ellen G. White commented on the above scenario:

> We ourselves owe everything to God's free grace. Grace in the covenant ordained our adoption. Grace in the Saviour effected our redemption, our regeneration, and our exaltation to heirship with Christ. Let this grace be revealed to others ....
>
> But there were many who desired the grace of heaven only to serve their selfish purposes. They recognized the marvelous power of Christ in setting forth the truth in a clear light. They heard the promise to His followers of wisdom to speak before rulers and magistrates. Would He not lend His power for their worldly benefit? ....
>
> God had given directions concerning the transmission of property. The eldest son received a double portion of the father's estate (Deuteronomy 21:17), while the younger brothers were to share alike. This man thinks that his brother has defrauded him of his inheritance. His own efforts have failed to secure what he

regards as his due, but if Christ will interpose the end will surely be gained. He has heard Christ's stirring appeals, and His solemn denunciations of the scribes and Pharisees. If words of such command could be spoken to this brother, he would not dare to refuse the aggrieved man his portion.

In the midst of the solemn instruction that Christ had given, this man had revealed his selfish disposition. He could appreciate that ability of the Lord which might work for the advancement of his own temporal affairs; but spiritual truths had taken no hold on his mind and heart …

In Christ's treatment of this case is a lesson for all who minister in His name. When He sent forth the twelve, He said, "As ye go, preach, saying, The kingdom of heaven is at hand. Heal the sick, cleanse the lepers, raise the dead, cast out devils: freely ye have received, freely give." Matthew 10:7, 8. They were not to settle the temporal affairs of the people. Their work was to persuade men to be reconciled to God … The gospel of His grace alone can cure the evils that curse society. (White, *Christ's Object Lessons*, pp. 252–254)

This is my reason for emphasizing the spiritual dimension of estate planning. I have carried a burden for donors to give for the right reasons so their gifts are accepted by the Lord. That way, these gifts can be used with efficiency and effectiveness to advance the mission of Christ to seek and to save the lost.

> *I have carried a burden for donors to give for the right reasons so their gifts are accepted by the Lord. That way, these gifts can be used with efficiency and effectiveness to advance the mission of Christ to seek and to save the lost.*

The injustice of the rich toward the poor, the hatred of the poor toward the rich, alike have their root in selfishness, and this can be eradicated only through submission to Christ. He alone, for the selfish heart of sin, gives the new heart of love …

Our Lord struck at the root of the affair that troubled this questioner, and of all similar disputes, saying, "Take heed, and beware of covetousness; for a man's life consisteth not in the abundance of the things which he possesseth. (White, *Christ's Object Lessons*, pp. 254, 255)

Era #3: The Apostolic Christian Church Model; the Spirit of Sacrifice

We know the first congregation of believers, after Christ's return to heaven, was fully committed to His mission to seek and save the world and prepare it for His return. As such, they were no doubt committed to the support of each other and all those who came along with an interest in their message, which was the gospel of Christ—not a social gospel of fairness and justice, but a mutuality of support in the Spirit. And they approached the ministry of the gospel in the pattern of Christ's ministry, of which the apostles had been a part.

Dr. Luke explained it this way:
And the congregation of those who believed were of one heart and soul; and not one of them claimed that anything belonging to him was his own, but all things were common property to them. And with great power the apostles were giving testimony to the resurrection of the Lord Jesus, and abundant grace was upon them all. For there was not a needy person among them, for all who were owners of land or houses would sell them and bring the proceeds of the sales and lay them at the apostles' feet, and they would be distributed to each as any had need. (Acts 4:32–35, NASB)

Ellen White commented on this passage:
As the disciples proclaimed the truths of the gospel in Jerusalem, God bore witness to their word, and a multitude believed. Many of these early believers were immediately cut off from family and friends by the zealous bigotry of the Jews, and it was necessary to provide them with food and shelter.
The record declares, "Neither was there any among them that lacked," and it tells how the need was filled. Those among the believers who had money and possessions cheerfully sacrificed them to meet the emergency. Selling their houses or their lands, they brought the money and laid it at the apostles' feet, "and distribution was made unto every man according as he had need."
This liberality on the part of the believers was the result of the outpouring of the Spirit.

> Their love for their brethren and the cause they had espoused, was greater than their love of money and possessions. Their works testified that they accounted the souls of men of higher value then earthly wealth.
>
> Thus, it will ever be when the Spirit of God takes possession of the life. Those whose hearts are filled with the love of Christ, will follow the example of Him who for our sake became poor, that through His poverty we might be made rich. Money, time, influence—all the gifts they have received from God's hand, they will value only as a means of advancing the work of the gospel. Thus, it was in the early church; and when in the church of today it is seen that by the power of the Spirit the members have taken their affections from the things of the world, and that they are willing to make sacrifices in order that their fellow men may hear the gospel, the truths proclaimed will have a powerful influence upon the hearers. (White, *The Acts of the Apostles*, pp. 70, 71)

The blessings of working to earn wealth; the evil of inheritance, per King Solomon:

> Even so, I have noticed one thing, at least, that is good. It is good for people to eat well, drink a good glass of wine, and enjoy their work—whatever they do under the sun—for however long God lets them live. And it is a good thing to receive wealth from God and the good health to enjoy it. To enjoy your work and accept your lot in life—that is indeed a gift from God. People who do this rarely look with sorrow on the past, for God has given them reasons for joy ...
>
> I am disgusted that I must leave the fruits of my hard work to others. And who can tell whether my successors will be wise or foolish? And yet they will control everything I have gained by my skill and hard work. How meaningless! So I turned in despair from hard work. It was not the answer to my search for satisfaction in this life. For though I do my work with wisdom, knowledge, and skill, I must leave everything I gain to people who haven't worked to earn it. This is not only foolish but highly unfair. So, what do people get for all their hard work? Their days of labor are filled with pain and grief; even at night they cannot rest. It is all utterly meaningless. So, I decided there is nothing better than to enjoy food and drink and to find satisfaction in work. Then I realized that this pleasure is from the hand of God. (Ecclesiastes 5:18–20; 2:18–24, NLT 1996)

The Spirit of Prophecy offers insight pertaining to the passage above:

> *The desire to accumulate wealth is an original affection of our nature, implanted there by our heavenly Father for noble ends.* If you ask the capitalist who has directed all his energies to the one object of securing wealth, and who is persevering and industrious to add to his property, with what design he thus labors, he could not give you a reason for this, a definite purpose for which he is gaining earthly treasures and heaping up riches. He cannot define any great aim or purpose he has in view, or any new source of happiness he expects to attain. He goes on accumulating because he has turned all his abilities and all his powers in this direction.
>
> There is within the worldly man a craving for something that he does not have. He has, from force of habit, bent every thought, every purpose, in the direction of making provision for the future, and as he grows older, he becomes more eager than ever to acquire all that it is possible to gain. It is natural that the covetous man should become more covetous as he draws near the time when he is losing hold upon all earthly things. (White, *Counsels on Stewardship*, pp. 148, 149, emphasis added)

We are called to be *reformers* of today's selfish system of making wills:

> Let it ever be kept in mind that *the present selfish system of disposing of property is not God's plan, but man's device. Christians should be reformers and break up this present system* ... formation of wills. Let the idea be ever present that it is the Lord's property which you are handling. The will of God in this matter is law ... Your heavenly Friend has entrusted you with property, and given you His will as to how it should be used. If this will is studied with an unselfish heart, that which belongs to God will not be misapplied. The Lord's cause has been shamefully neglected, when He has provided men with sufficient means to meet every emergency, if they only had grateful, obedient hearts. (White, *Testimonies for the Church*, vol. 4, pp. 482, 483, emphasis added)

Era #4: The Time of the End Era—All Belongs to God; with the Spirit of Sacrifice

During today's global atmosphere of fear and uncertainty of every kind, God's people are to shine as a beacon of light and peace like never before in the history of the world. Each one of God's people will adopt the manner of conduct that will carry him or her through the time of trouble that is creeping upon us. With Christ alive in us, we will have His mind, heart, spirit, will, selfless love, and faith. Praise the Lord from whom all blessings of such abundance come!

We are privileged to know we can expect individual guidance from the Lord. People have often asked me for advice on their inheritance plan: how should they distribute what they have in their will-plan, when should they sell their homes and give the proceeds to the cause, etc. Ellen White had the same experience and answered this way: "I would say to such, 'It may not be your duty to sell your little homes just now; but go to God for yourselves; the Lord will certainly hear your earnest prayers for wisdom to understand your duty'" (*Testimonies for the Church*, vol. 5, p. 734).

We all want to be prepared for the time of trouble, and Ellen White gave the following advice/instruction:

> Houses and lands will be of no use to the saints in the time of trouble, for they will then have to flee before infuriated mobs, and at that time their possessions cannot be disposed of to advance the cause of present truth. I was shown that it is the will of God that the saints should cut loose from every encumbrance before the time of trouble comes, and make a covenant with God through sacrifice. If they have their property on the altar, and earnestly inquire of God for duty, He will teach them when to dispose of these things. Then they will be free in the time of trouble, and have no clogs to weigh them down …
>
> I also saw that God had not required all of His people to dispose of their property at the same time, but if they desired to be taught, He would teach them, in a time of need, when to sell and how much to sell. Some have been required to dispose of their property in times past to sustain the advent cause, while others have been permitted to keep theirs until a time of need. Then, as the cause needs it, their duty is to sell. (White, *Counsels on Stewardship*, pp. 59, 60)

She also was instructed that we are required to make the advancement of God's cause prominent in our use of the resources He has placed in our hands, whether we are dead or alive, in poverty or plenty—giving Christ the preeminence in all things (See *Testimonies for the Church*, vol 2, p. 59; Col. 1:15–18).

> **Make Property Secure by Proper Will**—Those who are faithful stewards of the Lord's means will know just how their business stands, and, like wise men, they will be prepared for any emergen-

cy. Should their probation close suddenly, they would not leave such great perplexity upon those who are called to settle their estate. (White, *Adventist Home*, p. 396)

Ellen White also wrote, "Many are not exercised upon the subject of making their wills while in apparent health" (see *Ibid.*). When I was a professional financial planner and investment broker, I found that most people devote more time to planning their two-week vacations than they do to planning their financial strategy for old-age security. And the same is certainly true of God's people on the matter of creating their own will-plan.

This is perhaps the most valuable legal and spiritual counsel for making wills that comes from the pen of inspiration:

> Wills should be made in a manner to stand the test of law. After they are drawn, they may remain for years and do no harm, if donations continue to be made from time to time as the cause has need. Death will not come one day sooner, brethren, because you have made your will. In disposing of your property by will to your relatives, be sure that you do not forget God's cause. You are His agents, holding His property; and His claims should have your first consideration. Your wife and children, of course, should not be left destitute; provision should be made for them if they are needy. But do not, simply because it is customary, bring into your will a long line of relatives who are not needy. (White, *Adventist Home*, p. 397)

A fitting encapsulation for this whole discussion is one of my favorite paragraphs: "The offering from the heart that loves, God delights to honor, giving it highest efficiency in service for Him. If we have given our hearts to Jesus, we also shall bring our gifts to Him. Our gold and silver, our most precious earthly possessions, our highest mental and spiritual endowments, will be freely devoted to Him who loved us, and gave Himself for us" (White, *The Desire of Ages*, p. 65).

The comparative grid on the next page is designed to summarize the concepts of this chapter.

Family Support and Inheritance Plans ◆ 101

Summary of Socio-Economic Systems of the Old Testament, Apostolic Era, and End Time Church

Old Testament Era (Israel)	New Testament Era (Apostolic Church)	End-Time Church (E.G White's Concepts)
Defined in part by God's Absolute Ownership of All Property, which was publicly acknowledged	The Apostolic Church members held all property in common (in spirit)	The church exists in a world defined by a very inferior family and community support system as measured by the level of poverty
God gave property to each tribe and family and He gave instructions on its management and placed detailed restrictions on property sales	All who were owners of property would sell as needed and bring the proceeds to be used to help the needy ones	For all practical purposes, everyone on earth is part of a global complex society where we each fill a specialized niche and require a specialized education. Self-sufficiency is almost a lost art
Any sale of property was not to become a permanent transfer (the Jubilee system)	The over-riding goal that animated the community was the spread of the gospel. Personal gain was far from first in their thoughts; vanity and pride of place were not prominent drivers	The age is marked by a definition of human worth based on personal possessions and wealth. Accordingly, the age is also marked by a relentless pursuit of possessions by almost everyone, including members of God's end-time church
God supplied a complete set of resources (the land) for each family's self-sufficient support	The community was fairly close-knit and geographically concentrated	It is necessary that we part ways with society by acknowledging that God is the absolute owner of ourselves, our family, our money, and our possessions—whether we are dead or alive
God's people were farmers or skilled craftsmen with few if any poor or impoverished among them	God's people were still farmers or skilled craftsmen with few if any poor or impoverished among them	It is necessary that we make a covenant with God by sacrifice, placing all we have on His altar and earnestly ask God for duty. He will tell us when to sell or turn it in—whether during life or at death
God's system is the very best economic model of family support system since Noah's flood		The members of God's church in the final days will be as unified and focused – and persecuted – as were the members of the apostolic church – and they will likewise value the Lord's work over their possessions and wealth – dead or alive
At death, all property and other possessions transferred to the next generation to sustain the family support system given in trust from the Lord		At death, each true believer will have made a Last Will And Testament to honor the above covenant with God – that all belongs to Him dead or alive

This Comparative Grid is part of Chapter 3 in *The Joy of Giving Back to God: Accumulated Assets and The Great Controversy* by W. Robert Daum

Chapter 7

Why Estate Planning Is Important in the Great Controversy

The Lord has claimed us as His own and paid the price (see 1 Cor. 6:19, 20). However, the devil is still trying to hold onto our hearts, minds, and purses or wallets. Satan does all he is allowed to do to prevent God's people from pledging their accumulated assets, or at least a portion of it, to help fund and finish the work for Christ in this generation.

We know the Bible says the just shall live by faith. (See Hab. 2:4; Rom. 1:17; Gal. 3:11; Heb. 10:38.) We likewise know the just shall *die* by faith.

> *The Lord has claimed us as His own and paid the price. However, the devil is still trying to hold onto our hearts, minds, and purses or wallets.*

You must now, while alive, make diligent, faithful work, that after your death gifts and offerings may come into the treasury of the cause of God, which must be sustained ... Your treasure is loaned to you in trust and is the Lord's ... Said Christ to John, "Write, Blessed are the dead which die in the Lord from henceforth: Yea, saith the Spirit, that they may rest from their labors; and their works do follow them. (White, "Making Wills," *The Gospel Herald*, December 1, 1901)

How to design your will-plan is introduced in this chapter. We are discussing pertinent fundamental issues about the subject. Specific areas are added in Chapter 9 on the subjects of legal security for My Plan and its related legal documents. The spiritual design issues of faith, ownership, family, estate stewardship, and designing an inheritance plan are included in Chapter 14 of this book.

We hope and pray your prayerful consideration of each of these six principles will, with the help of the Holy Spirit, give you transparently clear thinking on how you want to design your own legacy inheritance plan—that you will be blessed with peace and your plan will be a blessing to your family's actual needs, both spiritually and with the assurance of your love for them and the Lord's work if or when you die. The legal and spiritual framework is intended to serve as a platform of spiritual and legal considerations for the design of your mission-driven legacy plan as a genuine Christian believer.

The purpose of a Christian's will-plan is to plan for our absence while continuing our support of Christ's mission to seek and save the lost—beyond the grave—so we don't have to sleep so long in awaiting Jesus' second coming. In order to design a will-plan that will gain the approval of heaven, we study the divine principles for this design and pray about it until we receive individual instruction on how to apply those principles personally. The state in which you reside when you die has a statutory will for you in case you have not created your own plan; and the state's will does not leave anything for the Lord's work. Therefore, as Elder Ed Reid says, the state's will always assumes we are atheists.

Does Jesus live in your heart? If you love Jesus with all your heart, strength, and mind (see Matt. 22:37), then, and only then, will you appreciate this information. Otherwise, you are likely to be offended by it. And it helps me to remember my love for Jesus can be no greater than is my love for the person I despise the most. Maybe that is why Jesus instructed us to love our enemies (see 5:44).

I understand the only way I can experience selfless love for those who disagree with me or are generally disagreeable is when Christ is really alive in my heart, mind, and spirit, replacing my life of self with His life. That happens when I follow Paul's example: "I die daily [to self]" and live by the faith *of* Jesus (1 Cor. 15:31; see also Luke 9:23, 24; Gal. 2:16–20).

My Personal Story on the Topic of Will Planning

The Lord came near to me at four different seasons about our personal/family estate plan documentation. After much joint study and prayer, Mary Jo and I got it done in each of the four seasons. That was in 1984, 1994, 2013, and 2022. Each time, the Lord visited me during my devotional time every morning for a week; then I got the message and decided to do it. Our plan documents included a last will and testament for each of us, a joint revocable living trust, a power of attorney for life management, and a health care proxy that included a living will. Having lost our daughter to the grave in 2010 made it essential to update the plan. Our plan documents were further refined in 2013 in general and in 2014 because of a new state law about how to deal with electronic-internet assets in our estate plan. Moving our life from our home in Massachusetts to a home in Michigan in 2021 and other pertinent considerations made it clear that we must update our will & trust plan.

After working as an estate planning consultant, both in my own business in California and in the church for a few years of the 1980s in Southern New England, the Lord appealed to my heart—coming near every morning for a week, prompting me to get our own will-plan done. He gave me these thoughts: "You have been promoting will planning for your constituent church members in Southern New England, and you must be a good example by getting your own plan in place." I concluded the Lord was asking me to be authentic—to "practice what I preach."

Each time, Mary Jo and I prayed for and received His direction about His will for our last will, which lawyer to use, etc. In the most recent case, I had decided to use an estate planning specialist who is a lawyer in Worcester, MA. However, when I prayed about it, the Lord directed me to a dear friend who is a brother in the church locally and equally qualified as a specialist. And that worked out very well.

Having a professional care for this—some call it "planning today for tomorrow"—we enjoy great peace. We know Jesus is coming very soon, but we don't know if we will be alive then or if our will/trust plan will need to be implemented. If the latter is the case, it would be a sin against God to not make provision for His work in our last will and testament or a living trust being used as a will substitute at our death.

Designing a will-plan is a very personal responsibility for each of God's children. The process is quite simple. Preparing an attorney packet of personal data seems to be a major chore for some. It consists of crafting a written report of your:

1. Personal data
2. Family data
3. Financial data
4. People to be involved as beneficiaries and fiduciaries
5. Plan of distribution of your property—how you want it done if your last breath was tonight

Why All This Effort Before Seeing a Lawyer?

Generally, lawyers get paid for their time and expertise. If you prepare such an attorney packet before you engage him or her as your representative, then much less time is required in your face-to-face engagement. Another advantage to doing this preparation is the opportunity to study and pray for the Lord's special guidance in your plan design. Most people I've assisted express appreciation for having so much personal and family and financial information assembled in one place. And I say, praise the Lord from whom all blessings flow!!!

I've assisted many hundreds of individuals or couples in such preparation, beginning with my twenty-eight-page confidential data form, EDIO (Estate Design Information Organizer), then by adding pertinent asset documentations such as deeds to real {estate?} property and financial account statements, plus related documents such as property insurance and tax bills. I refer to this as the creation of an "attorney packet."

When it comes to developing an updated plan or a new plan design for the distribution of your estate, you [either as an individual or as a couple] are faced with a difficult set of decisions to make. This is so because it is a most sacred journey if you wish to put God first in the final plan. I'm sure you don't relish the idea of spending time on your project of estate planning, but in fact, that just means your success will require a significant amount of time devoted to study and prayer, either as an individual or jointly together as a couple (if you are both legally competent).

Some have said to just think about doing this exercise is like thinking about going to a dentist and asking to have your teeth drilled. The difficulty of making the required decisions often causes people to keep putting it off rather than pray with a "thy will be done" spirit of surrender—until clarity comes to mind and heart.

Mary Jo and I have been through such an exercise in which we had different opinions about something. We knelt down in front of our living room sofa with the Bible, a Bible commentary, and carefully selected books by Ellen G. White spread out before us on our living room sofa with us on our knees to study and pray over. We looked up a number of pertinent passages we could think of or that the Lord brought to mind. We were successful in coming to a mutually satisfying conclusion, as led by the Lord of peace. Therefore, I do understand the difficulty of this part of your journey with Jesus.

Will-Plan Design—More Introductory Thoughts

1. Most importantly, when your will-plan is done, you must be completely satisfied that it is an honest expression of your will and not simply the wishes of another person or group—based only on your study and prayers. Why? Because you are accountable only to the living God of heaven for the design of your plan.

2. Designing your plan to dispose of your accumulated assets is often referred to as "estate planning," "legacy planning," "planning today for tomorrow." In any case, it is a snapshot in time that will probably need to be updated as time goes by. You should review it at least every five years to see if it is still the way you want it to be.

3. As you study the material in this book and ponder how to design your plan for the distribution of your assets after your death, you will have the very most satisfying outcome if you immerse your every thought and feeling in prayer to the Lord, along with considering the needs of His work and your family with a fully surrendered spirit, trusting that He knows best how to care for you and your loved ones.

4. Seek to know God's will for your will-plan—a most sacred journey that will bring order to your life and great peace to your spirit like nothing else can—for obedience to God's directions in the spirit of loving trust and loyalty to and support of His mission always gives that outcome.

5. Dwell time in the process is often very important. For example, Ellen White had her last will and testament drafted four times of which we know: signing a will document on October 16, 1901, August 14, 1906, and February 9, 1912; an unsigned will was drafted under her instruction in 1909. Reading those documents and her agonizing considerations suggests she went through a progression of thought that finally led her to a clear understanding of what she wanted to do that would harmonize with her sense of duty before God, her family, and church leaders. Of course, her greatest priority was to create a plan that would cause her work of ministry to continue after her death until the second coming of Christ—a most significant result at the time. You may look at this book's Appendix 3—Ellen White's Final Will of 1912 online at mystewardship.estate. And this book's Appendix 2 is on the same website. It is "The Making of Ellen White's

Will of 1912—Issues and Considerations." Appendix 4 is "Valuable Gems of Counsel from the Pen of Ellen G. White on Wills."

6. Ellen White's greatest struggle in making her final will was to select those church leaders as trustees of her estate who could be trusted to carry out her wishes. I expect she would have been praying very much for the wisdom of God to direct her in the design of her will plan. Today, the result of her final will is what we know as The Ellen G. White Estate, Inc., which has definitely fulfilled her plan design very well.

7. As to the cost of making such a plan, Ellen White was a widow when she lived near Angwin, California, where Adventist-owned Pacific Union College is located. She made her last will and testament after moving there from Australia. Her final will of 1912 was drafted by an attorney in San Francisco, California, at a cost of $25.85. At that time, a Seventh-day Adventist pastor's weekly wage was $14–$18. Today, it can also cost the equivalent of a week's wages or more, depending on the complexity of your estate and the time and expertise required to draft your documents.

God's Purpose for Wealth: "The one purpose above all others for which God's gifts should be used is the sustaining of workers in the harvest field" (White, *Counsels on Stewardship*, p. 36). "The desire to accumulate wealth is an original affection of our nature, implanted there by our heavenly Father for noble ends" (*Ibid.*, p. 148). Unfortunately, the devil has been sadly successful in getting people to use it for his purposes rather than for "noble ends." That is often true while the people are living *and* when they die.

The Lord does not propose to come to this world, and lay down gold and silver for the advancement of His work. He supplies men with resources, that by their gifts and offerings they may keep His work advancing. The one purpose above all others for which God's gifts should be used is the sustaining of workers in the harvest field. And if men will become channels through which heaven's blessing can flow to others, the Lord will keep the channel supplied. It is not returning to the Lord His own that makes men poor; withholding tends to poverty....

It is not the empty cup that we have trouble in carrying; it is the cup full to the brim that must be carefully balanced. Affliction and adversity may cause much inconvenience, and may bring great depression; but it is prosperity that is dangerous to spiritual life. (White, *Counsels on Stewardship*, pp. 36, 148)

The church in this generation has been endowed by God with great privileges and blessings, and He expects corresponding returns....

Through His people Christ is to manifest His character and the principles of His kingdom....

God imparts His gifts to us that we also may give, and thus make known His character to the world. (White, *Christ's Object Lessons*, pp. 296, 300)

People to whom the Lord has led me to serve by assisting them with their pre-lawyer preparation have often asked me what other people do about the distribution of their estates. This book contains a number of stories on both sides of the great controversy.

I hope you can see why your estate plan or the lack of one is important to your role and function in the cosmic conflict between Christ and Satan.

Section II

Completing an Estate Plan with the Assistance of a Seventh-day Adventist Denominational Organization's Planned Giving & Trust Services Department

Chapter 8

Availability of Professional Adventist Ministerial Assistance in the Will Planning Process

North American Division Trust-Certified Professional Seventh-day Adventist ministerial assistance may be available to you. Some conferences, ministries, and institutions operate a Planned Giving & Trust Services Department with comprehensive services, which is the place you should consider going for assistance with your planning process if you need a complete set of legal documents for your will-plan. Other denominational entities operate a minimal-services program by only offering the non-revocable charitable trusts and charitable gift annuity plans. In working in this line since September 1980, I've operated a program that embraced what I refer to as a "comprehensive planning service" or a "full-service department."

For me to do otherwise would be a disservice, but that is my personal and professional bias. This perspective was formed in me when I was a professional financial planner and investment broker in the early 1970s, after serving in managerial leadership in a Fortune 500 company where I worked from 1961–1970. For example, someone I didn't know called me and said he wanted to invest $100,000 in a mutual fund and wanted me to recommend the fund in which they would invest. I just could not do that unless they could answer some crucial questions.

My practice was to do comprehensive financial and strategic investment planning. I would meet with each client three or four times a year. I learned to know them better than they knew themselves in some instances. I wanted the clients to make their own investment decisions after surfacing their respective risk/reward comfort zones *and* understanding where the proposed investments would fit into their overall strategy for long-term and short-term goals and objectives. We also paid close attention to their income tax proforma annually in considering tax-sheltered investment options.

Of course, I've not assisted anyone with their general financial planning or making investment decisions since 1974. I lost all interest. More importantly, doing that would have been unethical and inappropriate because it would not have been a part of the scope of my employment with the church. I gave up all my licenses and registrations with the respective state and federal government agencies that had been required for my work from early 1970 to late 1974.

History & Policy

Seventh-day Adventist denominational organizations—in particular, the local conferences—have operated a Trust Services section of the Treasury Department since the early 1900s. In recent years, the General Conference in Session remade this service into a separate department and later renamed it the "Planned Giving & Trust Services Department." The purpose of renaming it was to give it an estate stewardship ministry role and function. My conviction is that we are not in this work as a church among God's people to provide a quid-pro-quo business service transaction but rather to conduct a spiritual journey for members and friends.

A crisis occurred with the investment of trust assets that caused the General Conference to create a set of Accreditation Standards for each organization that chooses to operate such a department, as well as Certification Standards for denominational employees to meet by an internal educational program. Said certification is sustained by internally conducted continuing education events. *Accreditation* of denominational organizations and *certification* of employees are determined by the North American Division Certification & Accreditation (C&A) Committee. Their decisions are based on reports from the General Conference Auditing Department. Selected financial auditors are recruited to become certified in trust services and conduct periodic audit reviews of each organization's operation of this department.

> *My practice was to do comprehensive financial and strategic investment planning. I would meet with each client three or four times a year. I learned to know them better than they knew themselves in some instances*

This program was launched by the General Conference in 1987. Various conferences, educational institutions, and ministry organizations have chosen to operate the program at a variety of levels. Others have chosen not to operate such a department. When choosing a denominational organization to help you, it is important that you ask not only what level of service they provide, but what type of accreditation they've earned.

The Accreditation Standards for Planned Giving & Trust Services Departments were significantly revised in 2017. In addition, requirements for certification of employees who staff these departments are set forth, as well. Job descriptions were created for planned giving consultants and for trust officers. An educational program was created to qualify and certify employees within these departments.

The General Conference Auditing Service examines each Planned Giving & Trust Services Department to verify accreditation and certification compliance. Those departments are granted either level A accreditation, level B accreditation, or no accreditation, based on a review of the audit reports by the NAD Certification & Accreditation Committee.

The requirements that a Planned Giving & Trust Services Department must meet depend somewhat on the level of service it has decided to provide. Policy provides a menu of different levels of service along with the accreditation standards for each. A full service model includes related fiduciary trust and estate accounting and preparation of tax returns—either by the in-house treasury department, or by outsourcing those responsibilities to the Western Adventist Foundation (WAF), a subsidiary of the Pacific Union Conference.

WAF has a large team of highly specialized personnel. They provide asset investment and record-keeping services, do tax returns, generate reports, and perform other fiduciary functions for client organizations. WAF also employs trust officers who provide ongoing client relationship services.

When you choose a Planned Giving & Trust Services Department that practices the *full service* model to assist in preparing your estate documents—rather than one that offers only limited service—you have an extra sense of security. It is reassuring to know that your documents are stored safely and your end-of-life plan will be professionally implemented when you fall asleep in Jesus to await His second coming.

Let us now consider a practical scenario. As a reader of this book, you might be asking, "Why would I want to contact a Seventh-day Adventist organization to assist me in creating my plans to take care of tomorrow—when I'm absent from friends and family? What might I expect there?" Those are worthy questions.

The trust services of yesteryear is not the same today. The name has changed to Planned Giving & Trust Services Department. This means it has gone from being viewed as a service to being a department of the church. It also means it is a fundraising arm of the church. A denominational organization that operates a full service department is the one that may assist you with your will-plan journey. It may be a very small conference or ministry or institution that you wish to benefit. But, don't assume that to be an indicator of their operational skill set in this area. If they have one full time employee dedicated to the department of Planned Giving & Trust Services, they can outsource the "back-room" technical functions of management to Western Adventist Foundation, which is a thriving corporation of the Pacific Union Conference of Seventh-day Adventists. They provide such services with a number of our organizations across the country.

It is the basis of my comfort when serving individuals as their Planned Giving Consultant, in which we work with independent lawyers to provide the legal services of advice and documents; while having the freedom of offering gift plan proposals that may include current revocable and NON-revocable gift plan models for your prayerful consideration and educational material on the spiritual dimension of such planning for your prayerful consideration.

To help you understand the function of a "Full-Service Department," I'm describing my approach with an example Letter From me to You About Estate Planning If you Asked me to Be Your Planned Giving Consultant. After personal greetings, my letter to you would include lines like these: "We are excited and *not alarmed* about the signs we see locally and globally that reveal the nearness of Christ's Second Coming. Isn't it simply wonderful to be alive to see what Martin Luther and all the other Christian Protestant Reformers longed to see? People all around us are expressing fear; I try to relate to them in a friendly, sympathetic manner and say, 'it will get worse and when it gets bad enough Jesus will come.'"

We know that Christ's Second Coming is both *certain and imminent*; what we don't know is which ones of us will be laid to rest before-time; and who will survive the great time of trouble to literally see Him come. If we are alive when He comes, we don't need a will-plan now. In that case, we will have given all we have to finish the work before we can no longer buy or sell.

However, since we don't know who among us will be laid to rest in mercy before the Great Time of Trouble, we know that If we are to be laid to rest aforetime, then we definitely need a legally valid will-plan that is up to date. So, based on what we do know, it is time for all of us to get our affairs in order. I humbly suggest that time is of the essence to get it done.

You can rest assured that when you go through the process and have it all done, you will rejoice with a great sense of relief and jubilation. God inhabits praise.

When it comes to developing a new plan design for the distribution of your estate, you are faced with a set of decisions to make; it is a *sacred journey* for those like you who wish to *put God first* in your plan; I'm sure that you don't relish the idea of spending time on your project of estate planning; but, in fact, that just means your success will require a significant amount of time devoted to study and prayer.

I might enclose with the letter or give to you the following CHECKLIST OF INFORMATION AND DOUCMENTS NEEDED FOR YOUR APPOINTMENT REGARDING YOUR WILL.PLAN—depending on the situation when the first visit resulted in an appointment for me to come back to see them for the purpose of beginning the process of assisting them in the effort to get their will-plan done, I have given it to them. The said CHECKLIST consists of the following:

I. <u>PERSONAL INFORMATION</u>

Name(s)

Address: Street/Box Number, City (Village or Township), State, Zip Code

Date(s) of Birth

Social Security Number(s)

Phone Number(s)

Occupation(s)

II. <u>FAMILY INFORMATION</u>

Living Children: Name(s), Addresses, Date(s) of Birth, and Social Security Numbers

Deceased Children: Name(s) and Date of Death

List of Children of the Deceased Child with Dates of their Births and Last Address.

If no Children, then the above information on Brothers, Sisters, and Parents.

III. DOCUMENTS

Wills and Trusts

Deed(s) for Property, Homeowners Insurance of Renters Insurance Policy

Property Tax Bill

Life Insurance Policy

Stock Certificates or Statement of Securities Account if held by your broker in Street Name.

Gift Tax Returns

IRA Statements of Accounts and/or Other Retirement Plans

IV. FINANCIAL VALUES INFORMATION

ASSETS: Values of Real Property, including Personal Residence (Your estimate), Bank Accounts, CDs, IRA Accounts, Other Liquid Account Values like Annuity Investments, Automobiles—Your Estimate.

LIABILITIES: Mortgage Balance (Approximate)

Automobile Loan(s) (Approximate)

Credit Card Balance

Other Debt

IV. PLAN INFORMATION—People to Include—Name & Contact Info.

Executor of Will – 1st and 2nd Choices

Trustee of Trust and Successor Trustee if Applicable

Guardian of Children—1st and 2nd Choices

Health Care Proxy (Power of Attorney) -- 1st and 2nd Choices

Power of Attorney for life Management -- 1st and 2nd Choices

Beneficiaries of Will-Plan – People and Agencies of Christ's Work

During a period of forty-plus years (approx. thirty-six in trust work and four+ as a professional financial planner and investment broker), I've worked with hundreds of family situations, advising them with the pre-attorney organizing of their information to create what I refer to as an "attorney packet" in their estate-planning journey. No two are alike; all are different.

While the emotional and spiritual dimensions of the Christian's will-plan are often the most difficult considerations, most Christians find them to be more important compared to all other considerations. We've included a number of stories of my experiences with family situations that reveal both sides of the great controversy in action as it relates to the disposition of accumulated assets.

All are different, with unique challenges that require an understanding of pertinent issues and options to consider and take into prayer. The process of planning today for tomorrow begins with you organizing your information for your attorney, particularly as they relate to your personal and family situation—including your values, priorities, and the goals of your personal or family life and mission—after you have studied and prayed until you receive individual instruction from the Lord.

> *One thing is absolutely certain: God will honor His promise to teach and guide you in the way you should go if you take it to Him in a teachable spirit, believing He has a plan for the design of your will and is eager to tell you about it.*

The struggle over how much to leave to children and how much to give to God's work is huge for some yet not so much for others. One family with adult children (parents in their fifties) created a plan that included a variety of ministry projects to be created upon their death, with one of their three children participating in the ongoing, long-term direction for each of the projects—matching a project with the interests and talents of each child.

Therefore, dear reader, this possible letter describes how my beloved wife and I designed our personal/family will-plan with our prayers to God. We prayed that His guidance would be real to us in our journey of creating an all-important, legally valid plan for our absence from this life. And He gave it to us clearly when we pressed our case before Him. We praise the Lord Almighty for such a powerfully precious blessing.

One thing is absolutely certain: God will honor His promise to teach and guide you in the way you should go if you take it to Him in a teachable spirit, believing He has a plan for the design of your will and is eager to tell you about it. Lay claim to His promise in Psalm 32:8–9 and pray the self-surrendered pleading, "Thy will be done," at each step of the journey. When He guides me with His eye, my thinking is always crystal clear and a big relief.

Individual Instruction in Your Preparations for the Biblical Time of Trouble

How do we relate to all that is going on around the globe? The following prayerful verse has become more and more meaningful to me: "Great peace have they which love your law: and nothing shall offend them" (Ps. 119:165). You probably know two-thirds of Christ's parables deal with money or possessions. Your faithfulness to Him in supporting His ministry suggests you really understand the import thereof and have an intimately saving relationship with Jesus. Please know we deeply appreciate your gifts and cherish our relationship with you.

With that said, it is in the context of these two relationships [between you and God and family and between you and God's remnant movement] that we share with you some thoughts on the services available to you in the Planned Giving & Trust Services Department. Preparing a will is a sacred journey for you as God's child because all we have and are belong to Him; and we are on a mission for Him. Making a will-plan that is approved by heaven requires an intentional design by each person who does a last will and testament inheritance plan.

One of the most prized bits of counsel of which I know has to do with the spiritual dimension of a will-plan design and offers each of us God's individual instruction. Here are a few pertinent excerpts:

Preparation for the Time of Trouble—Expect Individual Instruction

> Houses and lands will be of no use to the saints in the time of trouble, for they will then have to flee before infuriated mobs, and at that time their possessions cannot be disposed of to advance the cause of present truth. *I was shown that it is the will of God that the saints should cut loose from every encumbrance before the time of trouble comes, and make a covenant with God through sacrifice. If they have their property on the altar, and earnestly inquire of God for duty, He will teach them when to dispose of these things.* Then they will be free in the time of trouble, and have no clogs to weigh them down.
>
> *I saw that if any held on to their property, and did not inquire of the Lord as to their duty, He would not make duty known, and they would be permitted to keep their property, and in the time of trouble it would*

come up before them like a mountain to crush them, and they would try to dispose of it, but would not be able. ...

I saw that a sacrifice* did not increase, but it decreased and was consumed*. I also saw that God had not required all of His people to dispose of their property at the same time, but if they desired to be taught, He would teach them, in a time of need, when to sell and how much to sell. Some have been required to dispose of their property in times past to sustain the advent cause, while others have been permitted to keep theirs until a time of need. Then, as the cause needs it, their duty is to sell. (White, *Counsels on Stewardship*, pp. 59, 60, emphasis added [*emphasis in source]; see also *Early Writings*, pp. 56-58)

The Holy Spirit has given us even more advice on this delicate subject:

The Lord requires that those to whom He has lent talents of means make a right use of them, having the advancement of His cause prominent. (White, *Testimonies for the Church*, vol. 2, p. 659)

Make Property Secure by Proper Will—Those who are faithful stewards of the Lord's means will know just how their business stands, and, like wise men, they will be prepared for any emergency. Should their probation close suddenly, they would not leave such great perplexity upon those who are called to settle their estate.

Many are not exercised upon the subject of making their wills while they are in apparent health. But this precaution should be taken by our brethren....

Wills should be made in a manner to stand the test of law ... Death will not come one day sooner, brethren, because you have made your will. (White, *The Adventist Home*, pp. 396, 397, emphasis added)

Those who make their wills should not spare pains or expense to obtain legal advice and to have them drawn up in a manner to stand the test. (White, *Testimonies for the Church*, vol. 3, p. 117, emphasis added)

Consider all this, where should you begin? Here are my suggested steps for your planning:

1) Continually refresh your gift of yourself to God in full surrender of your mind (thoughts and feelings), heart (affections, values and passions), and will (choices, priorities and goals)—(see 2 Cor. 8, 9)

2) Make a covenant of sacrifice with God in which you place all you have on His altar; then listen for His still, small voice of individual

instruction in how to use what you have now and plan for its transfer, now and/or at the time of your death. If you have done this already, you might pray over it and see if it is time to refresh your covenant.

3) We should begin to finish the completion of the confidential EDIO data form so an overall estate plan design proposal may be prepared for you. We can begin to fill in the blanks of the form anytime you are ready. As we go through the form from section to section, we normally discuss pertinent issues and options for planning that might be of interest to you and create an estate design proposal that reflects your values and priorities. We will do a computer printout of the completed form for you to examine—it often takes three or more drafts of the EDIO to get it ready for your attorney. The job description of your attorney is included in chapter seventeen of this book.

4) We will then have a basis on which to prepare a plan design proposal to share with you. After we discuss our proposal, an adjusted proposal will be prepared for you to share with your attorney.

5) You can then go to your attorney to discuss issues and options as it relates to our plan design proposal and follow through the process with your attorney as described in other parts of this material.

My only sense of urgency when serving as your consultant is to assist you in carrying out whatever plan that you and the Lord decide on and get it done in a timely manner, at your pace—when you are ready to move from one step to the next. We focus on your agenda and timing at all phases of the process.

Here are some **suggested dos and don'ts** that have been meaningful to me:

1. **Do** make a covenant with God—prayerfully transfer ownership of all you have in relationships, plus all property and financial assets, to God, with the pledge to listen to His instruction for your conduct in the relationships and the use of the accumulated assets—whether dead or alive, in poverty or plenty.

2. **Do** make a legal inheritance plan that will honor God and your covenant with Him.

3. **Do** let God reveal His will to you for your will. Saturate each step of the process in prayers of self-surrender to His will.

4. **Do** feel welcome to call me to serve you in this project, if you wish. I'm available to walk you through the process. You don't need to have it all figured out before you call me.

5. **Do** know we will serve you on your timetable, at your pace, and on your agenda; we will respect your personal and family situation, with no manipulation. Our advice to you will have no tone of controlling you.

6. **Don't** allow the design of your will-plan to be dictated by anyone other than the Holy Spirit.

7. **Don't** allow convenience and inclination to keep you from praying about this.

This letter is sent for your prayerful consideration; I'd like to hear from you, if the Lord leads you to contact me.

Chapter 9

A Slice of History: A Variety of Operating Models for Planned Giving & Trust Services Departments at Seven Seventh-day Adventist Denominational Organizations (as of 2003)

This information is offered only as illustrations. The operating program of the Planned Giving & Trust Services departments of the Seventh-day Adventist Church in the United States is widely diverse in its purpose, mission, and focus from one conference, institution, and Ministry to another, as illustrated in the following seven examples. This is because an incoming new director of a given department always has the freedom to create and operate the program according to his or her preferences and skill set. Normally, their administrators are not in dialogue with the issues and options for such an operation. One conference president told me the wall between his office and the Trust Department might as well be ten miles thick.

This report is based on my random conversations with specific friends in person during the 2003 NAD Continuing Education Conference in Williamsburg, Virginia (these were circulated back to each respective organization for confirmation and/or corrections). My guess is each of them has been changed by now because of changing personnel:

All of our members need a will, and it is the church's responsibility to provide it at no cost to the member and with no donative conditions.

1. The declared purpose of the first department in this study is to provide estate-planning services to all church members and pay the legal fees with no requirement of a gift to the church, using the corporate legal counsel as donor counsel—apparently not using the Trust Services Department as a fundraising agency of support for the mission of the church.

    The focus is that all of our members need a will, and it is the church's responsibility to provide it at no cost to the member and with no donative conditions.

2. The declared purpose of the second department in this study is to provide legal documents to the church member with all related costs being paid by the department. The said legal documents include wills, general durable power of attorney, healthcare power of attorney, and a living will at no charge. The said legal documents and related legal services are provided by the denominational organization's retained legal counsel at the organization's expense. The organization's planned giving consultant does document delivery and supervision of document execution. The organization's legal counsel has no contact with the member in providing this service as corporate counsel for the organization.

    If the church member's plan calls for a revocable living trust, the member covers the cost. The member has the option to use the organization's retained legal counsel or seek their own legal counsel. The organization's planned giving consultant follows up by supervising document execution and asset transfers to the trust.

    The organization's retained legal counsel prepares all irrevocable trusts where the denominational organization is the trustee and a constituent entity of the organization is designated to receive at least 50 percent of the remainder benefit.

    The focus of the program is a spiritual ministry and fundraising for the ministries in the organization's territory and the church at large.

3. The declared purpose of the third department in this study is to provide estate-planning services to all church members without the members paying for their legal fees—with no requirement of a gift to the church—using the corporate legal counsel as donor counsel and offering various gift plan models for consideration. This is part

of the process of assisting members in filling out the will worksheet (confidential estate data form) for the legal counsel's use in making the necessary decisions of design in drafting legal documents.

The focus is to assist as many people as possible to get their wills done while hoping some will make a gift, using this department of the church with no conditions but minimizing the cost to the organization by not paying the normal cost of legal fees that would be charged by a lawyer, who should be an independent specialist.

4. The declared purpose of the fourth department in this study is to provide estate-planning services as part of a spiritual ministry to all members with no requirement of a gift, except a minimum of 10 percent of the estate as a fee-for-service when the denominational organization accepts fiduciary responsibility, using corporate legal counsel as donor counsel and paying the legal fees—emphasizing the spiritual principles of estate stewardship and encouraging prayer to know God's plan for one's will while looking for gift planning opportunities such as gift annuities and charitable remainder trusts.

The focus is a spiritual ministry with no responsibility for productivity in fundraising and no accountability with respect to the cost-benefit ratio.

5. The declared purpose of the fifth department in this study is to make estate-planning services available to all members while looking for non-revocable planned gift opportunities such as charitable gift annuities and charitable remainder trusts. There is no gift requirement for those who need a will-only plan. For those who need a living revocable trust, pour-over will, power of attorney, and health care proxy with *no fiduciary responsibility* for the denominational organization, the required gift is 10 percent of the estate (25 percent if the plan involves fiduciary responsibility for the church entity). Corporate legal counsel serves as donor legal counsel, with the organization paying the legal fees for all services. Many in the planned giving community at large view this approach as a "fee-for-service" program.

The focus is on estate planning services to as many of our people as possible while being alert to gift planning opportunities.

6. The declared purpose of the sixth department in this study is to provide *charitable* estate-planning services, preferably to our more senior members and friends, but ultimately to all who are authentic, heart-activated donors. The organization pays the legal fees for planning and related documents of *irrevocable* gift plans such as charitable gift annuities and charitable remainder trusts, as well as providing some assistance with payment of legal fees that are incurred by the donor for planning and drafting those *revocable* documents that provide the church a benefit that substantially exceeds the costs, using truly independent donor legal counsel.

    The focus is a spiritual ministry of emphasizing our mission, teaching the spiritual principles of estate stewardship, encouraging prayer to know God's will in applying the principles, and assisting donors to make planned gifts that are legally secure—outright and/or deferred gifts to support the mission of the church—the mission of Christ to seek and save the lost.

7. This seventh operating model is the one I've followed since 2001. Each of the denominational organizations I've served adopted it during my time of serving as their department leader.

    The declared purpose of this model is to provide *charitable* estate-planning services to our members and other friends who are authentic donors. The organization pays the legal fees for planning and related documents of *irrevocable* gift plans such as charitable gift annuities and charitable remainder trusts. Some assistance in paying the legal fees is provided for planning and drafting those *revocable* documents that provide the denominational organization a benefit that substantially exceeds the costs, using *only* donor legal counsel that is truly independent of the Seventh-day Adventist Church in its professional role and function in the practice of law.

    The focus is emphasizing the mission of (name of denominational organization) and assisting donors to make planned gifts that are legally secure—outright gifts and/or deferred gifts to support the mission of the organization.

    (For educational institutions: *to educate its students for generous service to the church and society in keeping with a faithful witness to Christ and the worldwide mission of the Seventh-day Adventist Church*; for an evangelistic ministry or conference: *to support the mission of Christ to seek and save the lost*.)

CHAPTER 10

Authorized and Unauthorized Practice of Law, Issues of Legal Security of the Will-Plan Design, and Documents If Contested in Court After the Trust-maker's Death

The following legal and economic issues might be considered for application as we reflect on the seven operating models defined in the previous chapter:

1. Conflicts of interest for lawyers in a dual representation function.

2. Unauthorized practice of law by a denominational organization and its employees. You may read "Appendix 1—Missouri Supreme Court Action on Unauthorized Practice of Law" by going online to mystewardship.estate.

3. Authorized practice of law by denominational employees who are lawyers—potential liability to the organization is another consideration.

4. Distinguishing corporate legal counsel duties from donor legal counsel duties is of significance.

5. The accelerated need of truly independent, competent legal counsel for appropriate representations of the interests of both the denominational organization and its donors.

6. Economic issues of the cost-benefit ratio for efficient support of the mission of the denominational organizations who operate the programs of planned giving ministry and trust administration services.

7. Purpose and mission of the department—estate planning services with no focus on fundraising for the support of its mission *versus* charitable estate planning services with an estate stewardship ministry—looking for gift plan opportunities that imply maturity within a timeframe of ten-to-thirty years.

8. Program design for the department based on its mission, purpose, focus, and identity.

9. Job description of the planned giving consultant.

10. Scope of services offered by the department.

11. Scope of employment by the church employees who make up the department as it pertains to the organization's insurance coverage for potential legal liability.

Securing the legal safety of your plan and legal documents that give them recognized definition and validity is of the utmost importance to you. Unfortunately, the general society of the United States of America has become increasingly litigious. And trial lawyers push that agenda hard against God's church. I read some years ago that the Trial Lawyers Association declared that their targeted growth opportunities would focus on religious organizations.

Many people have no qualms about bringing legal action to challenge a will or suing the church if there might be a credible case. In one case where I was the departmental director—and as such, I was the point man to deal with the case on behalf of my employer—a denominational organization was the defendant. The person who was the plaintiff brought a damaging lawsuit against the organization I worked for. The case took four years to settle. The person who sued us claimed to be a member of the church in good and regular standing, and said to me, "I don't want to hurt the church; I just want to collect on your insurance policy."

That person had significant affluence and influence within the denomination. The legal fees for us to defend the case were over $200,000. The first $50,000 was our deductible that was paid out of our church income, and our insurance paid the rest. Of course, such cases can cause the insurance premium to be increased in the future, which is a further injury to the church.

There are at least two significant considerations regarding the **protection** of your plan:

1. Your last will and testament document must be filed with the local probate court in a timely manner *after* your death. The laws that govern the amount of time after death for said filing will likely vary from one state to another. A probate judge monitors, supervises, and gives final approval of the work done by your nominated executor or personal representative in harmony with the specifications you made in your will document.

2. The *original* document (a copy is not admissible) must be filed at the court. Therefore, your decision on where to store the original document is quite significant. It must be stored in a secure place, safe from fire, flood, and would-be thieves.

The goal is to *prevent* the destruction of the original documents by those who do not like your plan when they see it, either before or after your death or, in some other way, take an action to make your plan of no effect. Therefore, you need to be careful and pray over the decision of where to store your will and related legal documents. Of course, you should keep a signed copy in your possession. Some have recorded a video at the time of signing the documents in which the husband and wife declare their intentions to be viewed by family at a later time.

The Seventh-day Adventist denominational practice generally is that when we store them, they are placed in a fire-resistant filing cabinet or vault that is kept locked when not in active use. And if the file is removed by an authorized employee in order to work on it at a nearby desk, the employee must sign the file-out with the date and time of removal and replacement.

People often choose to leave the documents at the office of the lawyer who drafted them. There can be problems of access when they are stored in a bank safe deposit box, depending on state laws. There are at least five possibilities:

1. Your documents could be destroyed (e.g., shredded or burned).
2. Potential executors (or personal representatives) who are to carry out your wishes as specified in your last will and testament might not agree with the decisions you made in your plan. They might disagree either about who you name to be the legal guardian of your minor-age children or with your preferred distribution of assets to family, friends and/or God's work. In this case, they can usually find ways to substitute their will for yours. Therefore, you need to pray until you know God's divine guidance in selecting the people who will serve in such roles and functions as executor or personal representative and power of attorney agent for life-management assistance for the donor.
3. Your plan could be challenged in court with a lawsuit against your will. A jury could decide it is not your will. I've seen it happen in a bitterly fought conflict.
4. If the person you name as your successor trustee of living trust does not agree with your plan to distribute a specific property or sum of money to a ministry or institution of the church, that distribution may not happen; there is no accountability to any person or court. I've *never* known of the church suing an offending trustee or executor in such a case.
5. There is one other method that is effective in defeating your plan, based on a few cases I've seen where our donor expressed a strong desire to leave a substantial amount to the Lord's work. The donor was very determined about it to the point of getting legal documents prepared for that purpose. However, family members didn't agree with that plan and took our donor to a lawyer of their selection to get new documents drawn for the donor to sign that left everything to them. In each case, the donor was quite senile and incompetent, probably with no or limited understanding of the reality of the family's thievery. In some cases, the family had no need but expressed hatred for the church.

Back to the Discussion About Legal Protection for Your Plan and Its Documents

Legal Representation of You

It is essential for you to have your own legal representation (a lawyer whom you select to be your attorney-at-law) to guide you through the legal process of preparing a set of legal documents: a will, perhaps a living revocable trust, a general durable power of attorney (POA) for life management, a health care proxy, and a living will, in which you name individuals whom you trust implicitly to act on your behalf when you cannot do those functions for yourself.

An employee of the denominational organization who serves you as a certified planned giving consultant and/or trust officer may assist you in organizing your data to share with your lawyer; that employee may also discuss issues and options of such planning to assist you to understand how to talk with your attorney about what you have and what you want to do with it at death. This normally results in a better quality of legal documents at a reduced cost of legal fees due to the attorney packet preparation and the professional guidance of the planned giving consultant.

Regardless of his or her professional qualifications, if an employee of one of our denominational organizations provides legal services to you by drawing legal conclusions about your fact case, offering you legal advice about what you should do, and/or drafting legal documents for your plan, that would raise a potentially high risk for the legally safe passage of your documents to the accomplishment of your purpose for creating them.

If such an employee of the church is a lawyer by training and admitted to the local state bar, he or she should not be your legal representative because that could potentially jeopardize the legal security of your plan if tested in a court of law. You should also avoid naming a Seventh-day Adventist Church pastor as your executor or POA. Generally, those functions are not included in pastors' "scope of employment" unless they are certified by the North American Division to also serve as an employee in the Planned Giving & Trust Services Department. Such employees are probably not covered by the church's Errors & Omissions insurance coverage for any legal action against them that might result from assisting you with legal matters. Regardless of those with whom you discuss your plan design— friends, family, or professional advisers—you should be consciously wary of their potential to exercise a conflict of interest and/or undue influence on their part—in their relationship to you and your planning process.

The concept of getting rich by suing someone for money has become all too popular. And the church is increasingly viewed as a "deep-pocket target."

Whenever you make a plan to distribute your accumulated assets, in all cases, it is essential for you to engage the services of a lawyer to represent you. The lawyer you select to do this work for you becomes your attorney (your legal representative) for this purpose. If your plan is challenged in court after you are no longer here, your attorney would represent you and defend your plan. If your attorney retires from practice before your death, then whoever takes over that legal practice would represent your estate in court and in the role of advising the executor as needed to settle your estate. If your lawyer is a solo practitioner, then your executor would need to use a lawyer of his or her selection. We have included guiding advice on how to select and work with a lawyer as your attorney.

"How to Select and Work with a Lawyer and Your Attorney's Job Description" are in Chapter 17 of this book, where you may learn the role and function of your attorney in his or her role and function of serving your wish to make a legally valid will-plan.

Your lawyer will study the facts of your case: your personal and family facts, financial facts (what you own and what you owe), along with your declaration of what you would want done with what you've got if you don't wake up the next morning.

Your lawyer will also supervise the signing of your new plan documents in your attorney's presence. This may occur in the lawyer's office or at the donor's place of residence. In a case where the denominational organization for which I worked was sued for multiple millions, the lawyer who defended us was assigned to us by the Adventist Risk Management office of the General Conference of Seventh-day Adventists. She was in her fifties, had never married, and her work was her life. She was well-seasoned in such cases. Her employer was a large law firm in a major city. That law firm's singular purpose at the time it was established was to defend organizations that were being sued. This lawyer specialized in defending organizations in will contest and/or trust cases involving estates and trusts. The case with which she was serving as our legal counsel involved a charitable remainder trust. One thing I had to do was to be examined with questions by the plaintiff's lawyer in what is called a "deposition." That experience confirmed the wisdom of my practice of keeping a written diary daily for decades. My diary was always detailed—like who I contacted by way of in-person contact or written letter delivered by the USPS or email or text, and the subject of communication with the amount of time the contact was engaged.

Our defense attorney told me it is common in court cases of a will contest for the plaintiff's lawyer to ask who supervised the signing of the will. The defense of our case would be seriously weakened in a will contest if our organization was a named beneficiary and denominational employees did the following:

1. Supervised the signing of wills and related documents.
2. Acted as a witness to the signatures of the donors.
3. Served as a notary public attesting to the signatures.

In my work with the intake of hundreds of will-plan cases for decades, I've never done numbers 2 or 3 above. However, I did supervise the signing of documents, though not in a lawyer's office. For example, I also explained the documents to the donors. I would walk them through a forty-page trust agreement, explaining the purpose and meaning of each paragraph during my first twenty years of this work.

Each of the Above Elements in Your Process of Planning Is the Practice of Law

It is very appropriate for Seventh-day Adventist denominational organizations to operate a Planned Giving & Trust Services Department. When this department has a "full service" operation, it consists of:

- Estate stewardship ministry—sharing emotional-spiritual principles (not rules).
- Comprehensive estate planning service.
- Trust administration services of fiduciary investing, accounting, and tax returns and reporting, either in-house or outsourced.
- Donor relationship ministry—to nurture and sustain the donors' consciousness of their favorite denominational organization or self-supporting ministry and its mission.

While the above legal services should be provided to you by a lawyer, *some* of the denominational organizations (conferences, institutions, and ministries) can and do provide valuable assistance to lots of people like you and me. Denominationally certified planned giving consultants and/or trust officers may assist you in the process of creating or updating your own will-plan design by assisting you in your effort to organize and prepare your pertinent information. The lawyer's fees might be less when you present your attorney packet to him or her.

For example, the planned giving consultant or trust officer may serve donor(s) in the following ways:

1. Provide you with spiritual principles of will-plan design with the encouragement to study and pray for the Lord's guidance in your use of the principles in your plan design.

2. Assist you in creating an attorney packet for you to take to your chosen lawyer. Such a packet generally consists of:

   a. A completed confidential data form that will provide your attorney your personal, family, and financial information, along with the names of people you wish to be involved as beneficiaries and fiduciaries.

   b. Copies of your financial account statements, title deeds for your real estate property, your property insurance documentation, and any other related materials about your assets and liabilities for the benefit of your attorney-at-law to know your planning issues and the appropriate advice you need to receive from him or her.

   c. Copies of your existing will-plan documents, if any.

3. If the planned giving consultant or trust officer assists you complete the confidential data form, he or she may educate you on the issues and options of plan design. For example, one cannot advise you to *do* a living trust but may share stories of how and why trusts have worked in other people's plans.

Legal security for will-plans is increasingly important because people are much more prone now than they ever were before to initiate a lawsuit if they don't like something. In the case of your will-plan, that would happen after your death to defend your plan in court. Therefore, it may be vitally important for you to tell your family about your plan—maybe after it is completed if you expect a high level of attempted influence by them.

Generally, we are a frugal people. Many of us adhere to the philosophy of "do it yourself." Hopefully, you would not exercise that approach with brain surgery. The process of will planning requires a lawyer who specializes in trusts and estates—providing legal expertise in both planning them and settling them after death. It has been my sad experience to witness some cases of very shoddy work of will-plan drafting.

A discussion of legal security in this context might include the following:

1. MEASURING STANDARD AND RELATED LEGAL ISSUES—of the legal services component of the Seventh-day Adventist Planned Giving & Trust Services Program. "Wills should be made in a manner to stand the test of law" (White, *Testimonies for the Church*, vol. 4, p. 482). Generally, we understand this to mean that the plans we assist our members to create must be done so they will

successfully withstand a potential legal challenge in a future lawsuit in court, such as a will contest.

Please consider the following issues with the above standard in mind:

A. Our Accreditation Standard #4 states, "All trusts, wills, and other legal documents are prepared by, or under the supervision of, legal counsel in such a manner that the attorney accepts responsibility for the documents."

NOTE: Generally, we understand this to mean that the independent attorney who accepts responsibility for the documents also accepts the accompanying potential future liability. Church policy requires that we have evidence that such retained legal counsel has liability insurance of at least $1,000,000 (see NADWP P 50 27).

B. Our Accreditation Standard #5. a. states, "A written opinion has been obtained from the [corporate] attorney regarding which activities Trust Services personnel may properly engage in and the risks that may be involved." We refer to this one as the "Permissible Activities Standard."

NOTE: We understand this to generally mean that while the independent retained attorney cannot guarantee the resulting outcomes, he or she will be committed to at least testify in our defense, if needed, in a court action if we follow his or her written opinions regarding our operating activities of the Planned Giving & Trust Services Department; and that said attorney's liability insurance will cover such event.

C. Our 2004 Massachusetts legal research and written legal memorandum includes a discussion of our said activities and their attending risks, along with prescriptions for managing such risks. One of the prescriptions for managing risks states, "Competent Counsel. The organization should take all appropriate steps to ensure that only competent counsel is engaged to perform legal services. Charitable gift planning is an area all too often practiced by those inadequately qualified to do so. In the event a gift fails due to inadequate counsel referred by the nonprofit corporation, the corporation itself could be the target of litigation by the donor or relatives who are harmed."

NOTE: The issue of liability in today's litigious environment compels the exclusive use of lawyers for donor counsel who are recognized as being capable of consistent excellence by virtue of their specialized credentials of training and experience with a reputation for outstanding quality of both their advice and "work product" in the area of estate planning; where appropriate, this includes the use of charitable trusts.

D. **Separation of Legal Service Duties** into two categories, with each category being served by different law firms, as follows—a plan for our program I decided to follow in 1999:

- Corporate Legal Counsel
- Donor Legal Counsel

This separation of duties should further reduce potential liability for the lawyer and the denominational organization, as follows:

I. Reduces or minimizes the potential of claims of conflict of interest against the organization's corporate attorney.

II. Reduces or minimizes the potential of liability claims against the church in the areas of:
- Undue Influence
- Conflict of Interest
- The church organization being viewed as the legal practitioner, thereby practicing law without the required licensing authority for such an operation.

E. Enhances and enriches the experience of our donors inasmuch as they can know with full satisfaction that their interests were fully represented in the process and the resulting will-plan documents truly represent their heart.

F. Written Legal Opinion. I received a letter in response to my letter to our legal counsel at the time, Attorney Fred Marcus, of Freeman, Freeman, & Smiley, LLP, at their Los Angeles office. Fred's letter produced clarity like I had never experienced before. (At the time, I was the director of Gift Planning & Trust Services for the Pacific Union Conference of Seventh-day Adventists. We had engaged Attorney Marcus and his firm to do the research for and to write our Written Legal Opinions on the eight issues of our program that are specifically required by denominational policy. The "Permissible Activities" opinion is the most crucial and difficult of the eight.)

In his letter of October 21, 1999, Attorney Fred Marcus wrote, in part:

While we have described in "Issue 1" [Permissible Activities of a Planned Giving Consultant] the conditions and the significant level of risk in which your retained Corporate Counsel may also serve as Donor Counsel in a "Dual Representative" role, this letter is in answer to your recently asked question of whether or not it is permissible in California for your Planned Giving Advisors [Consultants] to:

1. *Gather data from prospective donors, including information of a personal nature: family, finance, and goals; and*

2. *Prepare a suggested comprehensive Estate and Gift Plan Design with plan elements that are appropriate to the size of the estate and that are consistent with the donors' goals, including Charitable Gift Plan options.*

*While the activities of your Planned Giving Advisors described above could arguably be considered the unauthorized practice of law, we believe that the risk of such a finding is largely eliminated **if all of the following conditions are met**:*

1. *"The said plan design is submitted to an attorney who is serving as donor counsel;*

2. *"Said donor counsel must be competent and truly independent, with the freedom to accept or reject each element of the proposed plan design, or add other elements to it;*

3. *"Said donor counsel must have full responsibility for drafting any legal documents that may be used to implement some or all of the plan;*

4. *"Said donor counsel must not be concurrently serving as corporate counsel for the organization which employs the involved planned giving consultant and stands to gain a beneficial interest in the plan;*

5. *"Said donor counsel must not be captive to the Seventh-day Adventist Church (i.e., does not receive a substantial percentage of his or her revenue from one or more entities of the Seventh-day Adventist Church in the capacity of donor counsel of corporate counsel);*

6. "Said donor counsel may be paid by the church for the services of drafting the legal documents required to implement the particular part or parts of the plan design which provides for a beneficial interest to the church that is greater than the church's anticipated costs of establishing the plan and, when applicable, managing the plan, **so long as an appropriate conflicts waiver is obtained from the donor and the church.**

Marcus concluded the letter with this explanation of the benefits:

These conditions will also minimize the risk of legal action against the church for the activities of the Planned Giving Advisors in connection with conflicts of interest, private benefit and claims of undue influence.

I hope these comments are helpful to you. If you have any questions, please do not hesitate to contact me.

Signed by Fred J. Marcus, Esq. for FREEMAN, FREEMAN & SMILEY, LLP

Legal Foundation—This Written Legal Opinion of Fred Marcus, Esq. of California has served as the legal foundation of my work with donors in the operation of the Planned Giving & Trust Services Department of any given denominational organization, be it a conference, ministry, or institution. When I have shared a copy of the letter from Attorney Marcus with lawyers in other states, they have expressed full agreement with it, plus a high level of appreciation for it.

A Seventh-day Adventist lawyer and estate planning specialist, Dean Bouland, of Maryland, gave us the following legal advice for the legal security of the legal will-plan documents that are done for a donor as part of the work of a planned giving consultant at a denominational organization.

Attorney Bouland presented the following list of ten suggestions to encourage best practices at our continuing education meeting, which was held at the Columbia Union Conference offices in Columbia, Maryland, on October 8, 2008. Attorney Bouland's set of recommendations certainly harmonize with Attorney Marcus' opinion:

"Ten Suggestions"

1. The conference attorney should not prepare wills or trusts for donors.
2. Donors should have their own attorney prepare all legal documents.

3. If the conference refers a donor to an attorney, make sure that the attorney has not served as counsel for the conference in the past and do not assign the conference's other legal work to the attorney.

4. In dealing with contests over documents, you want the lawyer who drafted the document to be able to state in court that he or she represented only the donor and that he or she does not now and never has represented the conference. This will avoid a legal charge of conflict of interest.

5. If the conference insists on paying the lawyer's fee, make sure that the conference does not direct or regulate the attorney's services. All financial arrangements are disclosed to the donor. It is also a good practice to obtain the lawyer's written opinion that it is okay for him to accept payment from the conference when preparing documents for donors.

6. With the consent of the donor, have the conference's lawyer review all documents prepared for the donor by the donor's own counsel. The attorney for the conference can frequently offer suggestions to improve such documents.

7. If it is too good to be true it probably is.

8. Avoid the donor with grandiose plans but with little money. That donor may want to drag the conference into care-giving or other work to do for the donor.

9. Provide transparency to each donor about who each lawyer represents.

10. Follow the NAD policies which are designed to protect the planned giving program of the SDA Church.

The Lord's Double-Barreled Blessing

In the first twelve years of my work in trust services ministry, the most common question I received from people who had asked me to assist them in getting a will done was, "How much do I/we have to give the church in order to get your service?" My answer to that question was, "I do not work that way. My perspective is that whatever you give to the Lord's work is a spiritual journey, the same as what you give into the plate as it passes you at church on Sabbath. I'll be glad to share materials with you about the spiritual dimension of making a will-plan so you may study and pray for the Lord's instruction to you. And when you and the Lord figure it out, you let me know and I will share with you what we can do. I began thinking of my department as a limited resource for the financial and spiritual well-being of the church. In my thirteenth year (1992), I began the habit of praying, "Lord, please send people to me for this service who have a heart tender toward God and who have assets that the Holy Spirit might appropriate for a finished work." From that day until now, I've never heard that question again. And my role as an estate stewardship minister no longer included sharing materials about the spiritual dimension of will-planning during the interview process, because He brought people for the service who were *heart-activated, mission-driven, authentic donors* year after year. So very amazing!!!

The Lord brought people to me who sought to bless His work, whether they were in plenty or poverty, dead or alive. Therefore, the Lord's work has received millions of dollars from hearts that love Him supremely—gifts that probably qualify to be accepted by God and used by Him with efficiency and effectiveness—a great blessing toward a finished work. At the same time, none of the cases on which I worked ever wound up in court. There were two times when a family member uttered a threat at the funeral yet did not follow through on the threat. Praise the Lord!

I was also delighted when the Lord instructed me to adopt a new paradigm in my operation of the department because of the new legal foundation as given above. It resulted from a 1996 decision of the Missouri Supreme Court and a letter from our corporate legal counsel at the Pacific Union Conference of Seventh-day Adventists. (See Appendix 1 for the said court decision on authorized and unauthorized practice of law as it pertains to the work of an Adventist Planned Giving & Trust Services department by going to mystewardship.estate).

The changes in my operation of the Planned Giving & Trust Services program made a huge difference in the level of God's blessings. The proportionate number of genuine donors He brought to me for ministry and service was unexpectedly great. And many of them had substantial wealth with a strong donative intent. Praise the Lord again and again!

Here is what I learned about undue influence in this process:

Can Undue Influence be Defined?

"It is said the term undue influence cannot be given a definition that will serve as a safe and reliable test in every case, that each case depends to a large degree upon its own facts…not every influence exerted over a person can be undue influence" (Lynda Moerschbaecher, 1998, *Start at Square One*, p. 197).

Defining Clues of Undue Influence

"An influence is considered undue [when] exerted upon the grantor of a gift in order to override his/her will and make the act of executing the deed (or document) a mere mechanical performance" (*Ibid.*, p. 194).

"The court states that where a prior fiduciary relation exists, the court will "presume confidence placed and influence exerted ... A confidential and fiduciary relationship between [e.g., a pastor and member] gives rise to the presumption of undue influence" (*Ibid.*, pp. 194, 195).

"The court also states that it has held in the past that some influence may be properly used ... it is only when the testator's will is overcome is the result of the disposition invalid ... undue influence ... something excessive and unlawful, something which destroys free agency" (*Ibid.*, pp. 195, 193).

What May Create Suspicion of Undue Influence?

What conditions exist when undue influence can easily occur or be presumed to occur (even if it does not)? It might be indicated when dispositive provisions of a will differ from the natural order of things. While that may cause an adversarial legal action, it does not define undue influence.

Mild Influence is Not Undue Influence

"The court notes that 'even where solicitation is made for a specified bequest, this does not constitute undue influence unless it be so importunate, persistent, coercive or otherwise operates to subdue the will of the testator and deprive him/her of freedom of action.'" The court also stated, "Influence exerted merely by means of advice, argument, persuasion, solicitation, suggestion or entreaty is not undue influence" (*Ibid.*, p. 197).

When Might Undue Influence Occur?

The following list of situations illustrates areas to either avoid altogether or furnish with careful documentation with witnesses to be better able to rebut the presumption of undue influence.

After knowing all of this for several years, I spent a considerable amount of time visiting a couple at their home about an hour's drive from the office. He was in the process of retiring from pastoral ministry. We completed the data form, and it was ready to be given to their attorney. I had given them a considerable amount of material to read about the spiritual dimension of creating their will-plan. His affirming response to those materials caused me to be very surprised by the small amount of their estate that was to be designated for the Lord's work. If they would just increase it by a small incremental amount, we could pay a significant portion of the legal fees to get their documents done.

I asked our conference treasurer what he would think of me sharing that information with them. His response really took me back: "If you do that, you will automatically be guilty of undue influence." As I thought about that for about half a second, I realized he was absolutely correct.

Factors That Contribute to a Security Risk for Your Will-Plan

1. Confidential Relationship between you and a denominationally employed Planned Giving Consultant or Trust Officer.
2. Participation of the Planned Giving Consultant in procuring your will.
3. Unusually or unnaturally large part of the estate to be pledged to Lord's work.
4. The Donors' age and condition of health.
5. Existence of an opportunity to exert influence over the donor by the Planned Giving Consultant.
6. Unnaturalness of the objects of bounty (*Ibid.*, p. 198).

Conditions Ripe for Undue Influence

The planned giving consultant is considered an extension of the lawyer who serves his or her employing organization as both corporate legal counsel and donor legal counsel with respect to the same set of estate documents (dual legal representation).

Undue Influence and Conflict of Interest Exist or Are Presumed

Conflict of interest *exists* and undue influence is *presumed* when a planned giving consultant is working as an extension of the drafting lawyer, introduces a spiritual dimension, and asks for a gift to his or her employing organization during the process of assisting with the donor's estate design (dual legal representation).

Especially When the Planned Giving Consultant ...

- Prays the donor(s) will make a gift to God's work—in their presence,
- Delivers the data form to the lawyer,
- The lawyer doesn't contact the donor

- Planned Giving Consultant delivers documents and supervises document execution. Worse yet may be when Planned Giving Consultant serves as a witness and/or Notary Public.

We Don't Practice Law

We never:

- Draw legal conclusions on a donor's fact case
- Give legal or tax advice to donors as to what they should do
- Deliver documents with explanations and questions of suitability
- Supervise execution of documents
- Serve as a witness or notary public on documents
- Work in a dual legal representation program in which we are an extension of corporate legal counsel—never again!

Shifting gears, that's enough of what we don't do. What are we to do? What may we do?

Regarding major current gifts or major planned deferred gifts, it is estimated that most people have lost the mental agility to do this type of planning by ages 82–85. Although most of our work results in revocable plans, very few will change the plan that is done during the age span of 65–80, based on my experience.

What about donor influence? I seek to influence prospective donors to become heart-activated donors, using a mild form of non-manipulative, prayer-saturated influence, always striving to avoid undue influence by listening to and focusing on their life stories, sense of personal/family mission, and agendas.

We Always Educate and Minister to Hearts

- We walk through the confidential data form with the donor, providing information on issues and options of planning each section of the form.
- We always seek to understand the donor's planning agenda.
- We educate with respect to spiritual-emotional issues and a relationship with God.
- We educate with respect to technical, business, and legal issues.
- We discuss relational-family issues and needs at various levels.

- We may present an estate design proposal of our making, which may include a major gift to God's work, related to the donor's agenda and core-life mission—major gifts at death and/or during the donors' lifetime.

- Our primary goal is to educate folks enough for them to make informed design decisions for their legacy plan so they may explain it to their attorneys.

- Our secondary goal is transformational legacy planning—making spiritual transactions with heaven and sound business decisions by donors, rather than a simple business transaction with the church.

Note of guidance: In the "exercise of independent judgment and giving candid advice, a Planned Giving Officer may refer to law and tax, and to other considerations such as moral, economic, social, and political factors that may be relevant to the donor's situation. However, the PGO [Planned Giving Officer] may not give legal and tax advice" (*Ibid.*, p. 186).

When I made the presentation of this seminar on August 11, 2011, at a continuing education conference, a most important question was asked by an attendee: "When do you tell the donor how much they must give to the Lord's work in their will-plan in order to get your services?"

My answer was something like this: "I *never* tell anyone that information." If donors ask a question about that, I tell them, "Whatever you decide to give to the Lord's work in your will-plan is a sacred matter between you and the Lord. Such a gift or a pledge-to-give should be decided by studying the principles of the divine will design and praying for His instruction on how to *apply* those principles in your case that will give you peace. You might decide to claim God's promise of individual instructions found in Psalm 32:8–9. This should be a spiritually transformational transaction with heaven rather than a business transaction with the church."

For a bottom-line conclusion, let's highlight the prophet's descriptions of the future:

> The laws of the land will become more and more oppressive, as in the days of Noah. (White, *Manuscript Releases*, vol. 4, p. 78)
>
> Satan stirs them up, by a power from beneath, with an intensity that reveals his enmity to God and His laws. They enact human laws that are oppressive and galling. (White, *Manuscript Releases*, vol. 19, p. 162)

This book of memories is about my personal engagement in the professional experience of estate stewardship ministry as a planned giving consultant and trust officer. You may find more on this topic in "Appendix 1—Missouri Supreme Court Decision on Unauthorized Practice of Law" by going online to mystewardship.estate.

The seventh operating model at the conclusion of Chapter 9 is presented in a legal framework of considerations for your process of designing your will-plan. It is offered to you as "Guidelines for Legal Matters" (referred to herein as "Legal Security Issues").

To encapsulate this subject, my concerns are legal security of your will-plan design and the documents according to the law with legal carefulness and to encourage you to do your will-plan in a way that will minimize legal risks and maximize the safety of your legal documents while minimizing the potential success of people who would do a legal challenge of your documents in court after you are gone.

Chapter 11

My Experience as a Adventist Estate Stewardship Minister, a Planned Giving Consultant, and a Trust Officer

As a member of the family of God, each one of us knows we are one of a kind. God has a definite plan that is uniquely for you—a plan He designed to make you ready for eternal occupancy as a citizen of His kingdom, whether you are in plenty or poverty—whether you are dead or alive when Jesus returns for His precious bride, the remnant church.

I am writing about discovering God's unique plan for your life and how it relates to your accumulated assets, especially when making or remaking your will-plan. God has humble, penitent believers who make up His body. He is full of hope that you will be counted as one with Jesus and your family circle will be unbroken at that time. Evidently, Jesus prays on our behalf for such an outcome for each of us.

My Background

You might be interested in my experience with the Lord—His leading in my life and His blessings in my specialized ministry. I've enjoyed writing this material in the fashion of a memoir that will provide information you may use in practical ways. As such, I've

> *As a member of the family of God, each one of us knows we are one of a kind. God has a definite plan that is uniquely for you—a plan He designed to make you ready for eternal occupancy as a citizen of His kingdom.*

revealed my philosophy, style, and methods of operating the Seventh-day Adventist Planned Giving & Trust Services departments at various denominational organizations and how that changed over the years, telling several stories of my experiences in assisting people, as well as pertinent Bible stories. My employment by denominational organizations in this specialized ministry was from 1980 to the end of 2016.

Each such worker in Seventh-day Adventist denominational organizations operates the department according to one's own design. You may read my report of seven examples of Variations of Operating Models in this book. When I first entered the work of a trust services director at the Southern New England Conference in 1980, **I regarded trust services as another business operated by the church. However, the Lord converted my perspective to that of a spiritual ministry for His glory.** You see, I had just spent six years working at Loma Linda Foods, a business operated by the church (a General Conference institution at the time). Having worked as a professional financial planner and investment broker in the early 1970s, I was aware of bank trust departments, which also colored my thinking about this work in the church initially. My personal spiritual foundation and inspired spiritual covenant for planned giving ministry begins with the matter of *God's* calling.

The Lord made His calling to me explicitly clear after I had been doing this work nine years. In my role and function as the director of the two departments of Trust Services and Stewardship, I was at one stage or another of burnout all the time. I devoted about forty hours per week to each position. One morning, I got down flat on the floor at home and asked the Lord, "What is it you have called me to?" I also said, "Lord, people are telling me I should be a church pastor … Lord, You know I love the stewardship ministry most because that is a spiritual ministry. But I cannot handle this arrangement. I'm willing to be anything anywhere on earth or nothing."

The Lord came near in mercy and revealed to my mind that He had called me to trust services **ministry**. He went on to reveal to me that He had allowed me to be in the stewardship ministry leadership role of two conferences for six years so I might learn to apply His design of a spiritual stewardship ministry dimension to my responsibility in the denominational work of trust services. From the beginning of my learning to understand and do the work of stewardship ministry in the church, I was taught it is an **in-reach ministry** that seeks to save the lost in the church. My singular focus was shaped by being fully conscious of Ellen White's statement, which I read a few times before: "**not one in twenty [under 5 percent] whose** names are registered upon the church books are prepared to close their earthly history" (*Christian Service*, p. 41).

In my devotional time, the Holy Spirit convicted me when I read the words of instruction Jesus gave to His disciples: "Do not go into the way of the Gentiles, and do not enter a city of the Samaritans. But go rather to the lost sheep of the house of Israel" (Matt. 10:5–6, NKJV).

At the beginning of my work in trust services in 1980, I made the intentional assumption that the people who asked me to assist them with their estate planning would have studied the spiritual dimension and prayed to know God's plan for their will and I was there only to provide a technical service to assist them in establishing their plan with legal documentation. I soon came to understand that the reality is, in general, people give more thought to planning a two-week vacation than to this subject of planning for their absence from the earth—planning today for tomorrow.

That all changed in 1981 when I read Ellen G. White's counsel about how talking with the aged or invalids about their property "in order to learn what disposition they design to make of it" is a duty that "*is just as sacred as the duty to preach the word to save souls … Christian men should feel interested and anxious for that man's future good as well as for the interest of God's cause.*" She also mentioned we should not "stand by and see them losing his hold on this life and at the same time robbing the treasury of God" (*Testimonies for the Church*, vol. 4, p. 479, emphasis added).

My New Personal Covenant with God in 1981

The portions of the paragraph I've quoted above jumped off the page at me with convicting power, and the thought instantly formed in my mind: 'If my failure to make people aware of the spiritual dimension of estate planning and ask them to consider prayerfully a gift to the Lord's work results in those people being lost to eternity, I will be held accountable for their loss at the judgment bar.' Therefore, in 1981, I covenanted with God that whatever else I do, the spiritual principles (not rules) of estate planning will always be emphasized in my operation of Seventh-day Adventist Trust Services departments.

This new covenant I made with the Lord set me on a collision course between the matter of *it* (that has stayed with me since 1981) and the ethical and legal requirement to avoid the unauthorized practice of law and undue influence.

In answer to a lot of my prayers, the Lord led me into an operating program of the department that allowed for best practices to conform my work in planned giving ministry to suit my 1981 covenant with Him and minimize legal liability. This relief came in the form of the written legal opinion given to me by Attorney Fred Marcus in 1999 and was extremely valuable to me. This legal opinion was also supported by Attorney Dean Bouland, of Maryland, in 2008—as mentioned earlier.

Attorney Marcus, of Los Angeles, California, was our corporate legal counsel at the Pacific Union Conference. While I depended on his 1999 letter as my mainstay guide in the role and function of assisting God's people in their creation of a set of end-of-life plan documents, I always adhered to the necessity of selecting a local lawyer to serve our denominational organization as our Corporate Legal Counsel and to draft the eight essential written legal opinions for their legal jurisdiction, according to our denominational policy. While I always shared a copy of Fred's written legal opinion for California with the said local lawyer, he had to do his own research within the local state and, on that basis, formulate his own written legal opinion on the question of our permissible activities and the other seven issues.

The legal opinion of Attorney Marcus became essential to me and gave me huge relief from the ever-present tension with which I had lived from 1981–1999. The tension that kept me on my knees in prayer is the matter of my practice described above, the big difference being we would begin to depend on the member's legal documents to be drafted by a truly independent lawyer rather than on the denominational organization's retained legal counsel who worked in a dual-representation mode.

While there are many statements of counsel on making wills in the Spirit of Prophecy, the following excerpts are taken from a significant "bottom-line" statement:

> Many manifest a needless delicacy on this point. They feel that they are stepping upon forbidden ground when they introduce the subject of property to the aged or to invalids in order to learn what disposition they design to make of it. But this duty is just as sacred as the duty to preach the Word to save souls.... Should not Christian men feel interested and anxious for that man's future good as well as for the interest of God's cause, that he shall make a right disposition of his Lord's money ... Will his brethren stand by, and see him losing his hold on this life, and at the same time robbing the treasury of God? (White, *Counsels on Stewardship*, pp. 323, 324)

While reading the above passage, I was alerted that the design of our will-plans is definitely a salvation issue. The Holy Spirit's conviction was a "WOW!!!" moment that has stayed with me with great reality from 1981 to today.

The job description of an Adventist planned giving consultant and trust officer, either in print or by general understanding, does *not* include talking you into making a will-plan that conforms to the expectations of your consultant, the employing organization, or any other person or organization, **because**:

- God loves and accepts the person and the gifts of a cheerfully delighted donor whose heart is full of loving trust and grateful loyalty (see 2 Cor. 9:7; Gen. 4:5–7).

- *"God has the power to supply you abundantly,* so that, with all your needs supplied at all times, you may have something to spare for every work of mercy" (2 Cor. 9:8, Knox Version, emphasis added).

- "Whatever [you do that] is not of faith is sin" (Rom. 14:23).

- "*The offering from the heart that loves,* God delights to honor, giving it highest efficiency in service for Him. If we have given our hearts to Jesus, we also shall bring our gifts to Him. Our gold and silver, our most precious earthly possessions, our highest mental and spiritual endowments, will be freely devoted to Him who loved us, and gave Himself for us" (White, *The Desire of Ages*, p. 65).

- How could it be better *not* to give? Notice this valuable insight: "It were better not to give at all than to give grudgingly; for if we impart of our means when we have not the spirit to give freely, we mock God. Let us bear in mind that we are dealing with One upon whom we depend for every blessing. One who reads every thought of the heart, every purpose of the mind" (White, *Counsels on Stewardship*, p. 199).

- Studying the teachings on the formation of God-like *values* normally results in a passion for the pursuit of the mission of Christ to seek and save the lost. Part of my ministry as a planned giving consultant is to share such teachings with you and encourage you to study the principles to know His instruction—saturated in prayer—for the application to your personal and family plan for your end of life.

Evidently, it is the expectation of heaven that God's true children will make legally documented decisions about personal and family values and priorities, as we plan today for tomorrow. The focus of our prayers for the Lord's leading in our will-plan design should be given serious, prayerful consideration. It may also add to our sense of responsibility and need to really depend on the Lord for individual instruction in this sacred journey and its spiritual dimension.

My experience of serving as a spiritual and financial counselor to many hundreds of people during a period of a few decades for Seventh-day Adventist organizations, plus five years in a secular business as a professional financial planner and investment broker, has given me the following general perspective on God's people: A few people live as if their accumulated assets belong to Someone else, that being Christ, who is their Lord and Savior from sin to everlasting life. These people really live as if all they have belongs to God; and their planning today for tomorrow reflects the reality of that living experience in the core of their beings.

For me to work with people in their estate planning process is literally an experience of standing on holy ground.

For me to work with people in their estate planning process is literally an experience of standing on holy ground. This part of my journey with Jesus is most humbling and exciting.

How Do We Relate Estate Planning to Christ's Second Coming?

One lady said to me, "I had recent heart surgery. My husband and one son are dependent on me to care for them in their disabilities; my other two children are well able to care for themselves; but I must have a plan in place to care for these two dear men in my life because every night when I go to sleep, I don't know if I will wake up the next day or not."

This lady had just been through a major medical condition that encouraged this uncertainty to be a real threat to the two men for whom she was responsible to care. She also expressed the view that the second coming of Jesus is both very certain and very, very imminent. "We expect the rise in tyranny and anarchy in the USA to increase until it rolls us into the biblical time of trouble very soon [as predicted in Daniel 12:1]." She went on to say, "But we don't know who the Lord will, in mercy, put down to rest in the grave just before He comes; and who He will sustain to go through the great time of trouble. So, I must have a plan in place very soon."

In this journey with Jesus as the Lord of my life, I resonate most wonderfully with the message of the hymn, "My Lord and I":

I have a Friend so precious, so very dear to me,
He loves me with such tender love, He loves so faithfully;
I could not live apart from Him, I love to feel Him nigh,
And so we *dwell* together, my Lord and I.

Sometimes I'm faint and weary, He knows that I am weak,
And as He bids me lean on Him, His help I gladly seek;
He leads me in the paths of light, beneath a sunny sky,
And so we *walk* together, my Lord and I.

I tell Him all my sorrows, I tell Him all my joys,
I tell Him all that pleases me, I tell Him what annoys;
He tells me what I ought to do, He tells me how to try,
And so we *talk* together, my Lord and I.

He knows that I am longing some weary soul to win,
And so He bids me go and speak the loving word for Him;
He bids me tell His wondrous love, and why He came to die,
And so, we *work* together, my Lord and I.

(Shorey, Mary Ann. "My Lord and I." *Seventh-day Adventist Hymnal*, Review & Herald Publ. Assn., Hagerstown, MD, 1985, song 456. Emphasis added.)

Truly, it is wonderful to *dwell*, *walk*, *talk*, and *work* together with God. I have often discovered the great controversy or cosmic conflict in my work of His estate stewardship ministry. As you read the stories in this book, you might ask yourself, 'Is Christ the owner and Lord of who I am and what I've got?'

Purpose of Planned Giving & Trust Services Departments of Seventh-day Adventist Organizations

I have enjoyed the privilege of continuous employment by various entities of the Seventh-day Adventist Church in the department of Planned Giving & Trust Services, beginning September 1, 1980, and continued to be involved in regular part-time employment by denominational organizations until 2016, after my retirement in 2007.

Here's a suggestion: Ask yourself the question, '*Why* should the church spend tithe money to support such a department?' Some administrators might view it as a financial investment with the expectation of a financial benefit later. My answer, for whatever value you might find in it: The *purpose of Planned Giving & Trust Services* as a department of the Seventh-day Adventist Church is to conduct an estate stewardship in-reach ministry to save the lost of the church. It is like when Jesus gave instructions to His disciples, when sending them out to go to the lost sheep in the house of Israel (see Matt. 10:5–7).

Also, it is to assist our people in creating their documented will-plan in a planned giving ministry and operate a trust administration services system that will result in financial support for the mission of Christ to seek and save the lost—given by His people with the purpose of finishing His work in this generation by making major gifts (current and deferred gifts from income and accumulated assets)—gifts freely and cheerfully given by authentic, heart-activated donors. This has included estate stewardship ministry in my experience on a number of occasions. We hope and pray that such gifts are approved in the eyes of heaven:

1. **Gifts that are acceptable to God**, like the gift Abel gave (see Heb. 11:4; Gen. 4:3–5) and *unlike* the gifts Cain (see Gen. 4:1–8) and Ananias and Sapphira gave (see Acts 5:1–11), because "Whatever you do that is not of faith is sin" (Rom. 14:23) If you scan the reference listings under the word "Offering(s)" in volume 2 of the *Comprehensive Index to the Writings of Ellen G. White* (pp. 1909–1914), you may notice a number of listings in which she wrote about offerings that are *not* acceptable to God.

   My goal is to assist people in making gifts to the Lord's work that are acceptable to Him—gifts that will be guarded and used by Him efficiently and effectively to hasten the second coming of Jesus. That is only possible when gifts are given by a person who has a loyal heart of loving trust with a willing mind to God in an act of worship—in the spirit of praise and thanksgiving.

2. **Gifts that are affordable**—that the donors will not regret later and that will not disgrace the church by leaving the donors destitute at some time in the future, taking into account Medicaid planning.

3. **Gifts to support the mission of Christ to seek and save the lost** became my passion in 1992 (after twelve years of work in trust services ministry in three conferences), when I began work at Andrews University. The testimony of my boss, Dr. Greg Gerard, made a significant impact on me as he expressed his passion to raise money for the mission and honor of operating a Christian

fundraising ministry for that purpose. He helped me to see that planned giving ministry can be a significant component of the fundraising operation.

My work at Andrews University was joyful because of the strong motivation of loyal donors to give back to the mission of Christ. For many of them, this was the place where they found both the Lord and their spouses—those with whom they truly became one, in addition to being prepared to provide for their household support and an enriched lifestyle with beloved children.

4. **Gifts that are legally secure**—with minimum potential of legal liability to the church that *also* maximizes the potential to stand the test of law in court, thus maintaining the integrity and honor of the donor's plan in the end.

To accomplish such security, I refer donors to a list of choices in local legal counsel (lawyers) who are truly independent specialists, according to the needs and location of each donor. (I think of everyone with whom I work as a "donor" rather than according to the old paradigm references of "trustor" and "testator"—a significant component in my change of philosophy and focus from estate planning services to planned giving ministry). With that perspective, my donors became members of my ministerial flock in my heart and mind.

Legal security for your plan is one of the most important issues for you to prayerfully consider when you select a lawyer with whom to work in the preparation of your will-plan documents. This is due to the incredible increase in the seeming readiness most people have to launch a lawsuit when money is at stake. Legal security of your documents is the expanded subject of Chapter 10 of this book. For now, we are discussing it in connection with your need to select a competent, independent lawyer who will represent you for your will-plan now and after. My suggestions on how to do that is detailed in Chapter 17 of this book.

This means you must be served by a lawyer you select to be your attorney-at-law—a lawyer who represents your interests, not those of another person or organization. There was a time when our denominational organizations would have their lawyers serve their donors in this fashion, and the organizations would pay your legal fees. In that case, the organization's planned giving consultant would serve as an extension of the denominational organization's lawyer's legal practice, like a paralegal might function. In most of those situations, the lawyer never had contact with the donor except to write a letter that disclosed the attorney-client relationship with the denominational organization and encourage the donor to obtain advice from his or her own lawyer or sign a waiver.

Chapter 12

Donor Delight or Donor Chagrin? Stories of Assisting People in My Ministry: The Great Controversy in Action on the Front Lines of the Conflict

This chapter is about some of the relationships with our precious church members who sought my assistance with their end-of-life legacy planning. I experienced being with many who were or became authentic heart-activated donors, which has been my most cherished privilege. I enjoyed serving each of them because I came to love and regard each one as a member of my flock, carrying them on my heart prayerfully.

I'm sharing estate stewardship stories of actual cases that illustrate the great controversy in action relative to accumulated assets, including business interests, financial accounts, and various other forms of property, both real estate and personal. I've visited with hundreds of people in private sessions about what they have and what they wish to be done with it in their journey of planning today for tomorrow. Indeed, I've enjoyed the great privilege of such visits in New York, Ohio, Michigan, California, Arizona, Nevada, Hawaii, Tennessee, Florida, Wisconsin, West Virginia, and each of the six New England states: Connecticut, Maine, Massachusetts, New Hampshire, Rhode Island, and Vermont.

When I have asked, "How would you want your accumulated assets—your stuff—to be distributed if you knew you would not wake up tomorrow morning," **many people responded, "What do others do?"**

In the typical situation, I found they had not given it much thought, if any. Generally speaking, most people give more thought to planning a two-week vacation than they give to designing their will-plans. Of course, the unstudied default is to just leave it all to their natural heirs. I believe they were looking for ideas rather than wanting others do their thinking for them. Of course, we know dying and death—yes, even the process of planning to be absent from this life—is not the most pleasant subject about which to think. Therefore, the less time devoted to it, the better it will be when it is done. And that means it is natural to minimize the level of attention given to it when going through the process.

A completed will-plan is but a snapshot in time. It will need to be reviewed periodically and possibly updated to suit your changed circumstances and mindset. My goal with this book is to share the Lord's leading in the work of my specialized ministry as a certified Seventh-day Adventist planned giving consultant (assisting people with their planning, hopefully and prayerfully, with no tone of manipulation, undue influence, or conflict of interest) and certified trust officer (administrator of trusts and estates). Perhaps this will answer the question of what others have done. These are actual cases where I assisted men and women in their will-planning journey—stories of my journey with Jesus and His people.

The Bible contains a number of stories about real people that illustrate the great controversy theme: Christ vs. Satan; Truth vs. error; good vs. evil; selfishness vs. selflessness; and self-exaltation vs. humility. Some of the Bible stories that relate to stewardship of accumulated assets are included in the material (ref. Chapter 3). The target in the cosmic conflict is the control of human minds and hearts. In essence, will God be the master of mind and heart for you and me, or will our master be Satan or self? When self is one's master, it is actually Satan who is master.

> *A completed will-plan is but a snapshot in time. It will need to be reviewed periodically and possibly updated to suit your changed circumstances and mindset. My goal with this book is to share the Lord's leading in the work of my specialized ministry as a certified Seventh-day Adventist planned giving consultant.*

In these contemporary stories, you will find some of the characters to be authentic citizens of God's spiritual kingdom and others to be on the side of the dark kingdom in this snapshot of a time in their lives, from which they may yet turn away to live in His Light. Some of these are thrilling exhibitions of faith, and some are just plainly sad. Some exhibit great spiritual fulfillment while others exhibit financial security *and* spiritual fulfillment. For most people today, financial security is the most important consideration; some refer to it as "bank account faith."

For example, when I pray for them, in their presence or not, I don't pray for them to include a gift to God's work in the design of their will-plan. I only pray they will seek to honor God as their personal Savior and Lord and that their will-plan will enhance their relationship with Jesus—designed with heaven's approval.

This first story is most thrilling to me: Helen's Heart—Helen (not her real name) is one of my favorite people with whom I have worked. As the newly arrived director of the Planned Giving & Trust Services Department of a Seventh-day Adventist conference, I inherited the fiduciary (trust) responsibilities to manage about 280 revocable living trust files and about 1,100 will files.

One of those donors, Helen, lived about ninety minutes from the office. By the time I got acquainted with her, Helen was in a hospital. She was a delightful lady to visit and a wholehearted Christian. She had never been married and had no children. Helen was advanced in age—probably well beyond eighty; and she was still full of mental capacity.

I was the conference trust officer to manage her trust, and she signed a new General Durable Power of Attorney (POA), naming me as her agent. Her attending medical doctor advised me that she probably would not be able to go home. With her permission, I was given access to her bank accounts as a POA (not as a co-owner); I had her mail forwarded to me at the office and began signing her checks to pay household bills and other expenses. When it was time to admit Helen into a nursing home, I signed the paperwork for the financial responsibility in my capacity as her POA agent.

Helen had no close relatives, either relational or geographical. Her fellow Seventh-day Adventist church members were family to her—a most blessed relationship. Her beloved nieces and nephews lived in other states hundreds of miles from her and apparently knew little or nothing about Helen's life and the Seventh-day Adventist Church.

Helen's parents had fostered a close-knit set of family relationships between her and her siblings as they grew up and later, when Helen served as their mom's caregiver. At the passing of her mother, Helen inherited the house and its contents and lived there for many years, into old age.

Helen had come to live in the childhood home to provide care for the final chapter of her mother's life. Her siblings would all come with their children (Helen's nieces and nephews) to the home for family reunions from time to time, continuing good bonding memories with the home itself and each other. The time came when Helen was the only surviving member of her generation in that family before I came into the picture.

Helen's nieces and nephews apparently had not come to visit her for several years since their grandparents had died—when I arrived. Helen had transferred the title of the house to the conference in its role and function as corporate trustee of her revocable living trust; she had specified that her entire trust estate was to be distributed to the conference upon her death. I was also named by position as executor of Helen's last will and testament.

Customer care and the sense of fiduciary-stewardship responsibility for her as a person engaged me fully. As our dear donor and a member of my ministerial flock, I was compelled to stay in touch with Helen's progress at the nursing home. After some months of frequent visits to her bedside, her doctor gave me a written statement of his opinion that Helen would not be able to return home and could not manage her affairs of life (she had become incompetent); this meant her trust had become nonrevocable, and I was fully responsible for her business as her POA agent and trust officer. My Trust Administration Committee made all significant decisions, and my actions with Helen's checkbook were subject to review and audit by the General Conference Auditing Service.

I could have sold the house and its contents and used the money for her care. However, Helen continued to believe she would get strong enough to live independently at home again; therefore, I felt it would violate her best interests psychologically and emotionally to remove that possibility by liquidating her property.

Being conscious that Helen's property had been dedicated to God, I consulted my corporate legal counsel to be certain of my options. Going forward in prayer on my knees at each baby step, I selected a local moving van and storage company to pack up, haul, and store the household contents in their climate-controlled building. Then I felt that God brought just the right young couple to rent the house. We didn't require them to sign a lease or anything like that because we didn't know the future for Helen. About a year later, the tenants decided to buy their own place to live and moved out. Helen's cash to pay her monthly nursing home bill was about depleted, and she died—all in the obvious timing of our dear, merciful Father in heaven.

The memorial and funeral service were attended by Helen's nieces and nephews, with each one traveling a significant distance to be there (a day's drive). I clearly recall sitting with them at a table and sharing a meal in the fellowship hall of Helen's church. The church members were very hospitable to the family members. With the permission of the family members, I conducted a meeting with them, telling them that as their Aunt Helen's life was so focused on her saving relationship with and dependence on the living God of heaven, she wanted all she had to be used to proclaim the message of Christ to the world. I told them of my awareness of their relationship to the house and its contents because of their fond memories and sentimental attachment that were formed since their childhood.

We agreed that I would have the household contents on display for them to see on a Sunday of a three-day holiday weekend in the near future. Our plan was for them to all come back for that weekend and be able to return to their homes on Monday; and they would select the items they wanted upon mutual agreement.

Therefore, I had the moving van and storage company return the contents to the house and arrange the furnishings in each room as appropriate; I then had a qualified appraiser make a list of the household contents and assign a market value to each item. The Sunday on which they all came for the event, I gave each one of them a copy of the several pages of the appraiser's report. Some pieces of the furniture were expensive heirloom antiques.

I told them as a group (in so many words), "I know that each of you has an interest in selecting items to take home with you. Legally, the contents of this house belong to your Aunt Helen's church. However, I'm authorized to tell you that we believe the strength of your relationship as family entitles you to take whatever you want and as much as you want from here *without* paying money in exchange. I've given you the list so you can see the appraiser's valuation in case you decide to honor your Aunt Helen with a gift to the cause of God she loved. You are not required to pay any amount. If you decide to pay some amount, you are not required to pay the appraiser's suggested value, but rather whatever donation you decide."

At the end of the day, all of them had made their selections and loaded their vehicles; one made arrangements for the selections to be shipped by common carrier, and all but one had given me their checks for the full amount of the appraiser's suggested value. The other one expressed she was having difficulty with the idea of paying, and I told her she was free to go without any payment and I would not think less of her if she did. Before leaving, she gave me a check for the full amount like the others had done. Each one seemed to be fully satisfied, even delighted.

Helen's heart was full of joy during her journey because she gave her all back to God in self-denial and sacrifice. The Lord led in the estate sale for the balance of tangible personal property. He brought a buyer for the house at the appraised value. Truly, the Lord is my Shepherd. Truly, the Lord honored Helen's loving trust in Him, devotion to Him, and dedication of assets to be used for a finished work of His gospel commission. And I thought, *Praise God from whom all blessings flow*, with the following song in my heart and running over and over in my mind, even now as I write her story:

> Encamped along the hills of light, Ye Christian soldiers, rise,
> And press the battle ere the night shall veil the glowing skies,
> Against the foe in vales below, let all our strength be hurled;
> Faith is the victory, we know, that overcomes the world.
> Faith is the victory! Faith is the victory!
> O, glorious victory that overcomes the world.
>
> On every hand the foe we find drawn up in dread array;
> Let tents of ease be left behind, and onward to the fray;
> Salvation's helmet on each head, with truth all girt about,
> The earth shall tremble 'neath our tread, and echo with our shout.
> Faith is the victory! Faith is the victory!
> O, glorious victory that overcomes the world.
>
> To him that overcomes the foe, white raiment shall be giv'n;
> Before the angels he shall know His name confessed in heav'n.
> Then onward from the hills of light, Our hearts with love aflame,
> We'll vanquish all the hosts of night, in Jesus conq'ring name.
> Faith is the victory! Faith is the victory!
> O, glorious victory that overcomes the world.

(Yates, John H. "Faith Is the Victory." *Seventh-day Adventist Hymnal*, Review & Herald Publ. Assn., Hagerstown, MD, 1985, song 608.)

Story of an Eighty-year-old Widow

Some months after her non-Adventist husband died, an eighty-year-old widow called to ask me to visit her home to assist her in getting a will made. She had three adult children who were well off; she wanted the bulk of her substantial estate to go to the Lord's work, with small amounts going to her children. After we cared for that matter, I stopped to see her for a pastoral visit every few months because she lived alone. She always appreciated the visit.

This lady was most unusual in that she always had a wonderfully sweet spirit—never complained about anything. Living alone, she was always eager to visit and had lots of cheerful words to share. I enjoyed every visit and always looked forward to the next one because she talked faith, praising the Lord for His provision of all her needs and protective watchcare.

On one such visit, she matter-of-factly described an accident that occurred during her recent three-month visit to an out-of-state daughter her and family; the widow had fallen backward down the basement stairs from top to bottom, taking several weeks to mend. I was stunned by this trauma she had experienced, but she was okay with it.

Her home was about a two-hour drive from the conference office. One morning, I got to her home earlier than she expected. When she met me at the door, she asked me to wait outside while she got dressed. Afterward, she apologized, explaining that her prayer had taken two hours that morning—longer than usual because, as she said, "You know how it is: Satan is always there to give you thoughts that you don't want." Obviously, she *knew* the Lord; and the Lord knew her. She definitely knew His voice and how to gain the victory over the devil: in Christ's strength. Truly, the joy of the Lord was her strength.

This dear Christ-follower created an estate inheritance plan to honor the One she loved the most, in a spirit of loving trust in and grateful worship of Him, the One who held her in His hands in her struggles with a very long, difficult marriage to a non-believer; the One who had helped her raise her three daughters to share her values. In the time of the end of her life, everything worked out for the best because she always made the best of the way things worked out.

All I can say is, "Praise the Lord from whom all blessings flow," especially to those who wait on Him.

Another Widow

A local church founder and leader in her seventies, with over $900,000 of assets and no debt, asked me to assist her with a will-plan. After more than four years of prayer-bathed counseling with her, going through the process of educating her on the issues and options in will planning, while gathering her data to prepare her attorney packet, it turned out her eight children and numerous grandchildren were her most valuable treasure. The eight children were evenly divided in their loyalties: four lived for God; and four lived for Satan. Nevertheless, the design of the final distribution was to leave almost all of the estate to her eight children in equal shares.

In my agonizing with Christ one final time about this lady's heart, He reminded me of His words:

> He who loves [and takes more pleasure in] father or mother more than [in] Me is not worthy of Me; and he who loves [and takes more pleasure in] son or daughter more than [in] Me is not worthy of Me; And he who does not take up his cross and follow Me [cleave steadfastly to Me, conforming wholly to My example in living and, if need be, in dying also] is not worthy of Me. (Matthew 10:37–38, AMPC)

The Holy Spirit broke my heart by telling me her children were indeed her idols. While I'm not the judge of her or anyone else, I continued to carry a burden for this dear friend, longing for her conversion to Christ for years.

Karl and Judy's Story

Karl (real names not used) was a professional aerospace engineer—a retired corporate executive when I met him—very well off financially. His first wife had died, and he had married Judy. Karl had no religious background. Judy had divorced her first two husbands, living in rebellion against God since her teenage years. Her mother had prayed for her every day of those thirty years—praying she would come back to the faith of her childhood: the Seventh-day Adventist Church.

A health crisis led them to Jesus in full surrender at the foot of His cross. Karl suffered a serious heart attack. Judy stayed with him in the hospital all throughout his two-week care. They read *The Great Controversy* and *The Desire of Ages* by Ellen G. White and gave their hearts to God. They came home, called the Seventh-day Adventist pastor, and were baptized into Christ and His remnant church.

Making up for lost time, Karl and Judy went into high gear, working for Jesus in His spirit. The pastor taught them and others to give Bible studies. They went to many public places where large numbers of the community could be found, such as swap meets, beaches, and game venues. They handed out books such as *Steps to Christ* and *The Desire of Ages*, inviting each person to call them if they wished to join a Bible study group at their home and pointing to their contact information stamped in each book.

Visits to Family with the Gospel

Karl and Judy traversed the USA to visit each of their adult children and their families, enthusiastically sharing their newfound love for and peace and hope in Jesus. Can't you just imagine it? Then they returned home to their work for their dear Lord.

Planning Today to Take Care of Tomorrow

I first met Karl and Judy at a camp meeting. Upon learning of my ministry for Christ and His church, they wanted me to come to their home and assist them with their estate stewardship planning. It was a most joyous privilege to visit, hear their stories, and see the radiant love of Jesus in their faces. It was obvious that they had fully become citizens of God's spiritual kingdom.

Karl and Judy's Plan for Distribution of Their Financial Legacy

They told me their last will and testament should provide that, if they both died before Jesus comes and hadn't used all they had in the Lord's work, then all their remaining assets were to go to help the church finish the Lord's gospel commission.

Two Questions About Their Family

As a professional planned giving consultant, I asked them if any of their children had dependent needs. They said their children were well able to provide for themselves and doing well; they had apparently provided their children's preparation for life by way of a college education.

I asked Karl and Judy, "What will your children think of your plan to give all you have to God's work?"

They said, "After our visit to each of their homes, sharing our testimony with them, they will not be surprised, but we would like you to include a message for them in our wills." The message we jointly developed was more or less as follows:

> MEMORIAL REQUEST: Please arrange for the following message to be read by a minister of the Seventh-day Adventist Church at my memorial service for the benefit of my family:
>
> At this time, by the authority of the Holy Bible, I await the glorious second coming of Jesus Christ and the resurrection of God's people from the dead. I am awaiting Heaven not because I have lived a life deserving of Heaven, but because Jesus died for my sins and sent the Holy Spirit to open my eyes to see that the perfect life, the ultimate sacrifice and the glorious resurrection of Jesus Christ was the only answer for my sins; that Jesus was the only Person capable of ruling my life for positive results.

If my loved ones wonder why I have chosen to dispose of my estate in a way which gives all to my Heavenly Father, the following statement perfectly reflects my understanding: All things come of God. We have nothing that we have not received; and, more than this, we have nothing that has not been purchased for us by the blood of Christ. Everything we possess comes to us stamped with the cross, bought with the blood that is precious above all estimate, because it is the life of God. Hence there is nothing that we have a right to pledge, as if it were our own, for the fulfillment of our word. (White, *Thoughts from Mount of Blessing*, p. 66)

Having decided to put God first in my life as my loving response to HIS great demonstration of His love for me, to grant Him ownership rights to all I have, and having provided the needs of my family members during their years of dependence, how can I do anything but return to Him that which is His own?

Those who remain alive, don't weep for me; but rather rejoice, for I await the hope of His presence. My greatest desire and final request is that all whom I love totally commits their lives to Jesus, thank Him for dying for their sins and invite Him into their lives to fill them with His love and to rule their lives so we may enjoy eternal fellowship together in Heaven and in the Earth made new.

Karl and Judy realized the Bible promise for citizens of God's spiritual kingdom: "Blessed are the dead who die in the Lord when their works continue after them" (my paraphrase of Revelation 14:13). They knew Jesus and loved Him enough to trust Him with tithes, offerings, *and* with their legacy—indeed, with their whole lives.

Karl and Judy had not only taken hold of this message of Jesus; they had also let the truth as it is in Jesus take hold of them and completely transform their values and priorities, as well as allowed the Holy Spirit to give them the courage to consistently live their new life in Christ. Karl and Judy had fully come out

> *Karl and Judy had learned to know Jesus enough to trust Him; they had learned to trust Jesus enough to love Him; and they had learned to love Jesus enough to freely give their all to Him as an act of worship, in a spirit of thanksgiving and praise.*

from dwelling under the shadow of death and were dwelling fully in the light, ever moving onward toward the Light of their lives, Jesus Christ.

Karl and Judy had learned to know Jesus enough to trust Him; they had learned to trust Jesus enough to love Him; and they had learned to love Jesus enough to freely give their all to Him as an act of worship, in a spirit of thanksgiving and praise. Praise the Lord for their inspiring example as citizens of God's spiritual kingdom!

Jewel and George's Story

When I first met Jewel (real names not used), she was in her eighties. Jewel had lived the life of a widow for over forty years, raising her four children on her forty-acre farm while working a job in town. Jewel had a sweet Christian spirit and countenance about her; she never complained about anything, but rather was full of praise to the Lord for His loving care and merciful provision for her and her family.

For many years, Jewel had been the trusted treasurer of her Seventh-day Adventist church and had now given that over to someone else to do. Jewel had found a new life in marriage to George, a farmer whose wife had died a year earlier. She moved to his farm home, which was about a two-hour drive from her place. George had lived his life on the farm and was a hard worker. He and his first wife had raised five children. His youngest child had stayed in the Seventh-day Adventist Church with her husband and three young children. The oldest one, in her sixties, was bitter toward the church. The other three were also not living the message and mission of Jesus. Jewel had an estate plan with the conference and asked me to come and make up a new plan for both of them—a joint plan.

As I Visited the Home of Jewell and George…

We discussed various issues and options of planning. I mentioned the spiritual principles of estate stewardship while suggesting they pray over their family members and what they had, asking the Lord to reveal to them His plan for their will. George would have nothing to do with Christian estate planning. George said, "Blood is thicker than water" and intended to give all he had to his children. I wondered how thick the blood of Jesus was to George—that blood that was shed on the cross of Calvary for George.

Therefore, a plan was created that left all to each other for the survivor's life and then George's share to his children; some of Jewel's share would go to her children, and the rest to the Lord's work, honoring her covenant with God in loving trust. A few months later, Jewel received a nighttime visit from heaven. She told me later she was awakened by a visit from heaven with the instruction that she was to get out of that house and move back to her own house, even though she had rented it to someone else. And the move must be done right now.

George's house burned down one night with him in it, not long after Jewel had moved out. I learned from Jewel that George had not been faithful to God with gifts of tithes and offerings; he exhibited other selfish manifestations of his spirit.

Going to George's Funeral

As I prepared my own soul before the Lord to go and be part of the funeral service for George, I was reminded of the bitterly lost condition of most of his children and grandchildren. I pleaded the blood of Jesus and my great need of His help, asking Him to give me a soft answer that turns away wrath.

After the funeral, as the family gathered in a home for food and fellowship, George's oldest daughter expressed great hostility toward me because that for which her late mother had worked so hard was going to benefit Jewel for the rest of Jewel's life. The daughter threatened to see me in court. That was many years ago, and I never heard one word from her or her legal representative. Praise be to God from whom all blessings flow, including powerful answers to prayer!

Paul prescribed a divine test: "Examine yourselves, to see whether you are in the faith. Test yourselves. Or do you not realize this about yourselves, that Jesus Christ is in you?—unless indeed you fail to meet the test!" (2 Cor. 13:5, ESV).

The great controversy between Christ's claims on His people and Satan's attempts to prevent those claims from taking root in our hearts and minds, to be acted out by the power of our wills, is more evident in the way we design our last wills and testaments than in most other life events we face.

Adam and Evelyn's Story

The Lord does not slumber. A number of years ago, Adam and Evelyn (not their real names), a retired couple, attended my seminars at the annual nine-day camp meeting. After a couple of years of their attendance, they invited me to assist them in updating their old estate documents. They increased their charitable bequest portion of the plan substantially.

After Adam died, I assisted the widow in her desire to change the plan. Her plan reduced the charitable bequest portion to a very small amount. Her conversation about it revealed that she loved her family members more than she loved the Lord—a significant concern of prayer for me.

I had not seen her for several years before we saw each other attending a Bible study seminar at camp meeting. She asked me to sit down in the chair next to hers. She then shared with me that she had just recently read some of the materials I had left with them that presents spiritual principles of Christian estate planning and was taking them seriously. With a full heart, all I could say is, "Praise the Lord from whom all blessings flow!"

John and Joy's Story

A couple in their nineties with an estate of about $400,000 asked their pastor to have me come and meet with them in their home. They had a small, old home they had built. Most of their assets were cash in bank accounts. I assisted them in assembling an attorney packet of data and documents and select an independent lawyer to represent them, as well as took them to the lawyer's office. They both really believed and lived the truth of God's ownership of them and all they had.

Married over sixty years, John and Joy (not their real names) had no children of their own but still many relatives. Joy had been a very active Seventh-day Adventist Church member for several decades. John was a member of a Sunday-keeping church.

Here is their dialog with the attorney (independent legal counsel):

> Attorney: I'm glad to meet you, John and Joy. Why have you come to see me?
>
> Joy: The lawyer who did our old will has died. Our old will is obsolete, and we need to get our affairs in order.
>
> Attorney: What do you have?
>
> Joy and John: [described their holdings of property and bank accounts]
>
> Attorney: Tell me about your family.
>
> Joy and John: [shared names and locations of each of their siblings, nieces, and nephews]
>
> Attorney: What do you want to do with what you have got at the end of life?
>
> Joy: We want to give it all to the [local] Seventh-day Adventist Church.
>
> Attorney: Why would you want to do that?

>Joy: We have received everything we have, and we want to give it back to the One who gave it to us. It belongs to Him, not to us.

>Attorney: What do you think about this, John? What do you want to do?

>John: I agree with everything Joy has said. I want to give it to the [local] Seventh-day Adventist Church. We will make a cash gift now to my church to memorialize my family there.

>(That is when I left the three of them to complete this discussion and waited in the office lobby until they finished, because I wanted them to express themselves freely and fully, without any possible influence of my presence at the table).

The documents were completed accordingly. I took them back to the same attorney so he could supervise the ceremony of getting the documents signed with appropriate witnesses and a notary public. Within a few years, we handled the will probate as executor, using the same lawyer who served as the estate attorney. He had served as power of attorney in the final years of John's life. Joy died within a year of the document completion. John survived a few years, and the plan provided great benefits to our Lord's work in that city. John and Joy will be so glad to learn of it when they come up in the first resurrection.

Joy's statement, "We have received everything we have," sent a thrill throughout my body and mind because it reminded me of the following commentary:

>All things come of God. We have nothing that we have not received; and, more than this, we have nothing that has not been purchased for us by the blood of Christ. Everything we possess comes to us stamped with the cross, bought with the blood that is precious above all estimate, because it is the life of God. Hence there is nothing that we have a right to pledge, as if it were our own, for the fulfillment of our word. (White, *Thoughts From the Mount of Blessing*, p. 66)

A denominational worker (minister) and spouse, both over eighty, have an estate valued close to $1,000,000. Their able, educated adult children will receive 100 percent of the estate, not because there is any need by any of them, but apparently because of their sense that the wealth must be kept in the family, not to mention his statement that he could not trust the brethren in how the church would use it. Based on current evidence, at least one of the children will use the money in a manner that will definitely bring dishonor to God. I've often prayed for this retired Adventist minister, that he would come to know Jesus enough to trust Him with gifts to this denomination—this Bible-sanctioned movement—and love Jesus enough to feel compelled to give all to His precious bride, the church.

<u>Trusting the Brethren vs. Trusting God</u>—There was a time when I had a personal problem of not trusting church leaders to make wise use of my gifts—to be used for greatest efficiency and effectiveness in the mission of the church. However, the day came when I had come to know Jesus well enough to trust Him to direct me in giving, as well as trust Him with their use. Apparently, my love for Jesus had increased enough that nothing could keep me from giving to His precious bride.

My Good Friend Fred Smith

One of my most favorite people—and story—of the many hundreds I've known: Fred (real names not used) worked his way through the Seventh-day Adventist boarding high school in Mt. Vernon, Ohio, and college in Takoma Park, Maryland, with a student's job of working in their respective workshops, learning a valuable set of technical skills and the business of the trade.

Fred settled in a small town in New England with his bride, Beverly. They had two children, Susie and John. Fred bought a bankrupt business in a small town for $500 in 1944. His business grew, was doing rather well, providing a good living for his family. It had grown into a business with $500,000 in annual sales. His primary competitor in town was an immoral man who dealt in pornographic material and gave his employees an annual Christmas party with liquor flowing and lewd female entertainment. This man's business was also doing well, like Fred's was, with a similar level of annual sales: about $500,000.

God's Dialogue with Satan—One day, during this stage of life and business, in his personal devotional readings, Fred read Job 1, where the Lord asked Satan, "Have you considered [set your heart on] my servant Job, that there is none like him on the earth, a blameless and upright man, one who fears God and shuns [turns away from] evil?" (verse 8, NKJV).

Fred's mind also immediately went to Deuteronomy 28, where the first fourteen verses describe God's promised blessings for obedience: "The LORD will open to you His good treasure ... to bless all the work of your hand. You shall lend to many nations, but you shall not borrow. And the Lord will make you the head and not the tail; you shall be above only, and not beneath, if you heed the commandments of the LORD your

God, which I command you today, and are careful to observe *them*" (verses 12–13, NKJV).

Fred also recalled that the remaining fifty-four verses of the same chapter describe God's promised curses for disobedience: "The alien who *is* among you shall rise higher and higher above you, and you shall come down lower and lower. He shall lend to you, but you shall not lend to him; he shall be the head, and you shall be the tail" (verses 43–44).

In his prayer that morning, Fred reminded the Lord about the promise that He would make him the head and not the tail in response to obedience. And Fred asked the Lord if He could say to Satan of himself, like He had said to Satan of Job, "Have you considered My servant Fred?" Shortly after that discussion with the Lord, Fred was alone on a trip, flying across the country to attend a corporate board meeting for another enterprise. Having taken a favorite book, *Christ's Object Lessons*, to read on the plane, he was struck big time with two chapters: "The Lord's Vineyard" and "Talents," both of which he read that day. Upon returning home, Fred did two things about these reading experiences:

1. He asked his plant superintendent to read these two chapters. Then the two men *agreed* to read the two chapters *every month* and pray the Lord's blessing to bring a new level of excellence in the business.

2. He also began his weekly sales meeting the next Monday morning with a Bible reading and prayer, even though his most productive salesman was a secular Jewish man. To Fred's relief, this caused *no* problem, for which Fred praised the Lord with a heart full of loyal gratitude.

It was at that time that Fred was offered a very lucrative business opportunity to produce pornographic material (no doubt, this was a test by Satan), which he refused. Fred was not like Balaam, God's prophet who was offered a very lucrative opportunity to gain great wealth and prestige if he would curse God's people, Israel. Balaam prayed about it but eventually did what he wanted to do for the filthy lucre and lost his soul's salvation. By contrast, Fred didn't have to pray to know God's answer (see Numbers 22–24 for Balaam's story).

God began to increase Fred's business to the tune of double-digit growth each year—even more so in the years of a national recession. The last count of which I knew was his business had grown to over $30 million in annual sales; his rival had grown to $1 million. Therefore, my friend Fred experienced God's blessing of being the head and not the tail in so many ways.

Fred was asked to call for the evangelism offering at the annual conference camp meeting for several years. Speaking on an uplifted platform before thousands of people, Fred would testify about his experience of the Lord's faithfulness and blessings when we are obedient. He would share that he and his wife returned a tithe on their gross income, gave local church and world mission offerings, and then *gave all they could give* over and above that to the work of evangelism.

Fred gave 50 percent of his gross personal income and 10 percent of his corporation's net income to God's work for many years. His lifestyle of simplicity also reflected his belief that what he had received came from God, belonged to God, and would be returned to the Owner when he was finished here.

My friend Fred crafted his corporation so it could issue voting stock to the appropriate stockholders and non-voting stock to others. Then annually, he would give non-voting stock to a variety of denominational organizations.

Fred ultimately sold his business, and all of those charitable gifts of stock suddenly became very valuable and were converted to cash money. Fred became a full-time philanthropist after the sale of his business, funding world church projects, educational endowments, and evangelistic outreach events, which brought a big bonus of great joy to his life.

I believe the Lord's answer would be "Yes" to Fred's question, "Could You ask Satan, 'Have you considered my servant Fred?'" Fred gave money to support God's work locally and globally, but he first gave *himself* in full surrender of mind, heart, and will into God's hands to be shaped for service and security in Christ. Fred's story and others like it remind me of the following Bible text. Notice Paul's testimony regarding the call to generous giving:

> Now I want you to know, dear brothers and sisters, what God in his kindness has done through the churches in Macedonia. They are being tested by many troubles, and they are very poor. But they are also filled with abundant joy, which has overflowed in rich generosity. For I can testify that they gave not only what they could afford, but far more. And they did it of their own free will. They begged us again and again for the privilege of sharing in the gift for the believers in Jerusalem. *They even did more than we had hoped, for their first action was to give themselves to the Lord and to us, just as God wanted them to do.* (2 Corinthians 8:1–5, NLT, emphasis added)

I praise the Living God of heaven and earth—the only God of light and life, truth and justice, mercy and kindness, love and joy, and peace and happiness—with condescending grace toward the weakened human beings who populate this globe—for the privilege of seeing close up His character being lived out in Fred, like it was in Job of olden times—with an amazing level of loyal support and constantly positive influence for God as a Legacy of a most noble core life mission with financial blessings in the bargain, that he passed on to the benefit of God's work and to his family.

The Spirit of Prophecy comments on giving to God:

> *As born-again disciples of Christ, you and I are serving as foot soldiers of the cross in His army. As such, faith in Him may be the most important weapon of our warfare.*

> We are not to place the responsibility of our duty upon others, and wait for them to tell us what to do … The Lord will teach us our duty just as willingly as He will teach somebody else. If we come to Him in faith, He will speak His mysteries to us personally. Our hearts will often burn within us as One draws nigh to commune with us as He did with Enoch. Those who decide to do nothing in any line that will displease God, will know, after presenting their case before Him, just what course to pursue. And they will receive not only wisdom, but strength. Power for obedience, for service, will be imparted to them, as Christ has promised. (White, *The Desire of Ages*, p. 668)

Here are a few more case studies of the Lord's leading in my work. We know that, as born-again disciples of Christ, you and I are serving as foot soldiers of the cross in His army. As such, faith in Him may be the most important weapon of our warfare. The following stories of faith and a mutuality of two-way faithfulness between God and His daughter Ruth and son Jimmie are included here as exhibits of our greatest weapon. I'm also including a third story of Adam (real names not used), where there must have been some faith.

Ruth's Story

At over ninety years old, Ruth lived in the home of her youth. An only child, she was born there, cared for her aging parents in their final chapters of life, and inherited the house. As the new Trust Services director at the conference office, I inherited Ruth's file and decided to visit her at her home. Ruth lived alone.

The house was elevated above the state route upon which it looked down. The numerous steps to her front door from the edge of the road must have constituted about a sixty-degree climb. As she stood beside me looking out her front door, she said, "You see the church over there and the pond next to it (straight across the road from her house)? I was **baptized at age 16** in that pond and joined that church when it was a Baptist congregation."

Ruth continued, "**I was baptized again at age 36** into the Jehovah's Witness Church. Much later, my mother was in the nursing home here in town. We met a most wonderful Christian lady who came there one time each week to study the Bible and pray with us. She would even come by my home to pray with me. The leaders of the JW learned about my praying with her and sent some leaders from New York City in their black suits to visit me. They told me that I must stop praying with her or lose my church membership. I said to them, 'I don't see that in the Bible.'" As she told me about those leaders and their visit, she had no critical tone because she knew this was God's will for her, had forgiven them completely, and prayed for them.

Ruth continued her story: "**I was baptized at age 86** into the Seventh-day Adventist Church by Elder Bill Brace." The wonderful Christian lady whom Ruth loved to visit at her own home and the nursing home was a Seventh-day Adventist *Listen* magazine worker who loved people and loved to give Bible studies.

Ruth had worked in that small Connecticut town doing office clerical work as a single Christian child of God. When I met Ruth, she was carrying on regular correspondence with several friends in other areas; those whom she knew were in need received a cash gift with a letter of encouragement.

When Ruth was telling me about being baptized at the age of 16, she said, "I never got married because I could not find a young fellow who loved the Lord the way I did." And she lived a life full of service, with a cheerful and grateful spirit.

Conforming to my responsibilities, I visited her rather often. We made arrangements to be sure someone cared for her in every way during her final chapter of life. The time came when Ruth laid down her life to rest until Jesus comes again. She was a member of the family for whom the second largest city of Massachusetts is named. She had boxes of yellowed newspapers in her attic featuring stories of their annual family reunions. She told me when she was a young woman, about 1,500 people attended the yearly event, but now she said the whole family had almost died out.

Only one cousin came to Ruth's funeral at the church where she was first baptized; Elder Brace and I officiated (in 1984). After the funeral service, that cousin told me she had come with the idea of getting a lawyer to fight Ruth's estate distribution plan, but after experiencing "the way this was done, [she] decided not to."

Ruth gave 100 percent to the Lord's work—her one true love. While her death was a bitter loss to us, all we could say is, "Praise the Lord from whom all blessings flow." While her estate was modest, the funds would be used with utmost care and efficiency as directed by heaven because it came from a heart of love for Jesus that was loyal to His precious bride, the church.

Ruth had signed on to serve in the cavalry as a soldier of the cross of Christ, rather than to coast on a cruise; she lived a planned life that was full of the love of God, hope, and joy, regardless of the disappointing surprises life can offer up. She made it a life practice not to hold onto the negative experiences or be critical of another person, regardless of the situation.

Brother Adam's Vacant Home Lot

When I worked as the director of Planned Giving & Trust Services in a small conference in the early 1980s, a widower came to town to see me about his vacant, four-acre parcel of land that was adjacent to the conference office, as well as land where we held the annual ten-day camp meetings and other significant events. His parcel could be very valuable for parking of our increasing number of people coming to camp meeting year by year. He thought he might sell it to a party that was trying to get town approval to build a sixteen-unit apartment house there. I knew he was a Seventh-day Adventist Church member, about eighty years of age, who had just had a stroke. I also knew the appraised value of the land was $125,000. It had been Adam's (real names not used) home where he and his wife raised their family. The large home had burned down; we could still see some evidence of the burn-out and a small concrete pad.

I was hoping Adam had come to the conference to make an outright or at least partial gift of the land—a bargain sale, maybe. I had asked my Lord and Father in heaven to prepare my heart with His spirit, demeanor, and words. After he and I greeted each other and determined our agenda, I asked Adam what he wanted to do with the property. He coldly said he wanted to get every dollar out of it that he could. The Lord led; we made him an offer that he accepted: $15,000 cash and a $75,000 charitable gift annuity that would pay him $500 monthly for the rest of his life. He went away a delighted man, and the conference has made excellent use of the land for event parking, with a number of RV hookups.

Jimmie and Clare's Single-Minded Love for the Savior

After working in other locations, I returned to that same job sixteen years later. I noticed a couple I'd known before and wondered about them. They had a sizable lot where they had built a new home for themselves. It was adjacent to and on the opposite side of the conference office from the four-acre parcel in the previous story. By now, Jimmie and Clare (real names not used) were getting up in years and had retired during my absence. They had no children. Their lives revolved around their local church family and cheerful participation in the body of Christ, with ongoing responsibilities.

As I would see them outside for daily walks, I wondered about their finances and if they might benefit from a charitable gift annuity in exchange for their home property, like we set up to acquire brother Adam's land. The Lord laid it on my heart to pray for them, which I did regularly, asking Him for an opening to have a conversation.

After a few years of praying, I saw Jimmie at the post office. I was taking care of business for a member of Jimmie's church for whom I was the power of attorney agent. Jimmie talked to me, asking how she was doing and seeming to know I was serving her in that role (I never volunteer such information). He had certain responsibilities for his local church as a member. He knew I worked at the conference office.

Sensing the prompting of the Holy Spirit, I then asked Jimmie if he and Clare had a plan for their care, with an individual named in a legal document to act on their behalf if needed. He answered in the negative but was not ready to discuss it further. I continued to pray.

A few months later, he hastened over to the conference office building, "looking for Elder Daum." I was told about it upon my return from an appointment. I went to see him. He told me Clare had fallen and broken her hip, had surgery, had a stroke during her two-week stay in the hospital, was released from the hospital into the adjacent nursing home for rehabilitation, and had been there two months. He said the nursing home was saying she should go home, but she preferred to stay there for the social interactions she was enjoying.

Jimmie was deeply concerned about the financial aspects and said the social worker told him if she stayed long enough for Medicare to stop paying, he would have to pay $250.00 per day. He sounded frantic. All of this information was news to me; I had not heard any of it.

Therefore, I took him in my vehicle to the nursing home some twenty miles across the county. We met with the social services lady; she explained the picture to me more coherently. The nursing home had brought Clare to about 90 percent of her potential level of wellness; if she were taken home now and later needed to return to the nursing home, she could do that without having to be admitted again after a minimum of three days in the hospital. She emphasized that Medicare would pay for an additional thirty days if she had to return; she also advised that Jimmie needed to install handrails and a ramp at the outside entry doors of their home so Clare would have access to the home in a wheelchair or while using a walker.

Addressing the issue that was most troubling to Jimmie, I told him I would need to know about their finances in order to discuss his concern about paying the nursing home bill if Clare stayed there beyond the 100 days of Medicare coverage. We went to their home, where he showed me their account statements from the financial institutions in which they had assets. I then told him he could handle the nursing home payments with no sweat and not diminish his accounts to any significant degree, if at all; the worst thing would be it would slow down the growth rate in the value of the accounts. They were generous in their support of God's work, had no debt, and spent a small portion of their income for living expenses. They had a new car but didn't use it much.

I was there when Clare came home. Their friends at church had organized some volunteer ladies to keep her company on a rotating basis to get her settled at home so she would not feel the absence of the social setting at the nursing home.

When the volunteers quit coming, my prayers for her care were answered big time. We found a qualified caregiver who was available for a very reasonable hourly rate. We handled the payroll for her wages so the worker's compensation premium and the Social Security and Medicare taxes were both handled in conjunction with the payroll. The conference treated it as a "local hire" situation, like when one of our local churches or schools would hire a treasurer or janitor, for example, and send the money along with certain paperwork for each such employee.

Each time Jimmie received his mail, he would bring the bills to me for advice. Clare had always handled all of their finances; Jimmie had never written a check. My office secretary became accustomed to writing his checks for him to sign. Each quarter, he would have me calculate his income so he could pay his tithe and offerings to his church. Anytime he needed to buy an appliance or other need besides than food, I took him to stores for him to see his options and make a decision.

After a number of months, Jimmie decided he needed a power of attorney agent to care for their business. When he asked me if I would serve in that capacity, I told him I would be honored to do that, but such a decision could only be made by our Trust Management Committee; for them to make a decision, they would insist on knowing about Jimmie and Clare's last will and testament.

Jimmie found their will and showed it to me; it provided for 100 percent of their substantial estate to be distributed to three Seventh-day Adventist organizations in equal shares, one of which was my employer. Therefore, my Trust Administration Committee approved his request and he asked their lawyer to craft the documents. After serving them in that role a couple years, Jimmie told me he wanted to change their will so that 100 percent would go to my employing organization. As much as I appreciated that idea, I knew to step lightly; again, he called their lawyer, and the documents were done.

Jimmie and Clare didn't need the benefits of a charitable gift annuity like Adam did. Today, their home is being used as housing for a church employee and family, either as a parsonage or teacherage. Jimmie and Clare would be thrilled. Jimmie survived Clare. One time, when he was severely disappointed over an event in his relationship with his local church leaders, he told me about it in humble, non-judgmental tones, then said, "Oh well, my job is to just love everyone." That really touched my soul to its depths.

> One time, when he was severely disappointed over an event in his relationship with his local church leaders, he told me about it in humble, non-judgmental tones, then said, "Oh well, my job is to just love everyone." That really touched my soul to its depths.

I've never found any good substitute for or shortcut to providing customer care and service while going forward on my knees, seeking only their good. I knew when Jimmie came looking for me, that was Jesus answering my prayers. I've always enjoyed being the son of such mamas and papas of spiritual Israel—either as a son they never had or a substitute for a son who lives far away—and leaving the outcome to the Lord of my ministry.

Jimmie had grown up in a godless home. When he was nine years old, a car ran over him and almost killed him. He bore the marks of that event on his forehead to the end of his life. And the Lord led him to discover Bible truth and become a door-to-door literature evangelist. In the course of that activity, he met his wife.

Some words from a favorite song, "More Than Ever," come to mind right now. You can read the lyrics at 1ref.us/rdwgd3. Participating in stories like these leads me to value our merciful Savior and His sacrifice more than ever.

Vacant Lot Funded Retirement Income Enhancement Annuity

Henry and Karin Harper (not their real names) had just taken early retirement from their professions at ages sixty-two and sixty, respectively. They called for assistance in updating their old Last Will and Testament plan.

I met with them at their home and began the process of completing my twenty-eight-page data form. They mentioned a vacant lot they had owned for about thirty-five years. When a subdivision was being developed in a rural town, they bought a one-acre lot for $5,000 but never built there. This plan certainly enhanced their financial security; the question of spiritual fulfillment awaits the final answer. Now the desirable subdivision had been fully built out for a long time, except a very few lots such as theirs. Their lot had large trees growing there; they paid the annual property taxes and costs of weed control. When I suggested the idea of converting that lot into a life-income-deferred gift plan, they were very interested.

The flow chart below shows how the resulting plan worked. Henry and Karin are receiving about $625.00 monthly for their joint lifetimes—about $124.00 of it is tax-free for the thirty years of their joint life expectancy—a great retirement income enhancement for them; and the timing of the charitable deduction occurred in the year he exercised his S.O.P option with company stock, which created a tax problem for them that was solved by this gift plan:

The plan created a win-win-win situation that made the donors delightfully happy. We refer to it as an "income enhancement annuity." The following chart illustrates how it works:

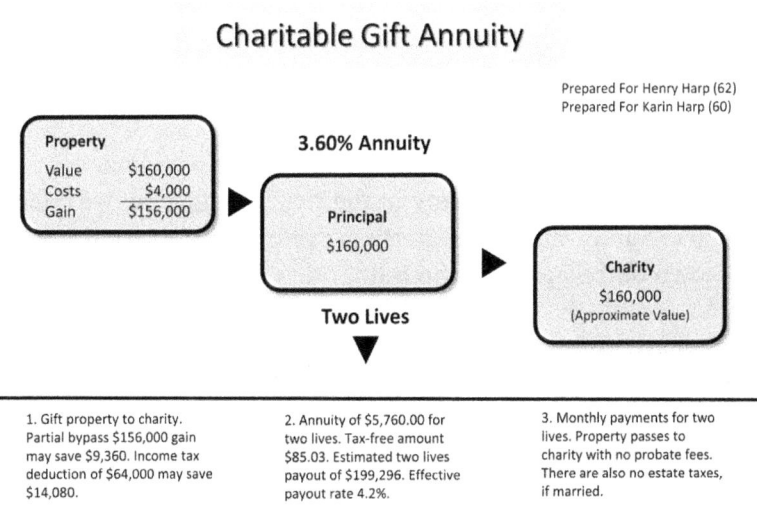

By now, you may be wondering how we got all the way to this result when we began with an unimproved vacant lot in a mature residential subdivision. **There were issues over which we studied and prayed, and we experienced the Lord's amazing leading**:

1. Marketability was the major issue. Was there a market for this lot? What was the market value? They thought it might be worth about $100,000–$110,000. Who could we ask for assistance p?
2. Finding an effective real estate broker was essential. Truly, the Lord led.
3. The lot would need to be engineered for septic system support and wetlands.
4. A water well would be required.
5. The lot would have to be surveyed.
6. The lot would have to be appraised.
7. The one-acre minimum lot size had doubled to two-acres since they bought it. Nevertheless, the town waived that for them.
8. We entered into an agreement between the donors and my employing organization:
   a. I/we would contract for all of the above listed services.
   b. My employing organization would advance the money to pay for them.
   c. The donors agreed to hold us harmless for any potential liability incurred by having contractors on the property.
   d. The donors agreed to reimburse us for our advances of money to pay for the services listed above.
9. Henry made it clear that he did not want to be involved in finding a buyer or caring for any of the steps outlined above. He took me to see and walk the property; he introduced me to the folks at the town office—about a three-hour drive from my office.

Here is what I did as a planned giving consultant on their behalf: This approach was based on a seminar by Charles Schultz at Crescendo Interactive, a software company, as well as a number of my similar experiences with such opportunities in Michigan, California, various New England states, and Hawaii. At each small step of the way, my trust management committee gave me most helpful advice and support and made the decisions with me.

1. Knowing each case is unique, I saturated this whole matter in prayer before doing anything, and again at each of the following steps—praying until I knew what to do first and next (at each step), with an overall sense of God's individual instruction for us.

   The example of King David inspired me in this. Three times, the enemy's army appeared against him; he "inquired of the Lord," and each time, the Lord gave David a different strategy and tactic, which resulted in victory (see 1 Sam. 30:1–10; 2 Sam. 5:17–25).

2. I called and asked the folks at the town office for the names of local banks and bank mortgage officers who were making home loans in the town.

3. I interviewed two such loan officers, asking them for names of the realtors who dominate the market there.

4. I interviewed two or three realtors, asking them:

   a. about their experience with the market in that town and their sense of values and market activity with vacant lots. I learned vacant lots are in very short supply, with a reasonable demand.

   b. if they would be willing to work with me on the basis of an informal listing. I told them about the property and that the owners had expressed an interest in making a charitable gift to my employing organization, the Seventh-day Adventist Church; I also told them we would only accept the property into our organization's name if/when we were rather certain of an imminent sale.

   After the interviews and prayer, I selected a realtor with whom to work—a choice that must have been ordered by the Lord, as you may notice in this narrative. We agreed that:

   a. she would treat this like any other listing, except she could not publish it on the local multiple listing

   b. I would sign a listing agreement only when it appeared we had at least one or more potential buyers

5. The next big step was to decide on a listing price. The realtor recommended an appraiser and gave me a few names. After interviewing two or three appraisers and praying for guidance, I selected one of them with whom to work, which again proved to be the very best choice.

In the meantime, word had gone around the community and I had at least two calls from other realtors. One of them sent me a list of comparable sales during the previous several years, which indicated the market value might be $60,000. That realtor was also an interested party; her husband was a builder who had an interest in building a spec house there. I called her later with the appraised value, and she retracted her interest.

The realtor I had chosen also had a husband who was a building contractor. After consulting with him, she said he offered to pay us $125,000 for the lot. Even though I was tempted, I told her we must get an appraisal before deciding on a price.

The appraisal came in at a range of $170,000–$175,000, which he acknowledged to be an unusually short range of value.

6. The next step was to have the lot surveyed. The realtor referred me to a local surveyor, which went very well at a reasonable cost.
7. **Then we made a difficult decision about engineering.** The realtor gave me the name and number of an engineer who is both competent and reasonable *and* had big-time credibility with all the applicable governing town committees, including the all-important Board of Health and Wetlands Commission.
    a. He identified and flagged the wetlands, reported to the town's Wetlands Commission, and obtained approval of his plan.
    b. He performed a perk test, reported the results to the town's Board of Health, and obtained approval of his plan.
    c. He drew a plot plan that detailed the elevation levels on a continuous basis, indicating the parameters of the wetlands, where the septic system would be installed, where the driveway would be created, and where the house would stand and its specific orientation. He described the number of bedrooms and the square footage of the house the septic system would support. He presented his drawing to the town's Building Committee and obtained approval for a building permit to be issued.
8. By the time all the foregoing steps were completed, the appraisal was legally stale by date, for our fiduciary* purposes. Therefore,

we took all of this most valuable information to the appraiser for a refreshed, updated market valuation. The appraisal now came in at $185,000–$200,000, and the appraiser told me on the phone he would personally write us a check to buy it for $175,000 if we could not get a better price for it.

9. We contracted with an attorney to represent the denominational organization in the acquisition of the property as a gift to us—a lawyer who is a real estate specialist in the state jurisdiction. He did the title search and scrutinized all the paper work on our behalf and advised us accordingly; and the deal was completed between him and the donor's independent legal counsel.

The realtor had done her excellent work of searching for a buyer. The property sold for $190,000 at the right time. The donors asked us to use that money to:

a. repay my employing organization for all our advanced property development and legal expenses.

b. make outright gifts to their local church for evangelism and their alma mater schools for Christian education.

c. fund a $160,000 charitable gift annuity agreement. We agreed on the deferred flexible model of gift annuities to safeguard any unexpected delay in the sale.

This piece of the donors' overall financial and estate plan certainly enhanced their financial security in retirement; as to their spiritual fulfillment, we encouraged them to keep this annuity on the altar of God in a covenant by sacrifice, asking Him for instruction on whether to or when to release their rights to the income from the annuity so the remaining balance would be put into His work before the time of trouble begins.

* a person to whom property or power is entrusted for the benefit of another.
* of or pertaining to the relation between a fiduciary and his or her principal
* a fiduciary capacity; a fiduciary duty.
* of, based on, or in the nature of trust and confidence, as in public affairs.

182 ◆ *Whatcha Gonna Do with Whatcha Got?*

The following story involved a retired couple—both were seventy-five years strong. They owned rental properties in the community where they lived; one was a residential duplex. Let's call the couple Adam and Eve Donor. **Their residential duplex was transferred to fund an income enhancement annuity:**

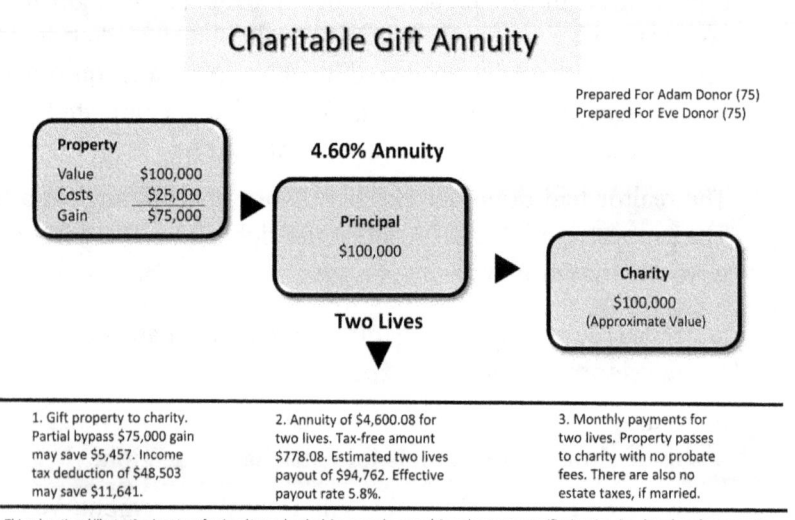

The flow chart above tells the story of what happened. Adam was weary of doing the maintenance work on the properties. The duplex had been totally depreciated in book value for income tax purposes. His income tax preparer had told him what his income tax bite would be if he sold it. He had an offer on the table for a few years from a long-term tenant but could not digest the idea of the income tax, so he had not sold it.

We met to update their estate plan documents, and I began completing the data form, becoming aware of this situation with the duplex. On my second visit to their home, I took some computer-generated illustrations of three optional plans that showed how they could give it to the Lord's work and continue receiving at least as much income as before, either in a charitable trust with variable income or in a gift annuity with fixed income guaranteed for their joint lifetimes, with no more property management work for which to care.

We had the property appraised and did the environmental due diligence, took title, sold it tax-free to the tenant, and began paying them with monthly checks—a win-win situation that made everyone happy. These are much simpler with improved income-producing property.

The next case is unique. Being in an urban commercial setting, the commercial warehouse caused a great concern about environmental hazards and toxic waste. Therefore, our due diligence was quite thorough on that issue. We are calling this couple John and Mary Donor; they were both seventy-five years old.

The flow chart below shows how it works with a cooperative market—again, a delightful win-win scenario, all saturated in prayer at each step of the way—a most unusual use of this form of the charitable remainder trust plans. We call this one "**annuity trust with warehouse**" because it was funded with a commercial warehouse in a choice location of a major city.

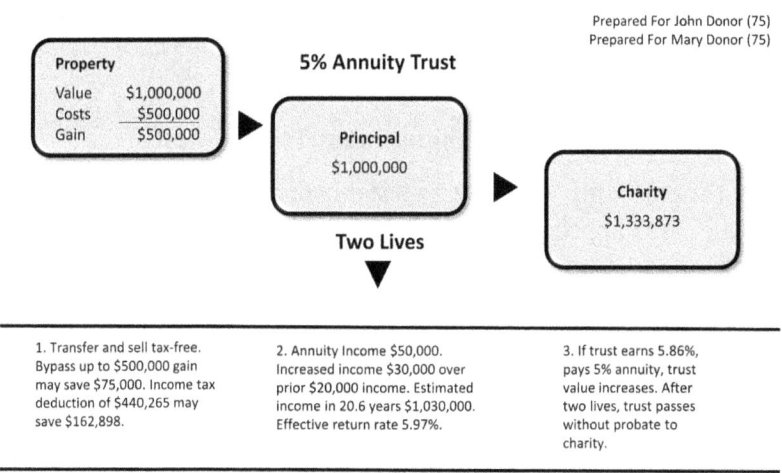

The Charitable Remainder Unitrust flow chart below illustrates how the charitable remainder trust plan may work for this newly retired couple. We are calling them Johnny and Merry Donor, if the market cooperates, and it did at the time. They were both sixty-five years old. We are calling this trust an "**income enhancement trust.**"

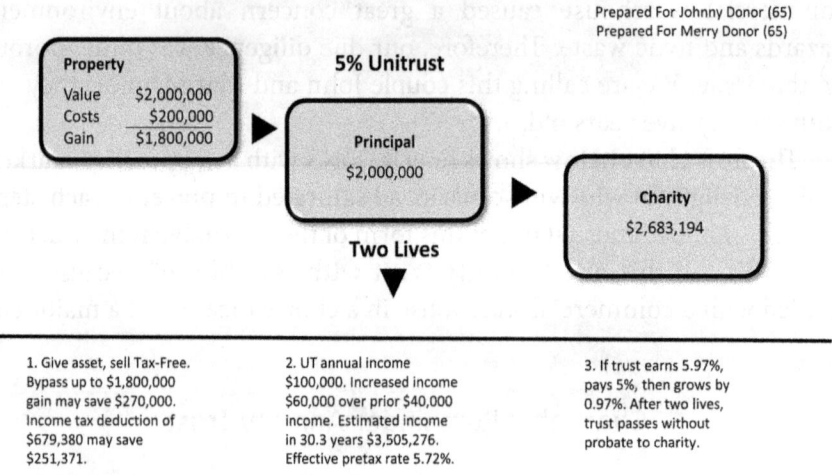

Income Enhancement Trust Notes

At the time Johnny and Merry established this trust, their joint life expectancy was approximately twenty-six years (at least one of them will live that long). They would have paid income taxes on about $1,900,000 of profit if they had sold the $2 million of stock in their own name. By transferring ownership of the stock to the trust, it was sold tax free. As the trustee of their own trust, they had given up ownership but continued to have control of the asset and its management.

They reserved the power to change the trustee and the remainder beneficiary. At the end of both lives, Johnny and Merry's trust will make a beautiful gift of the remainder value of its assets to the Lord's work *of their choice*, and the trust will be terminated.

Retirement Income Enhancement Unitrust (CRUT)

When Johnny and Merry Donor retired, they went on Social Security and Medicare. They had no other retirement income plan. They also sold their business in a tax-free stock exchange. They transferred 100 percent of the privately held C corporation stock of their business in exchange for publicly traded stock of a New York Stock Exchange corporation.

The stock they sold in their business caused them to realize capital gain income on a very large proportion of the sale. Their CPA told them they should do a charitable remainder unitrust and asked them, "Who is your favorite charity?" Johnny came to discuss this plan with me. I created three illustrations of options for our discussion.

Johnny insisted the trust should pay out at least 10 percent income to them. I told him I've managed dozens of these trusts with payout rates from 5 percent (the legal minimum) to 12 percent and that the most satisfied income beneficiaries of these trusts are the people with the lowest payout rate because the trust's investment income often exceeds the payout rate. Therefore, the trust asset value grows tax-free, so one's income from the trust grows accordingly. The income is reset each January based on the asset value. Often, the high payout rates remove capital from the trust so the dollar amount of payout decreases.

When Johnny and Merry met with their CPA for his advice, the CPA said, "You don't want to place yourself in a position of having to speculate with the investment of this kind of money—6.5 percent is a good place to be." Johnny agreed, so that is what we did.

Johnny and Merry funded the trust with $1 million of the publicly traded stock; the stock was sold tax-free because of the IRS tax-qualified nature of the trust, and they received a little over $5,400 per month.

At the end of the first year, the trust had paid income to them, and the asset value had increased substantially. They asked us to distribute from the trust assets a gift of $50,000 to their local church for a building project. This left the trust assets at more than the initial value of $1 million. Then they added a second deposit into the trust of $1 million of the appreciated stock; their income went to $10,800 per month ($130,000 per year) to enhance their Social Security income very nicely.

This piece of the donors' overall financial and estate plan certainly enhanced their financial security in retirement; as to their spiritual fulfillment, they were encouraged to **keep this trust on the altar of God in a covenant by sacrifice**, asking Him for instruction on whether to or when to release their rights to the income from the trust so the remaining balance can be put into His work before the time of trouble begins.

Ninety-four-year-old Man Used $450,000 to Fund a Charitable Gift Annuity

The next story involved a generous man of ninety-four years old. He declared he wanted to deposit some of his highly appreciated stock holdings into a gift annuity. A central question was whether he should transfer the stock to us and have us sell it with significant tax savings or if would it be to his tax advantage to sell the stock and transfer the cash.

The next two flow charts apply to this case. Normally, donors are advised to always transfer their appreciated asset to a charitable remainder trust or a charitable gift annuity before they sell it. However, one of my colleagues at one of our institutions was very thorough in exploring and explaining the options available to our donor. The stock's market value was $450,000. Apparently, the following chart had appealed to the donor.

Why did he want to do that? He may have been wearying of the stock market—the normal wisdom is that the equities market should be avoided by people of such an advanced age. And he may have wanted to avoid the low interest rates on savings accounts. One thing was certain: The donor wanted to make a gift to our educational institution and its mission of preparing young soldiers of the cross of Christ for service to the world's lost people. As he considered the features of a variety of optional solutions to satisfy his challenges and wishes, he decided on the charitable gift annuity.

This particular donor's tax advisor counseled him to sell the stock in his own name and fund the charitable gift annuity with cash from the proceeds of sale.

You may ask, "Why?"

And I would say, "Very good question."

Compare the next two charts, and you will see the reason for the income tax preparer's advice: He found the donor's income tax bracket was 48 percent on his ordinary income when he combined the federal and state income tax rates. This taxpayer needed all of the tax-free income he could get; and at his age, the income tax deduction provided a partial offset of the capital gains to be reported on an outright sale of the asset. If he had transferred the stock to the annuity, the stock would have been sold out of the annuity, with the proceeds going into the annuity account.

The first chart below shows how it would have worked in that case. His capital gain of $200,000 would have been included on his 1099 on a pro-rated basis at $17,070.56 annually, spread over his life expectancy of four-plus years, which would have reduced the donor's tax-free income dollar for dollar to less than half of his income from this annuity.

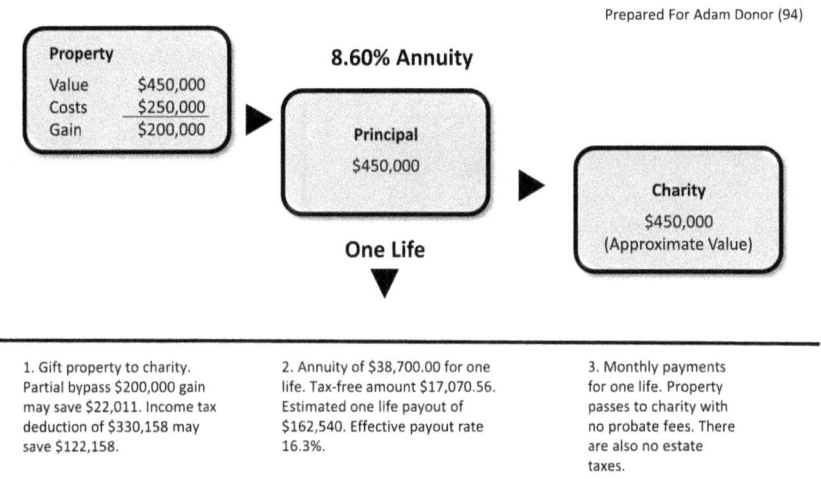

1. Gift property to charity. Partial bypass $200,000 gain may save $22,011. Income tax deduction of $330,158 may save $122,158.
2. Annuity of $38,700.00 for one life. Tax-free amount $17,070.56. Estimated one life payout of $162,540. Effective payout rate 16.3%.
3. Monthly payments for one life. Property passes to charity with no probate fees. There are also no estate taxes.

This educational illustration is not professional tax or legal advice; consult a tax advisor about your specific situation. See data sheets for assumptions.

In the next chart below, you can readily see the advantages of funding the annuity with cash rather than with the stock by comparing the amount of his tax-free annuity income from one chart to the other. He was able to maximize his tax-free income and have no capital gain income to be reported on the annual IRS 1099 income report.

1. His tax-free income from this annuity is about 80 percent of his total annuity income.
2. His charitable deduction of $330,158 leaves capital gain income to report on his income tax returns of $119,842, which is taxed at a much more favorable rate.
3. It's usually best to consult with a "multitude of counselors," as in the case of involving the donor's income tax consultant. I seek to be one of a team of the donor's advisors.

As you can see, this case was an exceptional one. It's important to remember that the usual advice, "Transfer your appreciated assets to an annuity or charitable trust before you sell them," is not best for *every* donor.

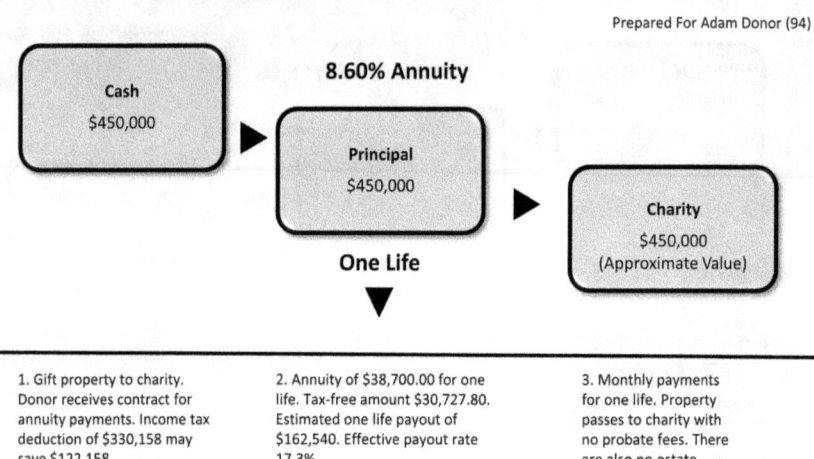

1. Gift property to charity. Donor receives contract for annuity payments. Income tax deduction of $330,158 may save $122,158.

2. Annuity of $38,700.00 for one life. Tax-free amount $30,727.80. Estimated one life payout of $162,540. Effective payout rate 17.3%.

3. Monthly payments for one life. Property passes to charity with no probate fees. There are also no estate taxes.

This educational illustration is not professional tax or legal advice; consult a tax advisor about your specific situation. See data sheets for assumptions.

Joe's Heart-Activated Gifts to God

In my work of planned giving ministry for the Seventh-day Adventist Church, Joe (not his real name), truly a godly man, called my office and asked me to visit and assist him in setting up a unitrust. He had already done that with another Adventist institution and wanted to do one that could benefit his local school. After we did one, he liked it so much that we did another, and then another—truly an exciting experience for this servant-minister. To watch Joe sign his name on the deed to transfer property to a charitable remainder trust in a spirit of gratefulness and worshipful praise to God—watching Joe enter into spiritual transactions with God that brightened his face with a heavenly glow—well, there might not be any better thrill for me this side of eternity. It was a "standing on holy ground" experience.

Joe was seventy-five years old and retired. He was a generous supporter of his local church and church school with tithe and generous offerings. He had a nice brokerage account of liquid assets and a beautiful retirement home, with several acres to work a great garden all year on a paradise island about 3,000 miles west of California.

Joe also had a few hundred acres in several contiguous parcels of land on the mainland he had held for over thirty years, with a cost of about $400 per acre and a market value of about $6,000 per acre. He consolidated parcels into a sizable block and subdivided it into various parcels to harmonize with the current realities of zoning laws and economics.

Joe then systematically transferred three parcels of land one by one, each into a charitable remainder unitrust.

- Fifty-plus acres of land in town given to provide about $500 monthly income to each of his five children for a specific term of years, and then the remainder to the Lord's work. He said, "That is their inheritance." Evidently, he had a plan to give the rest of his substantial wealth to the Lord's work.

- Twenty-six acres of vacant land in one town and twenty acres of orchard at the edge of another town to provide additional retirement income to Joe for as long as he lived—and then the remainder to the Lord's work—providing part of Joe's *financial security* during his retirement years; also providing him with a great sense of *spiritual fulfillment* in the knowledge that many young people would receive a Christian education because of these gifts to God.

> *To watch Joe sign his name on the deed to transfer property to a charitable remainder trust in a spirit of gratefulness and worshipful praise to God—watching Joe enter into spiritual transactions with God that brightened his face with a heavenly glow—well, there might not be any better thrill for me this side of eternity. It was a "standing on holy ground" experience.*

Joe made sound business deals with the church and beautiful spiritual transactions with heaven as a citizen of God's spiritual kingdom—transformational gifts to God as an act of worship in the spirit of thanksgiving and loving trust.

Joe told me he had lived the life of a hard-hearted professed Christian for forty-five years, teaching Sabbath School and serving in other roles as a leader in church before actually giving his heart to Jesus. Joe had been a Sabbath-keeping, health-reformed church member for all those years without receiving a heart of flesh on which the Lord could write His law of love, but then he fully surrendering his heart, mind, and will to God, and when he was finally converted rather than merely conditioned, he found a thrilling life by:

- Surrendering his heart and asking that all his affections would be framed by the cross of Christ, with the adoption of heaven's values as his values
- Surrendering his mind and asking for the mind of Christ to provide all his thoughts, with his priorities being based on Heaven's values
- Surrendering his will and asking for guidance and wisdom in every lifestyle choice, constantly bathed in prayer and based on biblical principles of simplicity and love for all people.

Joe became a citizen of God's spiritual kingdom when he allowed Jesus to take away his stony heart and give him a new, clean heart. He was then able to recognize all of his financial holdings belonged to God because he had been given eyes to see, ears to hear, and a heart to understand the spiritual realities of money and possessions.

I'm excited to be reminded of the following concepts and advice from the Spirit of Prophecy:

> The desire to accumulate wealth is an original affection of our nature, implanted there by our heavenly Father for noble ends. (White, *Counsels on Stewardship*, p. 148)
>
> When God entrusts man with riches, it is that he may adorn the doctrine of Christ our Saviour by using his earthly treasure in advancing the kingdom of God in our world. He is to represent Christ, and therefore is not to live to please and glorify himself, to receive honor because he is rich. (White, *Counsels on Stewardship*, p. 27)

Notice Jesus is apparently teaching us that we won't all receive the same level of return on our investment of money, time, and energy in our accumulation of assets:

> And he told them many things in parables, saying: "A sower went out to sow. And as he sowed, some seeds fell along the path, and the birds came and devoured them. Other seeds fell on rocky ground, where they had not much soil, and immediately they sprang up, since they had no depth of soil, but when the sun rose they were scorched; and since they had no root they withered away. Other seeds fell upon thorns, and the thorns grew up and choked them. Other seeds fell on good soil and brought forth grain, *some a hundredfold, some sixty, some thirty*. He who has ears, let him hear." (Matthew 13:3–9, RSV, emphasis added)

This parable of the sower provides a wonderfully compelling example to me.

Jesus explained His parable:

> "Hear then the parable of the sower. When any one hears the word of the kingdom and does not understand it, the evil one comes and snatches away what is sown in his heart; this is what was sown along the path. As for what was sown on rocky ground, this is he who hears the word and immediately receives it with joy; yet he has no root in himself, but endures for a while, and when tribulation or persecution arises on account of the word, immediately he falls away. As for what was sown among thorns, this is he who hears the word, but the cares of the world and the delight in riches choke the word, and it proves unfruitful. As for what was sown on good soil, this is he who hears the word and understands it; he indeed bears fruit, and yields, in one case a hundredfold, in another sixty, and in another thirty." (Matthew 13:18–23, RSV)

Jesus promised a phenomenal reward for sacrifice that He longs to give us:

> And Peter said, "Lo, we have left our homes and followed you." And he said to them, "Truly, I say to you, there is no man who has left house or wife or brothers or parents or children, for the sake of the kingdom of God, who will not receive manifold more in this time, and in the age to come eternal life." (Luke 18:28–30, RSV)

It is simply not possible to love God with our whole heart, mind, and spirit if we are focused on worldly pursuits of gain. "The love of Jesus and the love of money cannot dwell in the same heart" (White, *Counsels on Stewardship*, p. 157).

God withholds wealth from some people for their good.

> Some will have a hundredfold in this life, and in the world to come life everlasting. But all will not receive their hundredfold in this life, because they cannot bear it. If entrusted with much, they would become unwise stewards. The Lord withholds it for their good; but their treasure in heaven will be secure. How much better is such an investment as this! (White, *Counsels on Stewardship*, pp. 232, 233)

> It is not the empty cup that we have trouble in carrying; it is the cup full to the brim that must be carefully balanced. Affliction and adversity may cause much inconvenience, and may bring great depression; but it is prosperity that is dangerous to spiritual life. (White, *Counsels on Stewardship*, p. 148)

The mission of Christ is to seek and save the lost. **God's spiritual kingdom is established by Jesus.** "And I, the Son of Man, have come to seek and save those like [Zacchaeus] who are lost" (Luke 19:10, NLT). "Wherever your treasure is, there your heart and thoughts will also be" (Matt. 6:21, NLT).

Section III

Designing an Estate Plan Based on Sound Principles

Chapter 13

Will My Will-Plan Be in the Master Potter's Hands?

I grew up in the Ozark Mountains of Arkansas on a 400-acre farm; the farm had 100 acres of tillable crop land right along the White River; the house was about a mile from the river; the land in between was all trees and streams; our house was on frontage of a state highway: a gravel road to which they added pavement when I was nine. The river was always full of water, and somehow, the water stayed in the river, but lush vegetation grew along the riverbank. I now understand rivers are lined with clay to keep the water inside its banks. Therefore, I really love the powerful promise Jesus gave us:

> On the last day of the feast, the great day, Jesus stood up and proclaimed, "If any one thirst, let him come to me and drink. He who believes in me, as the scripture has said, 'Out of his heart shall flow rivers of living water.'" Now this he said about the Spirit, which those who believed in him were to receive; for as yet the Spirit had not been given, because Jesus was not yet glorified. (John 7:37–39, RSV)

Jesus was quoting from Isaiah 44: "For I will pour water on the thirsty land, and streams on the dry ground; I will pour my Spirit upon your descendants, and my blessing on your offspring. They shall spring up like grass amid waters, like willows by flowing streams. This one will say, 'I am the Lord's'" (verses 3–5, RSV).

Isn't it wonderful to realize you and I are like the river with Living Water (Christ alive in us) flowing through us to nourish those along the banks of our lives? We are the clay that is dead to self. I want to be so deeply embedded in Christ that self is completely dead. Someone said to have more of Christ is to have less of self. I want to be completely settled *in His hands*, with a fully surrendered spirit, mind, heart, and will. Notice the great help we can receive to find our way into His hands:

> The LORD gave another message to Jeremiah. He said, "Go down to the potter's shop, and I will speak to you there." So, I did as he told me and found the potter working at his wheel. But the jar he was making did not turn out as he had hoped, so he crushed it into a lump of clay again and started over. Then the LORD gave me this message: "O Israel, can I not do to you as this potter has done to his clay? *As the clay is in the potter's hand, so are you in my hand.*" (Jeremiah 18:1–7, NLT 2004, emphasis added)

Isn't it wonderful to realize you and I are like the river with Living Water (Christ alive in us) flowing through us to nourish those along the banks of our lives? We are the clay that is dead to self. I want to be so deeply embedded in Christ that self is completely dead

The potter takes the clay and molds it according to his will. He kneads it and works it. He tears it apart and presses it together. He wets it and then dries it. He lets it lie for a while without touching it. When it is perfectly pliable, he continues the work of making of it a vessel. He forms it into shape and on the wheel trims and polishes it. He dries it in the sun and bakes it in the oven. Thus it becomes a vessel fit for use. So the great Master Worker desires to mold and fashion us. And as the clay is in the hands of the potter, so are we to be in His hands. We are not to try to do the work of the potter. Our part is to yield ourselves to be molded by the Master Worker. (White, *The Ministry of Healing*, pp. 471, 472)

The Potter's *purpose*: to craft the beauty and usefulness that is in His mind for you and me. "The Son of Man came to find lost people and save them" (Luke 19:10, NCV). And He came to "destroy the works of the devil" (1 John 3:8, NASB1995).

The Potter's *power*: "For this reason the Father loves Me, because I lay down My life so that I may take it again. No one has taken it away from Me, but I lay it down on My own initiative. I have authority [power] to lay it down, and I have authority [power] to take it up again" (John 10:17-18, NASB1995).

The Potter's *patience*: He waits for us to allow self to be transformed. "Do not be conformed to this world, but be transformed by the renewing of your mind, so that you may prove what the will of God is, that which is good and acceptable and perfect" (Rom. 12:2, NASB1995).

The Potter's *presence*: "to save those who come to God through him. He lives forever to intercede with God on their behalf" (Heb. 7:25, NLT).

The Potter's *pressure*: His hands are on us as the clay, ever so gently shaping us for service and security in Christ while whispering His sweet, charming messages to us.

The Potter's *promise*: "I will ask the Father, and He will give you another Helper [Comforter], that He may be with you forever; *that is* the Spirit of truth, whom the world cannot receive, because it does not see Him or know Him, *but* you know Him because He abides with you and will be in you" (John 14:16, 17, NASB1995).

Is Your Plan In God's Hands?

What is your core life mission? Is your plan for daily living and dying in the hands of our dear Lord? Of course, we all agree that is the safest place, for His hands are most gentle, caring, and secure, and can be trusted implicitly to provide the very best outcome.

When the prophet Gad told King David the Lord was offering him a choice of three forms of punishment as a result of his sinful act, David replied, "I'm in a desperate situation! But let us fall into the hands of the LORD, for his mercy is great. Do not let me fall into human hands" (2 Sam. 24:14. NLT 2004).

While hanging on the cross, "Jesus, crying out with a loud voice, said, "Father, into Your hands I commit My spirit." Having said this, He breathed His last" (Luke 23:46, NASB1995, adapted).

Often, I pray, asking the Lord to take my spirit, heart, mind, and will into His hands to reshape me into the likeness of His gracious character. I acknowledge I'm the clay in His most noble hands, which are completely capable and safe. As such, I covet the grand privilege of being used as His vessel into and through which He can pour living water for the benefit of others.

I want my life to be in God's Hands more than in anything or anywhere else. Taking this life into my own hands, I will receive a counterfeit power from Satan, with *no* sweet love, joy, or peace, leading to a living drudgery and disaster, sooner or later, whether in plenty or poverty. **Life in Christ's Hands is full of hope, with His light, power, sweet love, joy, peace, comfort** (see White, *Early Writings*, pp. 54–56).

A rod in my hands will keep away wild animals,	Legacy
A rod in Moses' hands parted the mighty sea.	
It all depends on whose hands it's in.	Enables
A sling shot in my hands is a kid's toy,	
A sling shot in David's hands was a mighty weapon.	God to
It all depends on whose hands it's in.	Act in
Two fish and five loaves of bread in my hands is a couple of fish sandwiches.	Covenant with
Two fish and five loaves of bread in Christ's hands fed thousands.	You
It all depends on whose hands it's in. (Unknown Author)	

A legacy plan design or inheritance plan in my hands may include a gift to the church that represents a fee for service—a payment to the church for assisting with the plan—a business transaction with the church. In God's hands, my legacy plan design will spread the gospel across the region and care for any needs of my family that do not counteract the Potter's purpose, cut short His patience, exclude His presence and power, or remove His pressure through the crucible of affliction and trials.

In His hands, a legacy gift to God as part of your will-plan, given as an act of worship from a loyal heart and willing mind, as though it all belongs to Him, will be used by Him with great efficiency and effectiveness for His mission to seek and save lost people.

> Remember this—a farmer who plants only a few seeds will get a small crop. But the one who plants generously will get a generous crop. *You must each decide in your heart how much to give. And don't*

give reluctantly or in response to pressure. "For God loves a person who gives cheerfully." And God will generously provide all you need. Then you will always have everything you need and plenty left over to share with others. As the Scriptures say, "They share freely and give generously to the poor. Their good deeds will be remembered forever." For God is the one who provides seed for the farmer and then bread to eat. In the same way, he will provide and increase your resources and then produce a great harvest of generosity in you. (2 Corinthians 9:6–10, NLT 2004, emphasis added)

In His Hands

I urge you to put not only your plans for life and death, but to put *yourself wholly*, into the hands of our dear Lord.

When we are in His hands, which are so careful, caring, powerful, gentle, loving, and trustworthy, then we can know His *power*, *presence*, *purpose*, *patience*, and *promise*, which are all consistent with His Ten Commandments—His law of freedom (see James 1:25; 2:12).

The typical will-plan gives all or most of the accumulated assets to unbelieving relatives, and they are all spent in six months, with nothing much to show for it, except maybe a new car and a cruise. As soldiers of the cross of Christ, we signed on to serve in His cavalry, not coast on a cruise.

It all depends on the hands in which your plan is placed! What is your preference: an inheritance plan according to the world's custom or a transformational gift to God with heaven's blessing? As you can see, it depends on whose hands hold your plan. To whom are you ultimately committed?

Whom are you trusting to be your provider and protector? David prayed, "When my heart is overwhelmed, lead me to the Rock that is higher than I" (Ps. 61:2). Therefore, put your concerns, worries, fears, hopes, dreams, your family members—one by one, all of your relationships, along with all of the assets you have accumulated—put them all in God's hands in a covenant by sacrifice; then make a will-plan to honor that covenant in case you have to lay down your life in the dust of the earth before Jesus comes. That way, you have something left to be distributed into the hands of others so that your work may continue on until He comes. Additionally, you won't have to sleep so long before the resurrection. Place your plans in God's most capable hands in loving trust of Him to provide for you and your loved ones.

The Cosmic Conflict between good and evil is raging increasingly. Yes, it is true in the life of every person who enters the process of creating their own will-plan. Ellen White wrote, "I was shown the awful fact that Satan and his angels have more to do with the management of the property of God's professed people than the Lord has." The vast majority of the general population will die without an up-to-date, legally valid, plan in place. This is true also for most of God's professed people in our midst.

> **S**atan often plays upon [aged persons'] imagination and leads them to feel a continual anxiety in regard to money. It is their idol ... In this way they place themselves in continual want, through *fear* that sometime in the future they shall want. *All these fears originate with Satan.* (White, *Testimonies for the Church*, vol. 1, pp. 423, 424, emphasis added)

> For God has not given us the spirit of fear; but of power, and of love, and of a sound mind. (2 Timothy 1:7, AKJV)

> Peace I leave with you, my peace I give to you: not as the world gives, give I to you. Let not your heart be troubled, neither let it be afraid. (John 14:27, AKJV)

> Regarding the voice of God:

> Light comes to the soul through God's word, through His servants, or by the direct agency of His Spirit. (White, *The Desire of Ages*, p. 322)

> There are three ways in which the Lord reveals His will to us, to guide us, and to fit us to guide others. How may we know His voice from that of a stranger? How shall we distinguish it from the voice of a false shepherd? [1.] God reveals His will to us in His word, the Holy Scriptures. [2.] His voice is also revealed in His providential workings; and it will be recognized if we do not separate our souls from Him by walking in our own ways, doing according to our own wills, and following the promptings of an unsanctified heart, until the senses have become so confused that eternal things are not discerned, and the voice of Satan is so disguised that it is accepted as the voice of God.

> [3.] Another way in which God's voice is heard is through the appeals of His Holy Spirit, making impressions upon the heart, which will be wrought out in the character. If you are in doubt upon any subject you must first consult the Scriptures ... You should have an earnest desire to be pliable in His hands and to follow whithersoever He may lead you. (White, *Testimonies for the Church*, vol. 5, p. 512)

Jesus is clear on this avenue of knowing God's voice:

> To him the gatekeeper opens; the sheep hear his voice, and he calls his own sheep by name and leads them out. When he has brought out all his own, he goes before them, and the sheep follow him, for they know his voice.... My sheep hear my voice, and I know them, and they follow me. (John 10:3, 4, 27, RSV)

> Everyone who is of the Truth [who is a friend of the Truth, who belongs to the Truth] hears *and* listens to My voice. (John 18:37, AMPC)

> Your own ears will hear him. Right behind you a voice will say, "This is the way you should go," whether to the right or to the left. Then you will destroy all your silver idols and your precious gold images. You will throw them out like filthy rags, saying to them, "Good riddance!" (Isaiah 30:21, 22, NLT 2004).

> We cannot depend for counsel upon humanity. The Lord will teach us our duty just as willingly as He will teach somebody else. If we come to Him in faith, He will speak His mysteries to us personally. Our hearts will often burn within us as One draws nigh to commune with us as He did with Enoch. Those who decide to do nothing in any line that will displease God, will know, after presenting their case before Him, just what course to pursue. And they will receive not only wisdom, but strength. Power for obedience, for service, will be imparted to them, as Christ has promised. (White, *The Desire of Ages*, p. 668)

> We must individually hear Him speaking to the heart. When every other voice is hushed, and in quietness we wait before Him, the silence of the soul makes more distinct the voice of God. He bids us, "Be still, and know that I am God." (White, *The Desire of Ages*, p. 363)

God promised to instruct and teach us what to do—to guide us with His eye—if we ask Him in a teachable spirit, not in the stubborn spirit of a mule: "I will instruct you and teach you in the way which you should go; I will counsel you with My eye upon you. Do not be as the horse or as the mule which have no understanding, Whose trappings include bit and bridle to hold them in check" (Ps 32:8, 9, NASB; see also White, *The Desire of Ages*, p. 668)

As God's children, we are to *first* give ourselves to Him and then give our tithes, offerings, and major gifts as an act of worship in a spirit of thanksgiving and praise. Notice Paul's testimony:

> My friends, we want you to know that the churches in Macedonia have shown others how kind God is. Although they were going through hard times and were very poor, they were glad to give generously. They gave as much as they could afford and even more, simply because they wanted to. They even asked and begged us to let them have the joy of giving their money for God's people. And they did more than we had hoped. *They gave themselves first to the Lord and then to us, just as God wanted them to do.* (2 Corinthians 8:1–5, CEV, emphasis added)

Your starting point in the process is to give yourself to God in full surrender of your mind (thoughts and feelings) and heart (affections and passions—see 2 Cor. 8, 9). Surrender your will (choices) and make a covenant by sacrifice with God, placing all you have on His altar and then listen for His still, small voice of individual instruction in the use of what you've got now and at death—giving Christ the preeminence in all you are and do (see Col. 1:18).

The bottom line: study the Lord's design for your last will-plan and pray until you hear His voice of instruction on how to apply what you learn to your planning process. I personally wish to be found faithful in using the resources God lent me to rescue my fellow men for eternity. What do you think about that, dear reader?

Chapter 14

Designer Principles of the Spiritual Dimension in the Context of the Great Controversy in Action

How does one design a will-plan? In addition to the principle of legal security for the design of a will-plan and its related legal documents, we are also discussing pertinent foundational issues in the specific areas of faith, ownership, family, and estate stewardship with respect to how we relate to our accumulated assets. We also mentioned how to apply these principles to the planning process. Note, we said "principles," not rules. The legal dimension of the design for a will-plan is addressed rather extensively in Chapter 10.

As we write this material, we're hoping your prayerful consideration of each of the principles will contribute to your design of your own legacy inheritance plan and that you will be blessed with the Lord's gifts of personal guidance and peace. We're also praying that if you die before Jesus comes back for us, your plan will be a blessing to your family's actual needs, have a spiritual impact on them with the assurance that you love them, and further the Lord's work to the extent that the Holy Spirit leads you. The legal and spiritual frameworks are intended to serve as a platform of principles over which you to study and pray, seeking His instructions about how to apply the principles to the design of your own will-plan.

The purpose of my will as a Christian believer is to plan for my absence from the earth while continuing my support of Christ's mission to seek and save the lost, even beyond my grave, so I don't have to sleep so long awaiting His second coming. My goal is to design my will-plan so it will attain heaven's approval.

My personal story on this topic: The Lord came near during my devotional time morning by morning for a week at four different seasons, prodding me to get this done. He told me to do a will-plan set of legal documents. After working as an estate planning consultant, both in my own business as a professional financial planner and investment broker in California and for the church for a few years at the Southern New England Conference, the Lord appealed to my heart. He gave me these thoughts: 'You have been promoting will planning for your constituent church members in the conference, and you must be a good example by getting your own plan together.' I concluded the Lord was asking me to be authentic and "practice what I preach." Thus, we got it done the first time in 1984.

The Holy Spirit likewise urged me for a week at a time to update the plan; it was done in 1994 and again in 2004. Then it was necessary to update the plan again after the death of our daughter in 2010, and having moved again from California to Massachusetts made it more compelling to update again. Therefore, with the same Holy Spirit promptings as before, it was finally done again in 2013, and again after we relocated from Massachusetts to Michigan in 2021.

Each time, Mary Jo and I prayed for and received God's instruction about His will for our plan and which lawyer to use. In the most recent case, I had decided to use an estate planning specialist friend in Worcester, Massachusetts. However, when I prayed about it, the Lord directed me to a good friend who is a brother in the church locally and an equally qualified specialist in estates and trusts. That all worked out very well. Our state created a new law on how to deal with digital assets, so our attorney-at-law did simple amendments for our plan to include that provision in 2014. Having cared for that, we enjoy great peace.

Our dear Lord Jesus established a plan of succession by two bequests—a plan for His absence from His life on earth—as follows:

> *The purpose of my will as a Christian believer is to plan for my absence from the earth while continuing my support of Christ's mission to seek and save the lost, even beyond my grave, so I don't have to sleep so long awaiting His second coming.*

1. Peace I leave with you; My [own] peace I now give *and* bequeath to you. Not as the world gives do I give to you. Do not let your hearts be troubled, neither let them be afraid. [Stop allowing yourselves to be agitated and disturbed; and do not permit yourselves to be fearful and intimidated and cowardly and unsettled] (John 14:27, AMPC).

2. In John 19:25–27, Jesus provided for his mother's care by introducing Mary to the apostle John as being her son; and He introduced John to Mary as his mother for her care from that time on.

The Spirit of Prophecy offers commentary regarding us caring for our parents: "The same spirit will be seen in every disciple of our Lord. Those who follow Christ will feel that it is a part of their religion to respect and provide for their parents. From the heart where His love is cherished, father and mother will never fail of receiving thoughtful care and tender sympathy" (White, *The Desire of Ages*, p. 752).

Planning ahead by you and me is of utmost importance. Whereas the Lord knows the future, the process and design of one's plan must be continuously bathed in surrendered prayer—in the spirit of "Thy will be done," with our own wills neutralized.

The primary goal of the design of a will-plan is spiritual fulfillment. A secondary goal is financial security to the extent that it enhances the primary goal. You might ask how to do that. For me, there is only one way to do it: to **seek *individual* instruction from the Lord Himself for the design of your will-plan.** God promised to instruct and teach us what to do *if we ask Him in a teachable spirit*. He said to David, "I will instruct you and teach you in the way which you shall go: I will guide you with My eye. Be you not as the horse, or as the mule…." (Psalm 32:8,9a, AKJV)

Since the eye of Jesus is probably as bright as is the sun at high noon with no cloud in the sky, with it focused on my mind in laser-like intensity, I expect to receive immense clarity of instruction. And my expectations have never been disappointed. Indeed, His answers have come to me instantly, while I'm still in communion with Him on my knees, laid out with my face to the floor, or even driving solo, but only when I say, "Lord, you know what is in my mind and heart about this decision I need to make. You know what I'm thinking to do. But Lord, I don't trust myself, and I'm asking You to give me a neutral will and make me willing to be made willing to hear your will in this matter."

We will now look at principles of a will-plan design in a spiritual frame work.

Faith—Whatcha Do with Whatcha Got Is a Salvation Issue

Dear reader, we will now turn our attention to the principle of faith as most essential to spiritual fulfillment and appropriate financial security in the context of planning for our absence from this life.

Whenever you and I decide to be responsible for the design of our personal and family will-plan, it is helpful to acknowledge it is a *most sacred journey*, which means we are to intentionally devote time for study and prayer. The Holy Spirit will definitely lead us to the extent that we are able to sincerely pray, "Thy will be done."

Two Test Questions

1. Is Jesus living in your heart as you die to self daily? Are you converted or just conditioned as a professed Seventh-day Adventist Christian? Christ alive in our hearts—displacing ourselves from our inner thrones—is essential to being right with Jesus. He enables us to do right for God by the power of His presence inside of us. And this is true whether you and I are in plenty or poverty.

2. What is your plan design for the distribution of your accumulated assets when you take your last breath? Do you realize God has a plan for your will? That the devil does, too? This issue is at the very heart of *the great controversy in action*. Sadly, the evidence reveals it is a failed test for most of God's people.

Jesus said, "Where your treasure is, there your heart will be also" (Matt. 6:21, NKJV). David said, "If riches increase, *set not your heart on them*" (Ps. 62:10, emphasis added). How can you and I avoid setting our hearts on our riches? That is impossible to do in our own power. Yes, what we do with what God has entrusted into our hands is a salvation issue. That fact is illustrated by the following story—a true story of long ago.

Plenty or Poverty

Remember, right doing is the result of right being. Obedience to God is the result of being in a saving relationship with Him. Salvation is the root; obedience is the fruit. We cannot control our own hearts of self. We cannot even know our own hearts (see Jer. 17:9). Commenting on this verse, Ellen White said, "The lips may express a poverty of soul that the heart does not acknowledge. While speaking to God of poverty of spirit, the heart may be swelling with the conceit of its own superior humility and exalted righteousness" (White, *Christ's Object Lessons*, p. 159).

My observation of working closely with many hundreds of people on their finances during a period of forty-plus years tells me this liberating truth—this thrilling revelation of Jesus living in my heart—is not known by most professing Christians. I came to understand and experience this truth in my seventies, and I have been a professed Christian since I was eight.

The Lord's messenger observed long ago "that **not one in twenty [under 5 percent] whose names are registered upon the church books are prepared to close their earthly history**" (White, *Christian Service*, p. 41). Sadly, my experience indicates this has not changed for the better today.

A powerful story on family support and inheritance planning *without* Christ as Lord is forthcoming. It reveals the great controversy in action regarding estate and inheritance planning by one family in particular.

This true story was written out by Ellen G. White and published in the *Adventist Review*. I thought you would appreciate the certainty about God's design for your relationship to Him in the context of your money and other accumulated assets.

This story of one family White described in 1858 is based on what she saw in different visions over a period of years. I hope and pray, dear reader, that you sense God's blessing as you read it. The story was reported by her grandson, Arthur L. White, when he was in charge of the Ellen G. White Estate operation at the General Conference of Seventh-day Adventists. He was commissioned to write six volumes about his grandmother during the 1980s.

> In mid-March, [1858] while on the trip to Ohio, it seems that Ellen White sent to Uriah Smith a solemn message for the church, to be published in the Review. The two-column article, which made reference to several visions, appeared in the issue of April 15 under the title "A Warning." In it Ellen White reviewed the experience of a family of some means who had moved from New England to Illinois about the year 1855, there to engage largely in farming. There were three, the father, mother, and a grown daughter. Her article opens:
>
>> Brother Smith: As I consider the responsibilities and dangers of the people of God, I am led to fear for many, and I wish to set before them the following, which I consider a most solemn warning.

> As it became evident a few years since that the burden of the third message would be in the West, a brother, who had much of this world's goods, resolved to move west with his family, and thus introduce the work in the West.
>
> He went with one intention, his wife with another. His intention was to proclaim the truth, but her intention was to have all their means laid out in house and lands, that the means not only be secured, and kept from the cause of God, but that her husband's time be also employed in building, planting, sowing, et cetera.
>
> He was convinced of his duty to dispose of a portion of his means to advance the cause of God, but it was a great sacrifice for him to make, for he loved this world, and he was easily persuaded by his wife and daughter to gratify their desire and love of their earthly treasure and retain it. He disobeyed the call of God to gratify his wife and daughter, and was too willing to excuse or cover up his love of the world under a show of duty to his family …

While this family was professing to be looking for the coming of Jesus and to be a part of His peculiar people, Ellen White was shown that they were investing in large land holdings, showing that this world was their home and their treasure was here on earth. And the wife was holding the husband back from doing what he knew to be his duty. Wrote Ellen White:

> I was shown the wife of our brother, that she was engrossed in the spirit of this world, and loved and worshiped it; that she must unfasten her grasp, that she was a stumbling block in her husband's way, she was holding him back, and was unwilling that he should sell and give alms, also unwilling that he should go out to talk the truth to others. I saw that unless she got out of her husband's way, cut loose from the world, and distributed to the necessity of God's cause, the Lord would visit the family with judgment, and move her out of the way …

The message of warning was not heeded; while she was in the midst of making improvements to stay in this world, disease and affliction came, and her life record was closed. Soon after this James and Ellen White visited the place of their residence and found the husband struggling for freedom of soul. Ellen White was there given a vision, and light began to shine in upon the benighted father, but still the victory was not won:

> As our brother would come up to the point to give up the world, and get it out of his heart; as he would lay his farm upon the altar, and say he would sell a part, or all of it, then the daughter would act the same part the mother had done, to pull him back, and she would plead for their treasure here ...

There could be no mistaking that God was in earnest with those rich in this world's goods, who claimed to have surrendered their lives to Him and yet tenaciously clung to their earthly treasures:

> Before I left that place I was shown in vision that God had taken the mother away, ... and unless the father and daughter submitted to God, unless they cut loose from the world and had their affections weaned from it, God would step over the threshold again in judgment. I was astonished at what was shown me in vision.
>
> I saw that this brother loved this world more than he ever thought he did, and that it was a snare to him—it deceived him. I saw that he was so close and snug in deal, it really carried him beyond the bounds of strict truth and honesty. Said the angel, "The deceitfulness of riches causes many, many of its possessors to stumble over their riches to perdition, while only a few with the unrighteous mammon will make friends, and finally be received into everlasting habitations" ...

In the vision she was shown the selfish character of the daughter. If her father, whether he lived or died, should leave her a few thousand dollars, "it would be enough to ruin her, and displease God." All this, with anguished soul, she related to the father.

Again a vision was given to Ellen White aimed at saving the man. Of this she wrote:

> Last summer [1857] I was again shown this brother's case, that he was not moving fast enough, that he was not using his means to advance the cause of God as fast as he should. The next news I heard was that he was dead, and had left his large property to his daughter. Nothing was bestowed upon the cause of God ...

He was 51 years of age. In a subsequent vision, Ellen White was shown Satan's strategy:

> I saw that Satan had it just as he wanted it at his death, that nothing be left to the cause of God.... I saw that it was the design of Satan to keep all the means from the ranks of the truth that he could, and to use it as a stumbling block for souls. He is willing that those who profess the truth, and are snug, selfish, and covetous should have means in their possession, for they idolize it. They nourish it, and it will prove their ruin; for they lay up treasure on earth, and lose their treasure in heaven …

As Ellen White brought the account of this startling object lesson to a close, she gave the reason for hastening it into print:

> As I have seen that the reward of covetousness thus far upon this family should be a warning to the church, I cannot withhold from the people of God what has been shown me respecting them. (A. White, *Ellen G. White: The Early Years: 1827–1862* [vol. 1], pp. 375–378)

What is the role of faith's covenant with God for you and me in the design of an inheritance plan, which is to be made into a legally valid last will and testament and, perhaps, a companion revocable living trust? Let's consider some definitions as it relates to faith in this context. When you and I wade into the process of designing our personal will-plans, I believe we need to be conscious of Paul's admonition: "**Whatever does not originate *and* proceed from faith is sin** [whatever is done without a conviction of its approval by God is sinful]" (Rom. 14:23, AMPC). This is the reason prayer-saturated planning is so important.

What is faith? I really like Dr. Graham Maxwell's definition:

> Faith, as I understand it, is a word we use to describe a *relationship with God* as with a person well known. The better we know Him, the better this relationship may be. Faith implies an attitude toward God of love, trust, and deepest admiration. It means having enough confidence in Him, based on the more than adequate evidence revealed, to be willing to believe whatever He says, to accept whatever He offers, and to do whatever He wishes—without reservation—for the rest of eternity. (Maxwell, *Can God Be Trusted?* p. 46, emphasis added)

FAITH acknowledges God's gift of all the resources of heaven in the life and ministry of Jesus—the sacrifice and resurrection of Christ, the God Man, and His gift of faith to me as His child—empowering us to trust in His promises as both our Provider of all needs for life and godliness and Protector who weighs and sifts all trials that are headed toward us.

FAITH asks God for wisdom with no doubting (double-mindedness—see James 1:8) on how to apply spiritual principles to our personal legacy planning—to whom to give and how much to give them. Ellen White explained the key characteristic of such a man as "he who seeks to follow his own will, while professing to do the will of God" (*Patriarchs and Prophets*, p. 384).

FAITH asks, "How much do I need to give to my family? How much *may* I give to Jesus for a finished work in this generation?"

FAITH asks, "Have you prayed about it? Have you studied the divine will—heaven's principles on what to do with what you have accumulated? and have you prayed for instructions on how to apply those principles to your own will-plan design?"

FAITH requires us to make a covenant by sacrifice with the Lord, placing all I am and have on His altar and acknowledging that all I have belongs to Him absolutely, whether I'm dead or alive—in plenty or poverty.

Expecting Individual Instruction—In order to expect individual instructions from the Lord, it is of utmost importance for Christians to know the voice of God—to be eager and ready to listen to the "still, small voice." With this in mind, consider that …

FAITH requires us to get to know Jesus intimately, constantly abiding in Him.

KNOWING Jesus encourages us to trust Him with our whole lives, dead or alive; trusting Him for eternal life in the future and here and now with tithes and offerings pursuant to our vow of commitment; and ultimately trusting Him with all we are and have.

TRUSTING Jesus leads you and me to love Him with our whole hearts (affections, passions, ambitions, hopes, and dreams), minds (thoughts and imaginings), strength (physical body), spirit (attitudes), and wills (life's choices). And when Christ lives in you and me, we have the lofty privilege of having the faith *of* Jesus along with our faith *in* Jesus.

LOVE compels us to make a commitment to give, for we cannot love without giving.

LOVE becomes the spring of all commitment and action, including the use of resources—time, talent, influence, treasure, body-temple, and energy—to honor Jesus no matter what. I've loved the precious help found within the following insight for a long time: "When Christ dwells in the heart, the soul will be so filled with His love, with the joy of communion with Him, that it will cleave to Him; and in the contemplation of Him, self will be forgotten. Love to Christ will be the spring of action" (White, *Steps to Christ*, pp. 44, 45).

May God bless you, dear reader, with His special favor and wonderful peace as you come to know Him better and better. Yes, we can know Jesus by heart. I've also loved the insight of Peter's words for a long time. He offered the progression of experience in the development of our Christian characters:

> As we *know Jesus better*, his divine power gives us everything we need for living a godly life. He has called us to receive his own glory and goodness! And by that same mighty power, he has given us all of his rich and wonderful promises. He has promised that you will escape the decadence all around you caused by evil desires and that you will share in his divine nature. So, make every effort to apply the benefits of these promises to your life. Then your faith will produce a life of moral excellence. A life of moral excellence leads to *knowing God better. Knowing God better* leads to self-control. Self-control leads to patient endurance, and patient endurance leads to godliness. *Godliness leads to love* for other Christians, and finally you will grow to have love for everyone. The more you grow like this, the more you will become productive and useful in your knowledge of our Lord Jesus Christ. (2 Peter 1:2–8, NLT 1996, emphasis added)

My moral and ethical obligation to honor God in my estate inheritance plan is not a legalistic obligation. Rather, it's a matter of loving trust and grateful loyalty to my dear Savior, who is the Lord of my life—who is alive in me. I know that obedience to God is not what saves me for everlasting life. Obedience is the result of salvation. The fruit and not the root of salvation in Jesus the Christ. Perhaps my most favorite poem is given here as reflective of my personal testimony:

> If I ever heard the words that describe what He did for me,
> I know I would never forget;
> And if there are words to describe what He means to me,
> I just haven't heard them yet.
> But I love Him, I love Him, what more can I say,
> Though the words seem so feeble and small
> I love Him, I love Him with all of my heart

And to love Him is to give Him my all. (Herman Bauman, "I Love Him," emphasis added)

Ownership—How Does Ownership Impact My Will-Plan Design?

Dear reader, I hope and pray your faith in God, His faith in you, and His faithfulness *to* you will enable you to be faithful to Him in the exercise of designing your own inheritance will-plan. Amen! Now, let's consider the area of ownership.

It helps me to remember my love for Jesus can be no greater than is my love for the person I despise the most. Maybe that is why Jesus instructed us to "love your enemies" (Matt. 5:44, NKJV). I understand the only way I can love those who disagree with me or are disagreeable altogether is when Christ is alive in my heart, mind, and spirit, replacing my life of self as I follow Paul's example: "I die daily" (1 Cor. 15:31; see also Luke 9:23, 24; Gal. 2:16–20).

> *My moral and ethical obligation to honor God in my estate inheritance plan is not a legalistic obligation. Rather, it's a matter of loving trust and grateful loyalty to my dear Savior, who is the Lord of my life—who is alive in me.*

Biblical Evidence of God's Ownership

God gives to all life, breath, and all things (see Acts 17:25). "You shall remember the Lord your God: for it is he that gives you power to get wealth" (Deut. 8:18, AKJV).

It is according to the Bible that God **owns:**

- Each person alive on earth, believer and unbeliever (see 1 Cor. 6:19, 20; Ezek. 8:4 and *Christ's Object Lessons*, p. 326).
- Every wild animal of the forest and the cattle on a thousand hills (see Ps. 50:10).
- All the birds of the mountains and the wild beasts of the fields (see Ps. 50:11).
- The earth, with all that is in it (see Deut. 10:14).
- All the trees (see Ps. 104:16).
- All silver and gold (see Hag. 2:8).

- "The earth is the Lord's, and the fulness thereof; The world, and they that dwell therein" (Ps. 24:1).

Under the Jewish system the people were taught to cherish a spirit of liberality both in sustaining the cause of God and in supplying the wants of the needy …

The Lord sought to teach Israel that in everything He must be first. Thus they were reminded that God was the proprietor [owner] of their fields, their flocks, and their herds; that it was He who sent them the sunshine and the rain that developed and ripened the harvest. Everything that they possessed was His; they were but the stewards of His goods. (White, *The Acts of the Apostles*, pp. 336, 337)

Commentary on God's Ownership

As an acknowledgment that all things came from Him, the Lord directed that a portion of His bounty should be returned to Him in gifts and offerings to sustain His worship. (White, *Patriarchs and Prophets*, p. 525)

The Lord would have His followers dispense their means while they can do it themselves. *Some may inquire: "Must we actually dispossess ourselves of everything which we call our own?"* We may not be required to do this now; but *we must be willing to do so for Christ's sake. We must acknowledge that our possessions are absolutely His, by using of them freely whenever means is needed to advance His cause.* (White, *Testimonies for the Church*, vol. 4, p. 479, emphasis added)

All things belong to God. All the prosperity we enjoy is the result of divine beneficence. God is the great and bountiful giver. (White, *Testimonies for the Church*, p. 476, emphasis added)

All that man receives of God's bounty still belongs to God. Whatever God has bestowed in the valuable and beautiful things of earth *is placed in the hands of men to test them—to sound the depths of their love for Him and their appreciation of His favors.* Whether it be the treasures of wealth or of intellect, they are to be laid, a willing offering, at the feet of Jesus; the giver saying, meanwhile, with David, "All things come of Thee, and of Thine own have we given Thee." (White, *Patriarchs and Prophets*, p. 753, emphasis added)

Disposition of Accumulated Assets

What is the quality of your relationship with God? Have you entered into an intimate covenant with Jesus regarding your accumulated assets in a spirit of loving trust in Him and loyal support of His precious bride, the church?

Two Questions About Stewardship of Accumulated Assets

1. Are you aware of the counsel in the Spirit of Prophecy about a covenant relationship with God, which has to do with ownership of your assets?

2. Did you know we may receive individual instructions from God on the design of our will-plans? Oh friend, if not, a great blessing is in store for you.

Ownership Transfer

It is completely normal for the carnal heart to accept God's blessings of economic well-being and relate to those blessings in the spirit of Nebuchadnezzar, king of Babylon. He reveled in how great he was because of what he built and possessed (see Dan. 2–4). However, it is our privilege to make a transfer from the selfish heart to God's ownership. Here is a most precious, exciting piece of advice, and an invitation:

> **Houses and lands will be of no use to the saints in the time of trouble,** for they will then have to flee before infuriated mobs, and at that time their possessions cannot be disposed of to advance the cause of present truth. **I was shown that it is the will of God that the saints should cut loose from every encumbrance before the time of trouble comes, and make a covenant with God through sacrifice. If they have their property on the altar, and earnestly inquire of God for duty, He will teach them when to dispose of these things. Then they will be free in the time of trouble, and have no clogs to weigh them down.**
>
> **I saw that if any held on to their property, and did not inquire of the Lord as to their duty, He would not make duty known,** and they would be permitted to keep their property, and in the time of trouble it would come up before them like a mountain to crush them, and they would try to dispose of it, but would not be able. I heard some mourn like this: "The cause was languishing, God's people were starving for the truth, and we made no effort to supply

the lack; now our property is useless. O that we had let it go, and laid up treasure in heaven!"

I saw that a *sacrifice* did not increase, but it decreased and was *consumed*. **I also saw that God had not required all of His people to dispose of their property at the same time, but if they desired to be taught, He would teach them,** in a time of need, when to sell and how much to sell. Some have been required to dispose of their property in times past to sustain the advent cause, while others have been permitted to keep theirs until a time of need. Then, as the cause needs it, their duty is to sell. (White, *Counsels on Stewardship*, pp. 59, 60, bold emphasis added)

I remember reading this in the first year of being a member of the Seventh-day Adventist Church. It was so exciting to realize I could transfer my ownership responsibility to God for all of my stuff and relationships.

Making this covenant with God is vitally important for you and me to do in this sacred journey of designing and making a will-plan that is approved by heaven, yet there is one more thing that is first: We must give ourselves to God like the Macedonians did (see 2 Cor. 8:1–5).

The book *Counsels on Stewardship* was the first Spirit of Prophecy book I read when we joined the Seventh-day Adventist movement in 1974. I remember being serious about the above instructions.

I made a written list of all we owned and all our relationships. Then I got down on my knees and prayerfully transferred the title of ownership to God for each item, one at a time. It was a special relief to have Him take the responsibility for all of it. We have updated the covenant from time to time. And we continue to ask the Lord what to do with that which He has entrusted to us and when.

A Promise of Houses, Lands, and Family, Plus Eternal Life—in the Words of Jesus.

Jesus promised to reward us for the spirit of sacrifice and generosity:

Truly I say to you There is no man that has left house, or brothers, or sisters, or father, or mother, or wife, or children, or lands, for my sake, and the gospel's, But he shall receive an hundred times now in this time, houses, and brothers, and sisters, and mothers, and children, and lands, with persecutions; and in the world to come eternal life. (Mark 10:29, 30, AKJV)

A question was asked of me about this book, "So, how does it work to honor God in an estate plan when the donor has made a living by being the manager-operator of a business enterprise that is titled in his/her name and is to be passed on to a family member?" Examples might include a farmer or house builder or bakery or other retail activity, or a professional practice such as healthcare or legal practice.

My answer was that it depends on who the owner is according to Heaven's record. To honor God in the will-plan can only work by prayer of the one in charge of the operation. Is the owner a human person or has ownership been transferred to God in a prayer of dedication? It works very well when the operator is a bona fide steward, a heart-activated, mission minded servant of God who has literally turned over the ownership of all he or she has to God. I have known of such situations where a plan was devised to transfer operating ownership to a family member with payments being made into a trust—ultimately for the benefit of God's work.

Family—How Does Family Influence My Will-Plan Design?

The Super Struggle

I understand it will be a struggle for you to decide how to design your last will and testament plan. This is true for almost everyone, especially when it's done by a husband-and-wife couple. The greatest part of the struggle often revolves around how much to leave to the children or family and how much to leave to the Lord's work. There can be a rather wide difference of opinion about this between a husband and wife; sometimes, it can be contentious.

We believe all we have belongs to the Lord, whether we are dead or alive—in poverty or plenty; we also know a "large amount" is more dangerous than good for our children. It can be most hazardous to their spiritual life. I've observed that many times. The overriding concern and prayer is for our family circle to be unbroken when Jesus comes to take us home to spend eternity with Him.

For whatever value you might find in it, my perspective is that struggles to make decisions on how to distribute your accumulated assets may be made easier as you develop more information. The information helps when bathed in prayer. Information that often drives decisions for a positive outcome is usually derived from this time-consuming *process*, which brings relief and clarity:

In our personal and family life, my wife and I learned to listen to God in a spirit of loving trust—to recognize His voice and receive personal and individual instructions:

- When deciding on an invitation to another place of work.
- When deciding in which house to live.
- When deciding which car or mattress to buy.
- When making other significant financial planning decisions, including investments.
- When making health care decisions.
- When deciding how to design our wills to honor our covenant with God by putting all we are and have on His altar.

We often claim the following promise of God. When on my knees, facedown and prostrate before Him, driving alone, or in the shower, He always answers immediately.

"I will instruct you and teach you in the way you should go; I will guide you with My eye. Do not be like the horse or like the mule, which have no understanding, which must be harnessed with bit and bridle, Else they will not come near you" (Ps. 32:8, 9).

Since the Lord's eye is as bright as is the sun at high noon on a clear day, I take this text to mean His guiding light will focus like a laser beam to bring extraordinary clarity of thought to my mind *if* I come to him in a teachable spirit—not like the mule with a stubborn mind full of determination to do what I want to do.

I've often said to the Lord when praying, "You know what is in my mind and heart, Lord. You know what I want to do in this matter. You know what I've decided already. But Lord, I want to now surrender all of that to you so that I have *no will of my own* and you can write Your will into my mind and heart. I've talked to You about this—telling You what I plan to do and asking you to bless my plan; but now I'm ready to listen to You, for You are the Sovereign of my life and work." The Lord is faithful to His Word and has always answered immediately, placing new thoughts into my mind.

Money and possessions are where we live; they are life to us—deeply imbedded in the heart of all people in all cultures. Our manner of relating to them reveals whether God is our Sovereign Lord or not—whether we trust God with tithes, offerings, and our whole lives—putting all of our accumulated assets on His altar in a covenant by sacrifice.

For those who intend to put God first by saturating the will-plan process in prayer, the most important element is the emotional-spiritual area. We have special insight from the Spirit of Prophecy that may be helpful. It is better for us to assist our children to learn to help themselves "than to leave them a *large amount* at death." This is true because "children who are left to rely principally upon their own exertions make better men and women, and are better fitted for practical life than those children who have depended upon their father's estate."

The benefits are profoundly abundant when this counsel is followed. We have seen it in numerous cases where it is revealed that:

> The children left to depend upon their own resources generally prize their abilities, improve their privileges, and cultivate and direct their faculties to accomplish a purpose in life. They frequently develop characters of industry, frugality, and moral worth, which lie at the foundation of success in the Christian life. Those children for whom parents do the most, frequently feel under the least obligation toward them. The errors of which we have spoken have existed in——. Parents have shifted their stewardship upon their children. (White, *Testimonies for the Church*, vol. 3, p. 122, emphasis added)

What is a large amount? I never try to define that for anyone. Some people have told me $1 million is not too large for their children, while others have felt $100,000 is way too much; and some have said $10,000 is about right. It is a very personal, individual decision to be bathed in surrendered prayer for the very best outcome.

This depends partially on whether or not there are special needs for one or more of the children, which might indicate the need of a special needs trust for their benefit. It also depends on what you have already done to help them in their quest to get established in a home and career—considering the current status and potential of each one. I believe the decision is best when it is based on your sense of equity rather than on equality.

Some have set up plans to fund projects of ministry with one of their children participating in the direction for each of the projects—matching a project with the interests and talents of each respective child.

The Ultimate Considerations

By the end of life, many Christians are concerned about the following inheritance goals for their children when planning for an absence of parental influence, hoping and praying to be able to make the following transfers of *values, priorities, and assets* to them:

- Your love for eternity
- Your values of love to God and love for the lost of mankind

- Your value of love for Christ's body, the church
- Your values of initiative, integrity, and industry
- Enough of your money and possessions to send them a certain message of care yet not enough to neutralize the above values and priorities in them.
- Transfers to the Lord's work to honor the above values and magnify Him as the real owner of all we have—hastening the advent of eternity.

What is our duty to our Savior? Again, the great controversy is described:

Those who have property and *whose minds are darkened by the god of this world* seem to be controlled by Satan in the disposal of it. If they have true, believing children, and also children whose affections are wholly upon the things of the world, in making a transfer of their means to their children, they generally give a larger amount to those children who do not love God, and who are serving the enemy of all righteousness, than to those who are serving God. (White, *Testimonies for the Church*, p. 658, emphasis added)

> *It is common for many of the younger ones among God's people to accumulate great sums and declare they will not leave any of it to His work.*

It is common for many of the younger ones among God's people to accumulate great sums and declare they will not leave any of it to His work. I worked closely with a lawyer for a few years who spent her career assisting non-profit organizations with their fundraising programs involving estates and trusts. Occasionally, she had high-wealth people in her community come for her services. These were secular people who had heard of her extraordinary skills as a specialist with wills and trusts. As she interviewed them, she would tell them how much their children would receive from their estate when they die. In all cases, the clients' response would be, "That is too much. Our children could not handle that much in a responsible way."

Indeed, the great controversy is at play big time when it comes to God's people making plans for the distribution of their assets when they die. This God-inspired insight is worth our consideration:

They place in the hands of the unfaithful children the very things that will prove a snare to them and that will be obstacles in the way of their making a surrender to God. While they make large presents to the unbelieving children, they make very stinted gifts to those who are of the same faith with themselves. This very fact should startle the men of means who have pursued this course. They should see that the deceitfulness of riches has perverted their judgment. If they could see the influence operating upon their minds, they would understand that Satan had these matters very much according to his own purposes and plans. Instead of God's controlling the mind and sanctifying the judgment, it is controlled by exactly the opposite power. The ones who have been with them in the faith they sometimes even neglect, and are frequently very close and exacting in all their dealings with them; while they have an open hand to the unbelieving, world-loving children, who they know will not use the means they have placed in their hands, to advance the cause of God. (White, *Counsels on Stewardship*, p. 330)

The Lord requires that those to whom He has lent talents of means make a right use of them, having the advancement of His cause prominent. Every other consideration should be inferior to this. (White, *Testimonies for the Church*, vol. 2, pp. 658, 659)

It makes me sad to report I've noticed repeatedly that the **customs of the world** have come into the hearts of most—not all—of God's people as it relates to their accumulated assets—that, if put into words, would say, "All or most of what I have belongs to my family."

Unlike the faith question of the other group, normally, the two questions for this group is to ponder how to give as much as they can to family and wonder how much they are required to give to God's work in order to get the services of the church (referring to the church's services through a Planned Giving & Trust Services department).

What is the very best legacy parents can leave to their children? The pen of inspiration suggests it is "a knowledge of useful labor and the example of a life characterized by disinterested benevolence" (White, *Testimonies for the Church*, vol. 3, p. 399).

The only three valuable uses of money we should teach our children are that which is in harmony with the very best legacy we can leave to them. "By such a life they show the true value of money, that it is only to be appreciated for the good that it will accomplish in [1.] *relieving their own wants and the* [2.] *necessities of others, and in* [3.] *advancing the cause of God* (*Ibid.*, emphasis added).

Note: One modern definition of "disinte rested benevolence" is gifts that are made to God as an act of worship in the spirit of thanksgiving and loving trust in Him, with no strings attached.

What is our duty to our children? Well, when the counsel is taken all together, we find that our duty is overwhelmingly a spiritual one and upon us each day of our lives, with our estate planning being only the capstone of our lifelong spiritual efforts. What we also find is our duty to our Lord calls us to actions and commitments that are far, far away from the prevailing practice of designing a will that divides our assets among our closest relatives. In fact, doing so would, in some cases, be spiritually harmful to the recipient of the accumulated assets.

The bottom line is God calls us to be different from the rest of the world by honoring Him first and foremost and thereby be an example to our loved ones and to the world.

Jesus said, "He that loveth father or mother more than me is not worthy of me: and he that loveth son or daughter more than me is not worthy of me" (Matt. 10:37, KJV). "**This caution is not designed to lead us to disregard relatives or friends, yet the test comes to every soul, Will you receive Christ and acknowledge Him as your Redeemer**" (White, *The Gospel Herald*, December 1, 1901).

You may find more insight on the subject of family and what we owe our children in this context in chapter 6 of this book, where we discuss "Family Support and Inheritance Plans: Important Lessons for Today's Relationships with God and Family."

Estate Stewardship—How Does Estate Stewardship Affect My Will-Plan Design?

As we have established that all we have comes from God as gifts to us in trust, the following Bible verse is in play in this conversation: "It is required in stewards, that a man be found faithful" (1 Cor. 4:2). The word "steward" today would mean "a fiduciary trustee or manager"; and to be found faithful would mean proving oneself trustworthy, reliable, and knowledgeable. Those words seem to fit with this verse and work well for the topic we are considering in this brief discussion on estate stewardship.

The word "stewardship" means "the duties and obligations of a steward." It also means "conducting, supervising, or managing something; especially the careful and responsible management of something entrusted to one's care."

"The making of wills is a matter that we should consider carefully. We should not treat it as a delicate question that should not be introduced, fearing to create nervousness with feeble persons whose span of life is nearly run out" (Ibid.).

> *When people would see me at a church function like camp meeting or some other event, or perhaps at the Adventist Book Center, they would say something like, "Hi Bob, one of these days, I want to get on with the planning we started."*
>
> *I would respond with, "You are not accountable to me. That is the job of the Holy Spirit."*

The article quoted above also emphasizes our need to understand we are the Lord's responsible agents; all we have is loaned to us in trust. As we trade with it and acquire more, we then have more to invest for the Lord's cause. In the same article, Ellen G. White calls on us to set our houses in order. We should always live and plan as if time really is short, in recognition and acknowledgement that all we are and have belongs to God. Therefore, we need to be thinking of how we can liquidate and invest in a finished work rather than continuing to build up.

We are not responsible for our relatives because they all have a fair chance to live by their own industry. Our love for God will not diminish our love for parents or other relatives. "Do not spoil them by throwing responsibilities upon them, in the will that you make, that they know not how to manage" (Ibid.).

Mary Jo and I have been through such an exercise, in which we knelt down in front of our living room sofa with the Bible, a Bible commentary, and the "red books" spread out before us to study and pray over, looking up a number of pertinent passages of which we could think or that the Lord brought to mind. This exercise brought us more closely together as "one flesh" and gave us a greater level of mutual trust. Therefore, we do understand the difficulty of this journey, even more so as a widow.

The love of Christ leads His disciples to carry out His will and ways, expressed in the wills of His servants who are dead, waiting for the morning of the resurrection. **Our capital, entrusted of God,** is not to be recklessly signed away to men and women who would serve themselves and not Him. Giving to God's cause in our will-plan is *not* a business transaction with the church; rather, it is a spiritual transaction with heaven. In other words, we cannot purchase heaven (see *Ibid.*).

We are told that we parents have a responsibility to exercise the right God has given us when He entrusted to us the assets He expects us to use for His glory. That means the children are not to become responsible for the talents (assets) of the parents. Our parental role requires us to care for the disposition of our property while we have a sound mind and good judgment, with the Lord's guidance via surrendered prayer and the assistance of proper counselors who have experience in the truth and a knowledge of the divine will.

> If they have children who are afflicted or are struggling in poverty, and who will make a judicious use of the means, they should be considered. But if they have unbelieving children who have abundance of this world, and who are serving the world, they commit a sin against the Master, who has made them His stewards, by placing means [assets and money] in their hands merely because they are their children. God's claims are not to be lightly regarded. (White, *Testimonies for the Church*, vol. 3, p. 121)

We are further advised:

> Parents should have great fear in entrusting children with the talents of means that God has placed in their hands, unless they have the surest evidence that their children have greater interest in, love for, and devotion to, the cause of God than they themselves possess, and that these children will be more earnest and zealous in forwarding the work of God, and more benevolent in carrying forward the various enterprises connected with it which call for means. (White, *Testimonies for the Church*, vol. 3, p. 118)

> I was shown that the property left by the father had indeed been a root of bitterness to his children. Their peace and happiness, and their confidence in one another, had been greatly disturbed by it. Brother A Y did not need his father's property. He had enough talents to handle that God had entrusted to his management. If he made a right disposition of that which he had, he would at least be among that number who were faithful in that which is least. The addition of the stewardship of his father's property, which he had

covetously desired, was a heavier responsibility than he could well manage. (White, *Testimonies for the Church*, vol. 3, p. 127).

Unauthorized Transfer of Responsibility to Children

> I was shown that Brother X's course in dividing his property among his children was shifting the responsibility upon them which he should not have laid off. He now sees that the result of this course has brought to him no increase of affection from his children. They have not felt under obligation to their parents for what they have done for them. These children were young and inexperienced. They were not qualified to bear the responsibility laid upon them. Their hearts were unconsecrated, and true friends were looked upon by them as designing enemies, while those who would separate very friends were accepted. These agents of Satan were continually suggesting false ideas to the minds of these young men, and the hearts of brothers and sisters, father and mother, were at variance. (White, *Testimonies for the Church*, vol. 3, p. 129)

Hopefully, dear reader, you can see why I'm convicted that the process for each of us in coming up with our own will-plan **design** is indeed a spiritual journey and not to be taken lightly. I really hope and pray you will be challenged to take on this journey with Jesus as your Lord of all and, as you move forward, you will saturate the process in surrendered prayer that includes an authentic spirit of "Thy will be done."

Personal Application— How Do I Apply Design Principles to My Plan?

Planning is daunting for many of us because we are so task-oriented and often have other pressing tasks that take priority over looking ahead. Most of us are much more interested in our doings than in planning what we will do. The responsibility to design and execute my estate inheritance plan rests with me. And that is true for every child and disciple of God. The reality of doing the planning often requires an enormous effort to overcome inertia (the impact of some external force). I've assisted many church members begin the planning process, but so often, they take a long pause because they were not ready to answer the questions.

When people would see me at a church function like camp meeting or some other event, or perhaps at the Adventist Book Center, they would say something like, "Hi Bob, one of these days, I want to get on with the planning we started."

I would respond with, "You are not accountable to me. That is the job of the Holy Spirit." They needed to keep on praying. Most of them never got back to it—a disappointment to me over which I prayed.

When we consider that the vast majority of people in the world die without a legally valid will-plan—and it is very similar in the church—it is easy to understand the need of some help to overcome the inertia in order to get it done. One of the more common, powerful inhibitors to getting a will done may be overcome if you and I believe "death will not come one day sooner, brethren, because you have made your Will" (White, *Testimonies for the Church*, vol. 4, p. 482).

Inspired assistance is precious to me on the matter of planning. Let your prayer be, "Take me, O Lord, as wholly Thine. I lay all my plans at Thy feet. Use me today in Thy service. Abide with me, and let all my work be wrought in Thee ... Surrender all your plans to Him" (White, *Steps to Christ*, p. 70).

In order to design a will-plan that will gain the approval of heaven, we may study the divine principles and pray about it until we know how to apply those principles personally. "Many are not exercised upon the subject of making their wills while they are in apparent health. But this precaution should be taken by our brethren ... They should arrange their property in such a manner that they may leave it at any time" (White, *Testimonies for the Church*, vol. 4, p. 482).

Legal Issues in the Will-Plan Design

We have received great practical advice in the following two statements:

> Wills should be made in a manner to stand the test of law. (White, *Testimonies for the Church*, vol. 4, p. 482)

> Those who make their wills should not spare pains or expense to obtain legal advice and to have them drawn up in a manner to stand the test. (White, *Testimonies for the Church*, vol. 3, p. 117)

The phrase "stand the test of law" simply means you need to have your will-plan documents done in a way that will assure their legal security in case someone chooses to challenge it by bringing legal action against your plan in court; it happens all too often in today's litigious society. I've witnessed the eruption of greed glands in one member of a family to the surprise of the other family members.

As we noted earlier in Chapter 10, we included the subject of legal security for your plan design and documents. We continue to talk about designing your inheritance plan in this chapter.

Give-it-twice plans are available in a variety of forms. Would you have ever thought it? You might be interested in the following special insights after your prayer of faith about it. Ellen G. White gave the following counsel, which we may apply to **life-income plans** such as a charitable gift annuity plan and a charitable remainder trust plan (not revocable). Revocable living trust plans may also be written with a give-it-twice orientation.

> There are *those among us who have a surplus of means*, but they think they need it to sustain themselves. *Let matters be arranged that these persons shall have interest on their money as long as they shall live, and let them donate the principal to the cause and work of God.* Thus, they will return to the Lord that which is His own. Carefulness should be manifested in this respect. *Christians should not be negligent to place in the Lord's treasury the means which should carry forward His work while time shall last.* His entrusted goods should reach the highest accumulation, for the kingdom of God is to be extended, and the interests of His kingdom increased by a wise disposition of His means to make known the unsearchable riches of Christ. (White, *Australian Union Conference Record*, December 1, 1900, emphasis added)

> We wish that all who are becoming old and feeble would *make a wise disposition of their means*, giving freely back to God that which is His own. *Some need the interest on their money to support them while they live. These can lend their money at reasonable interest to our publishing or medical institutions, and make arrangements that it shall be used in missionary work after their death.* Wise and faithful men should be chosen as their stewards, and clear and thorough work done to *ensure the use of their means in the very way that they wish*. Then they will know that their treasure is to be used to warn the world of its coming doom. *We have no time to delay* (White, *The Gospel Herald*, December 1, 1901, emphasis added)

The process of creating an estate plan design can be time-consuming for various reasons:

1. Your plan design is best decided by your exercise of organizing the pertinent data of your fact-case (personal, family, and financial information), including monetary values of assets, how titles

are held, and any beneficiary designations, like in a life insurance policy, annuity investments, and IRA accounts, as well as the completion of your Confidential Estate Data Form (EDF). This process is designed to serve the purpose of your personal/family will-plan. Normally, this is appreciated by and enlightening for those I've served in this process.

2. You may explore issues and options such as business decisions to be made and technical methods that are available for your plan, which are different for everyone.

3. Your prayer-saturated study of pertinent spiritual principles while seeking divine illumination with clarity of thought in your mind about the pertinent issues.

4. Praying for divine guidance with a teachable spirit—asking the Lord how you are to apply all you have learned to the design of your plan so it is approved when evaluated through the eyes of heaven.

With that said, what do we do to prepare for crafting a will-plan?

1. **Ownership and Faith-Stewardship**—Acknowledge God's ownership of all you are and have. The Bible and Spirit of Prophecy will tell you the truth about that. **When you and I design our will-plans to honor our covenants with God,** we acknowledge all we are and have belongs to the One who placed it in our hands in a trust relationship.

2. Study God's design principles for your last will and testament plan.

3. Pray for God's personal instructions to you individually on how to apply His design principles in your case—considering what He has entrusted to you, your family's needs, and your interests in His work. Claim God's promise to teach and guide you with individual instruction. The promise I love to claim is Psalm 32:8–9.

4. Make a will-plan accordingly with the services of a qualified lawyer.

Planning issues and options vary from one person to another and may include any or all the items listed below, as they pertain to your individual fact-case based on your questions and what you already know—always based on your agenda for your process of planning today to take care of tomorrow:

- Technical issues and methods of planning
- Legal and business issues
- Business ownership structure of your life work, if applicable
- Family issues—their spiritual and financial situations and any special needs of a family member for whom you are responsible
- Relational issues—family, work, community, church, and God
- Emotional-spiritual issues
- Your values, priorities, and goals in life, both now and after you die
- Your core mission in life
- What assets you own
- How you hold title to your accumulated assets
- How you acquired your accumulated assets
- What you want to do with what you have while living and after death
- Whom you want to benefit from what you have during your life and after death
- Whom you trust to carry out your plans if you become disabled or die.

For the overwhelming majority of people who die in the United States of America, they die without a legally valid will; this is true in the church and around the world. For the Christian, this is a sacred responsibility before the Lord, even as sacred as the practice of returning tithe to Him. Those who fail in either area are labeled in the books of heaven as thieves robbing God. To die without having made a covenant with Him—placing all we have and are on His altar, followed by making a last will and testament to honor that covenant—is, in fact, robbing God.

What is robbery? A Christian brother recently shared the following thought: "A thief is one who takes something of value from another under the cover of darkness, when and where the thief is not observed. A robber is one who gets right in front of the victim and takes it by force." In that case, the one who is not faithful to God by returning a faithful tithe is a robber, as declared in Malachi 3:8-9. The same is said to be true of making a will that does not honor Him. However, all gifts to God must be voluntary acts of worship in the spirit of thankfulness and loving trust in Him along with grateful loyalty to His cause, so that the gifts and giver are accepted by the Lord. Jesus died to preserve our religious freedom in all matters of life and death.

I recommend you make a covenant of sacrifice with God in which you lay all on His altar and plan to listen for instruction. This is the very first thing for you to do in this sacred journey of designing and making a will-plan that can be approved by heaven. And yet, there is one more thing that should be first before you do that.

As God's children, we are to *first* give ourselves to Him and then give our tithes, offerings, and major gifts as an act of worship in a spirit of thanksgiving and praise, as the Macedonia people did (see 2 Cor. 8:1–5).

In our personal and family lives, my wife and I learned to listen to God in a spirit of loving trust and recognize His voice, receiving personal and individual instructions, as mentioned before.

We often claim the following promise of God. When on my face, prostrate before Him, He always answers immediately. "I will instruct you and teach you in the way you should go; I will guide you with My eye. Do not be like the horse or like the mule" (Ps. 32:8, 9).

Given the information in this book, where should you begin the process of getting from here to there? Here are some ideas that may serve as a brief overview summary of the process from start to finish—steps in the process of Christ-centered, values-based plans to take care of tomorrow today:

1. I suggest your first step in this journey is to refresh the gift of yourself to God in full surrender of your mind (thoughts and feelings), heart (affections, values, and passions), will (choices, priorities, and actions), faith (in loving trust in God and loyal support of Christ's precious bride, the church), and spirit (attitudes toward all people and institutions). Study 2 Corinthians 8–9.

2. If you have not already done this, make a covenant of sacrifice with God in which you place all you have on His altar and then listen for His still, small voice of individual instruction in how to use what you have now and plan for its transfer—now and/or at death, whether you are in plenty or poverty—pursuant to the instructions given to Ellen White for us in *Counsels on Stewardship*, pages 59–60 (quoted above).

3. Study the principles of the divine will for your will.

4. Pray to God—asking how to apply the principles to your planning for life and death—pleading for the Lord's mercy and light, bathing all your concerns and questions in prayer, seeking the pure wisdom from God's mind until you know His best plan to apply the principles to your personal and family case.

5. To the extent of your interest in values-based planning, answer the values questionnaire of your choice to assist you to surface your core values regarding your family members and your relationship to your accumulated assets and liabilities. A variety of such questionnaires are available for values-based planning to care for tomorrow today.

6. Your family mission statement may be created to assist in the design of your plan.

7. Complete the Estate Data Form (EDF). Normally, as I've gone through the form from section to section, assisting donors complete it, we discuss pertinent issues and options for planning that seem to be applicable to their cases. This assistance is designed to prepare them to communicate effectively with their attorney.

8. The donors' income planner is developed as an impact study to discover your income needs, the possible impact a life-income gift plan option might have on your life, and the cost of taxes to achieve your goals of financial security and spiritual fulfillment.

9. When the EDF and financial impact study are completed, then the consultant will have a basis on which to assist you in your creation of an overall estate design proposal. Hopefully, the proposal will perfectly reflect your values and priorities. After a full discussion of the plan design proposal with you, your consultant will prepare an adjusted proposal for you based on your review and discussions.

10. You should then select a lawyer to work with if you have not already done so.

11. You would then visit and share your EDF and tentative plan design with the lawyer you choose to represent you. Your attorney would read it. Then you would want to discuss your list of issues and options.

12. Your attorney will then draft legal documents as a "draft for discussion purposes" for your review and feedback.

13. Review the documents as a draft; ask questions to be sure you have a good understanding.

14. Give your feedback to your attorney so the final draft will be exactly what you want—a genuine reflection of your will. He or she then makes final changes to your plan documents and prepares them for your signatures.

15. Sign your new plan documents under the supervision of your attorney, either at the attorney's office or your place.

16. Decide where to store your signed originals of the new documents and who should have a copy of them. Remember, only an original will is of any value to the court, so safety is an essential consideration.

17. Consider your options for ongoing trust and estate management competencies with an organization of the church or other institution where a sizable team of specialists is available to care for the fiduciary functions of investing, accounting, tax returns, and other related trust management functions.

18. Continue to live your plan as a purpose-driven Christian—a living, walking, talking, breathing disciple of Jesus—bringing the light of hope, courage, joy, and selfless love to those with whom you have contact.

I've often referred the friends I'm serving in the process to a list of choices in local legal counsel (lawyers who are candidates to represent them in the process—lawyers who are truly independent specialists, according to the needs and location). The advantage of this approach is that those of us who serve as planned giving consultants for the church are not functioning as an extension of the denominational organization's corporate legal counsel in the role of a "paralegal," in which we would not be allowed to suggest a gift to God's work because that would be a serious conflict of interest on our part. Therefore, we are *free* to function in the role of planned giving minister rather than as an extension of a lawyer's practice.

The sense of freedom is most exhilarating. We are free to present comprehensive estate design proposals to you as a prospective donor that may include gift plan models to benefit the Lord's work as an option for your prayerful consideration.

There is freedom to being a spiritual minister. We are free to share with you the spiritual estate stewardship principles of Adventist legacy planning as part of our consulting process, without being guilty of a conflict of interest or undue influence, as long as we do it with *no* manipulative tone or manner.

You may freely establish a plan that truly represents your will because our proposal is evaluated for you by a truly independent lawyer, without the unsaid psychological pressure on the lawyer or you to be obligated to establish a gift plan to benefit the denominational organization that is represented by your planned giving consultant.

You have the advantage of greater assurance of the legal security of your will-plan documents with this process. Additionally, you will find the greatest amount of satisfaction with our valuable service of educating you on the pertinent issues and options—spiritual issues, business issues, technical legal issues, asset issues, relational issues—and assisting you to organize your estate design materials with your personal, family, and financial data and goals for the plan—all in one place for future reference.

If you are like everyone else I've served since 2000, you will become enthusiastic about our services, not because you paid nothing for an estate plan (you will pay), but because of the truly objective nature of the process and the resulting high-quality plan that should "stand the test of law."

Your sense of urgency for this project should be to study and pray for the Lord to assist you in making the indicated decisions and get it done in a timely manner, yet at your pace—when you are ready to move from one step to the next—with a focus on your agenda and the Lord's leading and timing.

> *We know Christ's second coming is both certain and imminent, yet we don't have a clue which of us will be laid to rest beforehand and who will survive the great time of trouble. Therefore, perhaps we could say time is of the essence for such planning in just about everyone's case.*

We know Christ's second coming is both *certain and imminent*, yet we don't have a clue which of us will be laid to rest beforehand and who will survive the great time of trouble. Therefore, perhaps we could say time is of the essence for such planning in just about everyone's case. You can rest assured that when you go through the process and have it all done, you will rejoice with a great sense of relief and jubilation. God inhabits praise.

The only sense of urgency from the denominational consultant is to assist you to carry out whatever plan you and the Lord decide to design and get it done in a timely manner. The timing and pace are dependent on your readiness to make the required decisions.

We also know it is the Lord's plan to prosper His people: "The desire to accumulate wealth is an original affection of our nature, implanted there by our heavenly Father *for noble ends*" (White, *Counsels on Stewardship*,

p. 149). Stewardship is a responsibility and privilege of faith. "It is required of stewards that one be found faithful" (1 Cor. 4:2, NASB).

It has been my most happy privilege to work with God's people who are like that—those who:

- Make transformational gifts, not simply transactional gifts.
- Make *honest* gifts—not as a fee for service, but with a genuine interest in helping fund a finished work.
- Make gifts to God as an act of worship with a willing mind in the spirit of love, loyalty, and thanksgiving to Him—in loving trust that He will *provide* all their personal and family needs and *protect* them now, later and forever.
- Make gifts that are acceptable to God (unlike the gifts that were given by Cain or Ananias and Sapphira) because "Whatever you do that is not of faith is sin" (Rom. 14:23) and "The offering from the heart that loves, God delights to honor, giving it highest efficiency in service for Him" (White, *The Desire of Ages*, p. 65).
- Make gifts that are affordable—that will not disgrace the church by leaving the donors destitute at some time in the future—that take into account Medicaid planning and other practical considerations.
- Make gifts that are legally secure, with minimum potential of legal liability to the church, and maximum potential to "stand the test of law" in court, thus maintaining the integrity of the donor's plan in the end.
- Make gifts to support the mission of Christ to seek and save the lost.

   "If we live, we live to the Lord, and if we die, we die to the Lord; so then, whether we live or whether we die, we are the Lord's. For to this end Christ died and lived again, that he might be Lord both of the dead and of the living." (Rom. 14:8, 9 RSV). "Don't waste what is holy on people who are unholy" (Matt. 7:6, NLT).

We are also advised about our standing before God in this regard with our relationship to others who are also in the faith:

   Many manifest [reveal] a needless delicacy on this point. They feel that they are stepping upon forbidden ground when they introduce the subject of property to the aged or to invalids in order to learn what disposition they design to make of it. But this duty is just as sacred as the duty to preach the word to save souls. Here is a man with God's money or property in his hands. He is about to change his stewardship. Will he place the means which God has lent him to be used in His cause, in the hands of wicked men, just because they are his relatives? Should not Christian men feel interested and anxious for that man's future good as well as for the interest of God's cause, that he shall make a right disposition of his Lord's money, the talents lent him for wise improvement? Will his brethren stand by and see him losing his hold on this life and at the same time robbing the treasury of God? This would be a fearful loss to himself and to the cause; for, by placing his talent of means in the hands of those who have no regard for the truth of God, he would, to all intents and purposes, be wrapping it in a napkin and hiding it in the earth. (White, *Testimonies for the Church*, vol. 4, p. 479)

Final thought: As you study and ponder how to design a plan of distributing your assets after your death, I plead with you to immerse every thought and feeling in prayer to the Lord—along with the needs of His work and your family—seeking to know His will for your plan. This is a most sacred journey that will bring order to your life and great peace to your spirit like nothing else can.

See Appendix 1 online at mystewardship.estate, where you will find the *Missouri Supreme Court Decision on Unauthorized Practice of Law*. It is vitally important to this discussion, in my opinion, which is based on my years of experience.

It is rather common for church members to ask us for a legal document for themselves, such as a will, power of attorney, healthcare proxy, etc. Please understand that is a no-no. When you do that sort of thing, you place the denominational organization in potential legal jeopardy if it complies with your request.

The practice of law includes "the preparation of legal instruments and contracts by which legal rights are secured"; thus, the denominational organization should not draft documents for donors that secure legal rights. When the donor signs a document drafted by a denominational organization or lawyer that secures legal rights without preparation or review of the document by the donor's own truly independent legal counsel, the denominational organization runs a risk of potential legal damages.

For clarification, when a denominational organization offers sample forms or documents as a courtesy to a donor in care of his or her independent legal counsel for use in transferring a gift, the organization is not preparing *executable* documents for the donor that secure legal rights. The denominational organization will make it clear in communications with the donor and/or his or her legal counsel that sample documents are provided as a courtesy and may or may not suit the needs and specific situations of the donor. The denominational organization may not render advice as to its suitability.

The donor and his or her advisor must determine which document(s) and provisions are suitable for the donor. At the specific request and direction of the donor's legal counsel, the denominational organization may prepare a document, which counsel may then use to execute a gift transaction. Such a document should be accompanied by a cover letter indicating that the attorney requested the preparation of the document for his or her use. It is best to send such a document to the donor's attorney electronically so the donor's legal counsel may edit it in any way.

If sample forms or documents are provided for charitable remainder trusts, the denominational organization should distribute the most up-to-date forms available. It should also disclose all known options to the donor and his or her advisor upon request, including the right to amend the remaindermen and the right to remove the trustee.

Dear reader, here you have my completed presentation on the spiritual and legal frameworks, which offer you my definitions of key principles to consider and pray about when you decide to create your own design of a will-plan set of documents.

Section IV

Designing an Estate Plan Apart from Denominational Assistance—Concepts and Vocabulary

Chapter 15

What Is a Will?

Now we will turn to a description and vocabulary of wills and trusts and how they work in general terms. You will read about a variety of issues in drafting a will document in this chapter, and in the next chapter, we explore trusts and annuities regarding the basic use of those concepts. A document that is universally known as a last will and testament is the most basic, common method for an orderly transfer of accumulated assets to your designated beneficiaries after death, according to your wishes. And yet, way more than half of deaths occur without a legally valid last will in place. That is true in the Christian church as well as in the world. It is even true of lawyers as a group.

A will is a snapshot in time; as time continues to flow forward, you experience changes in your family, assets, and values, priorities, and goals. Therefore, it is normal to review it and possibly update it from time to time, especially when there is a death or birth or if you move from one state to another. A will is state-specific because estate and trust laws vary from state to state. The importance of doing it well and storing the documents safely cannot be overstated because recent statistics have revealed that most wills are not ever processed after the death of the testator(s).

> *Way more than half of deaths occur without a legally valid last will in place. That is true in the Christian church as well as in the world. It is even true of lawyers as a group.*

A will is a legal document that is properly signed and witnessed and includes the following information:

- Who I am? (my identity)
- What do I have? (in general terms, a list of your accounts and properties are not listed in a will)
- What would I want to do with what I have if I don't wake up tomorrow?

Intestate: a word that is used to describe the legal status of you and your affairs if you die without a legally valid will. Transfers of property and your other assets may be done at a much greater cost and probably not according to your wishes.

Disadvantages of Dying Intestate

You forfeit all control, benefits, and privileges given below. When there is no will, the state where you are living when you die has a law that describes how your assets are distributed.

The State Writes Your Will

Every state has a law of intestacy that determines how your assets are to be distributed if you have no legally valid will when you die; in many states, it goes to your spouse, then children, then parents, then brothers and sisters. Therefore, when you relocate to a different legal jurisdiction (state), you need to have your plan documents reviewed by a qualified lawyer to see if it would be effective in your new state.

> Should you die without a will, the state's laws of intestacy and descent and distribution come into play. Your possessions will pass on to your relatives:
>
> ➤ whether or not you want them to receive it
>
> ➤ whether or not they need it
>
> ➤ whether or not they would make good use of the money.
> (G. Edward Reid, *It's Your Money! Isn't It?*, p. 107)

Are you okay with being considered an atheist in the eyes of heaven? "If you die without a will, the state assumes that you are an atheist, because in no case will it give any of your estate back to God through a church or other charitable avenue" (*Ibid.*).

Other disadvantages of no legally valid will-plan:

- May be much more costly to settle your estate

- State law specifies the distribution of what you have
- Probate court selects a guardian for your minor children
- Probate court selects an administrator (executor) who is paid handsomely from your assets
- Probate court determines any special needs of family
- No provision is made for God's work to fulfill your covenant with Him

The great controversy is in play big time. Satan's game plan is to prevent God's people from making a Christ-centered will-plan. The devil's success in this means a setback in the fulfillment of God's mission to win us for His eternal kingdom. The following testimony of God's Spirit reveals the reality and consequence of our unfaithfulness in this matter:

> I was shown the awful fact that Satan and his angels have had more to do with the management of the property of God's professed people than the Lord has. Stewards of the last days are unwise. They suffer [allow] Satan to control their business matters, and get into his ranks what belongs to, and should be in, the cause of God. God takes notice of you, unfaithful stewards; He will call you to account. (White, *Testimonies for the Church*, vol. 1, p. 199)
>
> *The cause of Christ is robbed*, not by a mere passing thought, not by an unpremeditated act. No. By your own deliberate act you made your will, placing your property at the disposal of unbelievers. After having robbed God during your lifetime, you continue to rob Him after your death, and you do this with the full consent of all your powers of mind, in a document called your will. What do you think will be your Master's will toward you for thus appropriating His goods? What will you say when an account is demanded of your stewardship? (White, *Testimonies for the Church*, vol. 5, p. 155, emphasis added)

Probate: a word that is used for the process by which assets are gathered, used to pay debts, taxes, and expenses to settle your estate, and distributed to the designated beneficiaries. Again, if you have a legally valid will at the time of your death, the beneficiaries you included will receive the benefits of your intentions; if not, then the beneficiaries are those listed by position in a state's common will.

Testate: an old-fashioned word that still has legal significance. It is used to describe the legal status of your affairs when you die *with* a legally valid will in place.

Advantages of testate—benefits and privileges of a legally valid will:

- You specify the distribution—what goes to who
- You nominate a guardian of your minor-age children, if any
- You nominate an executor ("personal representative" in some states)
- You can create trusts
- You can give to the Lord's work
- You control the transfers of your stuff

You may notice the word "nominate" in two items of the above list. That means you are making your preferences known. The judge makes the final decision and appoints the individuals who will serve in those roles. The judge will give careful consideration to your nominations, but other interested parties may present a challenge about any nomination. If minor-age children are fourteen or older, their choice of guardian will exercise a strong influence on the judge in some states. Such minors have the legal power to decide for themselves in some states.

Executor (male); Executrix (female); Personal Representative (gender-neutral):

These titles are used in the courts to designate the one who is *nominated* by a testator or testatrix (you) to carry out the terms of your will after your death when there is a legally valid will to be processed through the local probate court. When there is no will, the judge appoints an administrator or administratrix to do the same: distribute everything according to your state's will design.

Who should be the executor of your last will? You might want to notice the following testimony of God's Spirit:

> **God has made us all His stewards, and in no case has He authorized us to neglect our duty or leave it for others to do** ... If we leave others to accomplish that which God has left for us to do, we wrong ourselves and Him who gave us all we have. How can others do *our* work of benevolence any better than we can do it ourselves? **So far as practicable, God would have every man an executor of his own will in this matter, during his lifetime.**
> (White, *The Retirement Years*, pp. 94, 95, bold emphasis added)

> *Dying charity is a poor substitute for living benevolence.* Many will to their friends and relatives all except a very small pittance of their property. This they leave for their supreme Friend, who became poor for their sakes, who suffered insult, mockery, and death, that they might become sons and daughters of God. And yet they expect when the righteous dead shall come forth to immortal life that this Friend will take them into His everlasting habitations. (White, *Testimonies for the Church*, vol. 5, p. 155, emphasis added)

Why is a will so important? Are your affairs in order? "Thus says the Lord, Set your house in order, for you shall die and not live" (Isa. 38:1; 2 Kings 20:1).

Significance of Order in Our Lives

When the Lord's Word tells us to put our affairs in order, I take that seriously. When the medical doctor tells a patient to go home and put his or her affairs in order, we know what that means, right? Order, even in the smallest details of life and work, brings with it a sense of peace that we would never have when we are surrounded by a mess. When we are in the presence of confusion and chaos, it creates great tension within our beings of which we may not be aware.

"For God did not give us a spirit of timidity (of cowardice, of craven and cringing and fawning fear), but [He has given us a spirit] of power and of love and of calm *and* well-balanced [well-ordered*] mind *and* discipline *and* self-control" (2 Tim. 1:7, AMPC, * phrase supplied).

When Jesus was resurrected on that fateful Sunday morning, He rose up in His tomb and folded His linen cloth (see John 20:5–7). Could His sense of order be an example for us? The following commentary nails it for me:

> [Peter and John] saw *the shroud and the napkin*, but they did not find their Lord … *The graveclothes were not thrown heedlessly aside, but carefully folded, each in a place by itself* …
>
> *It was Christ Himself who had placed those graveclothes with such care.* When the mighty angel came down to the tomb, he was joined by another, who with his company had been keeping guard over the Lord's body. As the angel from heaven rolled away the stone, the other entered the tomb, and unbound the wrappings from the body of Jesus. But *it was the Saviour's hand that folded each, and laid it in its place. In His sight who guides alike the star and the atom,*

> *there is nothing unimportant. Order and perfection are seen in all His work.* (White, *The Desire of Ages*, p. 789, emphasis added)

> There is order in heaven. There are rules and regulations which govern the whole heavenly host. All move in order …

> God loves purity, cleanliness, order, and holiness. *God requires all His people who lack these qualifications to seek them and never rest until they obtain them. They must commence the work of reform and elevate their lives, so that in conversation and deportment their acts, their lives, will be a continual recommendation of their faith and will have such a winning, compelling power upon unbelievers that they will be compelled to acknowledge that they are the children of God.* (White, *Our High Calling*, p. 230, emphasis added)

What is the purpose of a last will and testament?

- To go forward (indicates futurity)
- To determine by choice
- To give or dispose of property by will

However, to answer a common question, the provisions of your will-plan of distribution cannot be exercised by anyone other than you as long as you are breathing. It even says that in the Bible, albeit with respect to spiritual life and the death of self: "For where a testament is, there must also of necessity be the death of the testator. For a testament is of force after men are dead: otherwise it is of no strength at all while the testator lives" (Heb. 9:16–17, AKJV).

The original will is required (a copy is not acceptable) to be registered with the probate court. Normally, the state required a will to be registered with the local probate court within a set number of days after the death of the testator (the one who made the will). It should be kept in a safe, secure place of storage until the death of the testator. The rules of care are specific and very important.

Contents of a Will

In the first part of a will, the drafting lawyer will normally include the following features:

- Declaration that you are of a sound mind.
- Revoking of all previous wills you may have signed.

What Is a Will? ◆ 243

- Declaration that your executor shall not be required to post a bond.
- Name(s) of your spouse and children, if any.

Your will describes your intention for the distribution of your *Tangible Personal Property*—your household contents, automobiles, and recreation vehicles—*not* including cash, financial accounts, or real estate property. The "rest, residue, and remainder" of your assets, including real estate property if any, are then distributed *without* a listing of those assets in the will.

If your will is a companion to a revocable living family trust, this provision in the will simply declares the trust's existence and says something like, "I give all the rest, residue, and remainder … to the then Trustees of The [your family name] Revocable Family Trust." Your will shall then add the name(s) of people you trust to carry out your wishes when you are not alive for them to consult. Such people are referred to as "serving in their individual capacity as a fiduciary" (a position of trust).

Requirements of a legally valid will-plan:

- Legal age.
- Your status of citizenship is important to the legalities of a plan.
- You must have legal mental capacity to make a will-plan—at least a lucid interval when signing the document.
- You must know what you have, who your heirs at law are, and what you want to do with what you have got, all at the same moment.
- You must have an intention to transfer property and your other assets.
- You must plan with freedom from fraud, undue influence, duress, and coercion.
- The will must be properly executed (signed), with your signature as the testator added among witnesses. In many states, if your witnesses' signatures are notarized, it becomes a self-proving will, which means when you die, the court does not require an affidavit to be signed by your witnesses.

Advantages of a Legally Valid Will-Plan

- You specify the distribution.
- You nominate the guardian of your minor children, if any.
- You nominate the executor of your will.

- You may create trusts and name the trustee.
- You may give to God's work via your plan so your gifts continue to support your interests thereof.
- You may still keep your assets on the altar of God for further instructions from Him after you make a will.
- You may have a sense of spiritual fulfillment and financial security that gives you unparalleled peace.

An executor (many states now use the gender-neutral term "personal representative" in place of "executor or "executrix") is nominated in your will to carry out its terms. The judge makes the election after you die and your original will document has been admitted to (filed with) the local probate court.

There is inspired counsel for those wondering, *Should I be my own executor?* "By becoming their own executors, they could meet the claims of God themselves, instead of shifting the responsibility upon others" (White, *Testimonies for the Church*, vol. 4, page 480).

Regarding Christian plans, "That which many propose to defer until they are about to die, if they were Christians indeed they would do while they have their strong hold on life. They would devote themselves and their property to God, and, while acting as His stewards, they would have the satisfaction of doing their duty" (*Ibid.*).

It is essential to engage a qualified team of advisors to assist you in your process of creating your will-plan and related documents. Central to the team is someone to walk through the confidential data form to organize your information; next is your choice of an attorney who specializes in estates and trusts in your area.

Possible team members of your will-plan advisors when you organize your information for the drafting lawyer might include:

- Lawyer who is a personal friend or another selection.
- Certified public accountant with estate planning expertise
- Certified financial planner
- Trust officer of a bank
- Planned giving consultant or trust officer of a denominational organization
- Trusted friend with estate planning expertise

Chief Justice Warren Burger was a trained lawyer who served as the Chief Justice of the United States Supreme Court from 1969 to 1986. He wrote his own will—never a good idea for anyone. It was a one-page document—the ultimate in simplicity. Never good!

Judge Burger typed it himself at age eighty-six. He died on June 25, 1995, at age eighty-seven. He provided that his estate be distributed as follows: one-third to his daughter and two-thirds to his son. While his will was not fatally flawed, Judge Burger's will left out important ingredients that would have made it hassle-free and much less expensive to settle:

- No power to sell real estate.
- No waiver of bond for the executor.
- The costs and fees of the estate settlement were significantly higher because of going through probate to sell real estate and posting a bond for the executor—and *no* living trust to avoid probate.
- The "hassles" of probate were no doubt made worse because the will was not "self-proving." This means the witnesses' signatures were not notarized.
- No tax planning, which resulted in $450,000 of taxes—a lot more money at the time than it would be today.

Chief Justice Warren Burger was a trained lawyer who served as the Chief Justice of the United States Supreme Court from 1969 to 1986. He wrote his own will— never a good idea for anyone. It was a one-page document— the ultimate in simplicity. Never good!

Bequest—a court term that refers to a gift left to a person or organization at death. It may be specified in your will as a:

➤ Fixed amount of money

➤ Specific property

➤ Percentage of the residuary

▶ Contingent gift to be made if a specified event occurs. For example, you might name your child to receive a bequest if the child is living. Then you might add that if the child has died before you do, that bequest gift would go to a contingent beneficiary.

Two sample wording options are given below to illustrate how the bequest language might be written:

1. Fixed Amount of Money (sample wording of a bequest): "I give THE SUM OF _____dollars ($_____) as a charitable gift to _____, a non-profit religious corporation, with its principal office located at _____ to be used to establish or be added to the _____Family Memorial Endowed Scholarship Fund to train young warriors (ministerial students) for the mission of Christ to seek and save the lost" (The wording may work similarly in a last will and testament or a living revocable trust).

   Percentage of the Residuary (sample wording of a bequest): "I give _____percent (_____%) of the Rest, Residue and Remainder of my estate to the _____, a nonprofit religious corporation, with its principal office located at _____, to be used to fund evangelistic outreach meetings as determined by its governing board or committee" (Again, the wording may work similarly in a will or trust).

Methods of transferring property after death—not by will:

- Transfers of property are made by operation of the law, depending on how the title is held (e.g., tenancy in common or joint tenants with right of survivorship)—without regard to any provision of your will.

- Totten trust, POD (payable on death), or TOD (transfer on death)—the asset on deposit in a bank, credit union, or brokerage company is transferred after death to your named beneficiaries on the signature card of a bank or other documentation. **Your will has no jurisdiction over such accounts.**

- Trusts—transfers are made to a living trust during your lifetime, and the trustee transfers the assets of the trust to your beneficiaries after your death, hopefully according to the instructions you have included in your trust. **Your will and the probate judge has no jurisdictional legal standing over these assets.**

- Life insurance and annuity contracts—transfers are made after your death according to your beneficiary designations. If you are advised to include these assets in your probate, you may designate your estate as the beneficiary. Otherwise, your will has no jurisdiction over these assets.
- Pension plan death benefits—including IRA, 401k, 403b, and other similar tax-deferred accounts. These assets are transferred after your death according to your beneficiary designations—the same as described in the above paragraph on life insurance. **Again, your will has no jurisdiction over such assets.**
- Business agreements by contract—may include provisions for the transfer of assets outside your will, such as your interest in a business or other enterprise. Many such cases are served well with a buy-sell agreement.

Real Estate Properties Transfer at Death by Operation of Local State Laws; How Does It Work?

The following explanations may or may not be accurate in your state. It is necessary to check it out with your own local lawyer:

1. *Tenancy in Common*

    May be any number of individual owners.

    Undivided interest—property is not divided.

    Interest of a deceased owner passes according to either that owner's will or the owner's beneficiaries.

2. *Joint Tenants with Rights of Survivorship*

    May be any number of individual owners.

    Undivided interest—property is not divided.

    The interest of a deceased owner passes to the survivor(s).

Hazards of assigning children as joint tenants with parent(a):

- Potential liability may result from a divorce.
- Potential liability may result from a liability claim (such as an automobile accident or business failure).
- If the child dies before the parent does, the value of the property may be included in the child's estate.

Working with lawyers (see chapter 17 for what you need to know):

1. Select a competent specialist in estate planning
2. Initial contact is made to interview the candidate to discover costs and comfort, with no obligation or payments of fees.
3. Since lawyers usually charge by the hour, every minute you take with him or her is valuable.
4. Plan to use the attorney's time efficiently by thorough preparation of information and documents that might be helpful for that person to review before giving you legal advice and drafting your documents.

Checklist of issues to prepare for the process of your will-planning journey:

- Form of securities title
- Form of business entities
- Business transfer issues
- Property transfer issues
- How is my property titled? What is the form of title?
- Beneficiary designations for life insurance, annuities, and IRA-type accounts
- Do I need a living trust or only a will?
- What costs can I avoid regarding court fees and taxes?
- What if I don't plan properly?
- Will I make a gift to my church as a part of my will-plan?
- Whom will I choose to advise me?
- How much will it cost me?
- How would God have me distribute what I have if I don't wake up tomorrow morning?

List of Fiduciaries

A fiduciary is a person or corporation you trust to carry out your wishes. You will want to prepare lists of the name, address, and phone information for the:

- <u>Guardian</u> for my children's person and assets
- <u>Executor</u> for my will
- <u>Agent</u> to name in my <u>power of attorney</u>
- <u>Agent</u> to name in my <u>health care proxy</u>
- <u>Trustee and successor trustee</u> (individual or corporate) if I establish a trust

Lists of other people:

- Children's names, addresses, phone numbers, dates of birth, social security numbers, occupations, and family statuses.
- Grandchildren's names, addresses, phone numbers, and dates of birth.
- Parents, brothers, sisters—names, addresses, and phone numbers.
- Names of any other people who will benefit from your will or might have legal standing to file a claim against your estate.

Checklist of financial information:

- Inventory of what you own—value of your holdings
- List of your assets and their values—property and financial accounts
- Bank name and account number and balance on deposit for each account
- Real estate—list each property, its assessed and market values, and how it is titled
- Life insurance—list the insurance company, face value of death benefit, cash value, primary beneficiary, secondary beneficiary, policy number, policy owner
- Pension plans—IRA, 401k, 403b, etc.—list the owner, value, primary beneficiary, and secondary beneficiary
- Value of business assets and good will
- Inventory of what you owe—to whom and amount
- Inventory of what others owe you

Checklist of Documents:

- Titles for automobiles, boats, trailers, and recreational vehicles

- Deeds for properties
- Statements for all of my bank, brokerage, 401k, and other IRA-type accounts
- Current will, trust, power of attorney, and health care proxy, if any
- Existing wills, if any
- Life insurance policies, if any
- Annuity contracts, if any

The Foundation of All Estate Plan Documents

The will is considered to be an essential foundation of an effective plan. A will is a snapshot in time, representing your knowledge, assets, and family situation at the time. Therefore, it is wise to review your will to be certain it continues to reflect your desires regarding your future stewardship and distribution of your assets.

Legal Fees for a Will

Often you get that for which you pay. As an example, Ellen White paid attorney Theodore Bell $25.85 for her 1912 will; that was more than one week's wages for an ordained Seventh-day Adventist minister at the time. **Motivators for Making a Will—What Commonly Causes Most of Us to Get on With It?**

I've observed that it takes some major event in one's life to instigate a sense of need at the level to overcome the inertia that holds one back from the task—an event such as:

- A death among your family or friends.
- A planned significant trip—overseas, long-term, etc.
- Anticipated major surgery.
- Diagnosis of a major illness.
- Any form of crisis—a fire, loss of job, and etc.
- A spiritual awakening—considering one's ultimate stewardship.
- A personal testimony of one you respect.

The Spirit of Prophecy contains specific advice that may be a motivator for some:

Many are not exercised upon the subject of making their wills while they are in apparent health. But this precaution should be taken by our brethren. They should know their financial standing, and should not allow their business to become entangled. They should arrange their property in such a manner that they may leave it at any time. (White, *Counsels on Stewardship*, p. 328)

In our personal case, the Holy Spirit was my motivator. The fact that I've been assisting people get their wills done for over forty years (thirty-six years of this specialized ministry as an employee of Seventh-day Adventist organizations, plus about five years as a professional financial planner and investment broker) should be helpful, but the line of resistance reminds us that we are no different from the proverbial shoe cobbler whose children went about barefooted. Water still runs downhill—again, following the line of least resistance.

It never would have happened for Mary Jo and me if the Holy Spirit had not prompted me morning after morning for about a week each time we have done it: 1984, 1994, 2004, 2013, and 2022. The Lord came to me during my devotional time of study and season of prayer with specific instructions to get it done.

Another motivator may be the possibility of living a longer life. Notice the statistics in the box below; they come from a study in the United Kingdom. This information was supplied by Elder Jeffrey Wilson, retired General Conference director of the Planned Giving & Trust Services Department:

The will is considered to be an essential foundation of an effective plan. A will is a snapshot in time, representing your knowledge, assets, and family situation at the time. Therefore, it is wise to review your will to be certain it continues to reflect your desires regarding your future stewardship and distribution of your assets.

> # MAKE A WILL—LIVE LONGER!
>
> Average **Age of Death** in the UK:
>
> - People **without a will: 69**
> - People **with a will: 79**
> - People with a **will & charitable bequests: 82**
>
> Source: Richard J. Radcliffe, Chairman of Smee and Ford, UK AFP Conference, San Diego, CA, March 2001

Advantage of a Will-Only Plan

Court supervision is necessary by operation of law with a will-only plan. This can be an important assurance of having your wishes carried out under the supervision of a probate judge, especially if you expect problems from one or more family members.

Disadvantage of a Will-Only Plan

Court supervision means your will and all proceedings of paying your bills and distributions to beneficiaries become part of the public record that is available to anyone who wants to know. The probate court process may take an inordinate amount of time. I've had cases where I served as executor. The court took many months to give me the letters of authority so I could deal with the decedent's assets and carry out the terms of the will. Funeral homes become very upset when waiting for payment because of such delays.

In one state where I worked for several years, the probate court would run out of money and close down for a few months, which means it had an even greater backlog of work on hand when the funding was renewed by the calendar, allowing "next year's budget" to become available to pay the employees of the court.

If the executor has to manage property during the waiting period, best practices require the property to be insured like it was before it became vacant, which can cost an unusually large amount of money. I had one case where the house had been abandoned for several years on an extra parcel of land that was part of the estate. The insurance company would only insure it for a limited amount of time, and the premium was over $2,000 for six months. In that case, the personal residence of the testator had to also be managed. We had to care for the yard work and maintain the utilities and security of the property against vandalism for a number of months. Then winter snows came, and we missed the good selling season.

A one-page will can be challenging. It may be perfectly legal but not qualify as "best practice." I've seen them a number of times. A one-page will might authorize the executor to carry out all their duties by making reference to the appropriate state law by title and number but without listing those powers. The ten-page will spells out those statutory powers of authority so the will-maker can read powers they are granting. The same difference occurs when the will-plan involves a revocable living trust. I've seen three-page, five-page, and eight-page trusts. I've replaced many of those with thirty-page, forty-page, and even up to seventy-five-page trusts, depending on the complexity and size of the estate.

For a more complete set of vocabulary, refer to Appendix 6 at mystewardship.estate.

The following chart might be a helpful illustration. In it, you may view the pathway your assets travel when your will has jurisdiction over them. Titles for all assets that are in your name travel through the probate court process. There may be other assets under your control that are not in your name at or at least exclusively. We will discuss that topic further in the next chapter.

Asset Transfers after Death

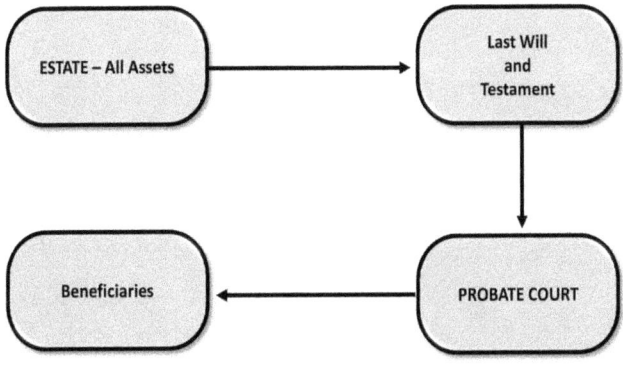

We have focused on the will in the foregoing section. The chart above illustrates the method of transferring your assets that are subject to your will. Assets that are subject to your will-plan are those where the title is in your name and are not subject to being transferred by any of the other methods given above. They are transferred after your death; your will has no power over your assets as long as you are breathing. You might wish to compare the simplicity of the above chart with a similar chart in the next chapter.

Chapter 16

What Is a Revocable Living Trust?

A revocable living trust (RLT) is a legal entity; some say it is similar to a corporation in that it has a life that may live on after your death. Best practice in a number of states suggests a preference of using an RLT as part of the will-plan; and the trust-maker would be named as one's own trustee and, as part of the trust agreement, designate a successor trustee who would take over when you cannot manage your assets anymore. That may happen if you become disabled, die, or voluntarily resign from being trustee in writing. It does not save you from legal liability that may occur due to accidents or disasters that involve assets of the trust. It does not save you on taxes, either income or estate.

What Is the Vocabulary of Trust Ownership?

You, as the "owner" of your trust, are the "trustor," "settlor," "grantor," or "trust-maker," depending on the preferred nomenclature in the customs of your state or the lawyer who drafts the trust agreement document.

Principal or Corpus—consists of the assets for which you transfer the ownership title to your revocable living trust.

Beneficiaries—income beneficiaries receive income; remainder beneficiaries receive what is left in the trust when it terminates; normally, a trust terminates after the income and assets are all distributed and the trust is empty. Such distribution usually happens after the death of the trustor or surviving trustor (if it is a joint trust)—that is commonly the case when the trust-makers are a husband and wife as joint owners.

However, if you withdraw all assets of the trust in order to make it through the health care maze (nursing home) that often happens near the end of life, you may wish to leave $10 in it. If you still want the trust's distribution provisions to be in effect when you die; this would be very important if you have a pour-over will as a companion to the trust. If you terminate the trust, there is no place to which your will's executor can send the assets—assets that were not already transferred to the trust. I've seen this happen, and it is unfortunate. The problem is people go on thinking they have a valid plan in place, but in fact, they have no plan at all, and they may not have the mental capability to restructure a new will-plan.

Revocable Living Trust (RLT) May Serve as a Will Substitute

Revocable living trusts are popular because they allow your estate to be managed and distributed without going through the probate court process; therefore, it is often referred to generically as a "will substitute." In that case, your will is drafted as a companion to your trust; it takes on the character and is referred to as a "pour-over will." This means whatever assets you have *not* transferred to the trust while living gets transferred to the trust after death. This eliminates confusion about your intentions because the ultimate distribution of your assets is only specified in one document: the trust.

> *The problem is people go on thinking they have a valid plan in place, but in fact, they have no plan at all, and they may not have the mental capability to restructure a new will-plan.*

In general, most revocable living trusts are created with the trustor as the trustee. The costs and delays of probate is such a problem in some states where almost everyone has a revocable living trust. Having served as an executor of numerous wills and trust officer to close out these trusts after death, both in various states, I much prefer the trust plan with a pour-over will, for several reasons.

The trust document provides for a successor trustee to take over when the initial trustee resigns, becomes incompetent, or dies. The named successor trustee is often a corporate entity such as a bank or an Adventist denominational organization. It is sometimes an individual person who is a member of the testator's family. It could be a personal friend or the lawyer who drafted the trust agreement for you. The successor trustee provides professional management of trust assets and income for the benefit of the trustors as long as at least one of the trust-makers is living. In either case, you will have an authorized party paying all your bills, including those for medical care and other life-care arrangements.

How Do Revocable Living Trusts Work?

When you buy property, you will want to remember to have it titled in the name of the trust. For example, in my personal case, it reads like this: the name(s) of the seller(s) "Grants to W. Robert Daum and Mary Jo Daum, Trustees of The Daum Family Trust u/d/t dated June 10, 1994, and recorded in Book ____, Page___ of [property address]." The date of our June 10, 1994 trust has been kept with each new amendment to the trust document to avoid withdrawing assets and transferring them again to the new trust.

A trust may be revoked or amended at any time as long as you are mentally competent. Our updated trust document of 2013 is an all-new trust "Amended and Restated in its Entirety"; it had been amended before. I prefer not to have "a patch added to a previous patch." That can create strange confusion after I'm gone. Therefore, we now have an "Amended and Restated in its Entirety" trust. It continues to carry the date of June 10, 1994, to assure continuity of assets that were or may have been previously assigned to the trust and not withdrawn from it.

We used the following language as advised by our lawyer for the secondary (or contingent) beneficiary of my life insurance policy and for my IRA account (the primary beneficiary for both is my wife): "The Trustees then serving under The Daum Family Trust dated June 10, 1994, as amended on [a given date], or later."

Trusts—Now and Later

Trusts that are created during your lifetime are known as "living trusts." Assets are transferred to a living trust at the time it is created and as assets are bought and sold in the name of the trust during the natural course of life.

Trusts that are created under the terms of a will, to be established after you die, are known as "testamentary (after death) trusts."

Let's now consider other assets you may own jointly—or over which you may singly have control—but that will probably not be subject to your will.

Advantages of a Living Revocable Trust

It allows for the orderly, timely payment of your bills and distributions of your assets to your designated beneficiaries after your death, as you have directed in the trust. The trust is a private document: it never becomes part of the public record at the County Court House like a will does. The cost in time and money to get this end-of-life process handled is very little, when compared to the cost of probate court processing in several states where I've worked.

Disadvantages of a Revocable Living Trust

The cost of legal fees to create the plan documents is considerably greater than a will-only plan is. You may ask, "What possible *dis*advantage is there with avoiding probate?" One disadvantage is there is no legal oversight provided for the distribution of your assets to be certain it is done according to your stated wishes as declared in the trust document.

When parents name their children as successor trustees and the children don't appreciate the parents' desire to direct some of their assets to God's work, it may not happen. Indeed, I've known of cases where the church would have been much better off if there had been a will-only plan with probate court supervision because of such family dynamics. I've not known of an Adventist organization to initiate a lawsuit to enforce their donors' wishes; I would be very surprised if it ever happens.

Notice in the chart below the distinction of "Lifetime Asset Transfers." You remove money from your "probate-able" estate by operation of law when you put it into life insurance policies or financial accounts such as an IRA, 401k, 403b, and pay on death (POD—bank accounts) or transfer on death (TOD—stock accounts). Those assets are transferred after your death by "beneficiary designation." You may designate your trust or have it go directly to beneficiaries.

The same is true of real estate assets. Joint tenants with rights of survivorship (JTWROS): You may have multiple names on a deed to real estate property and have it ultimately go to your trust; it is very common to transfer a property title to the trust when the trust is created—real estate and brokerage accounts—and change the beneficiary designations accordingly.

Asset Transfer Design Options

Lifetime Asset Transfers *

- *Insurance IRA P.O.D Accts.
- *Real Estate JTWROS or Life Estate

ESTATE – All Assets

*Living Revocable Trust

If a Pour Over Will

After Death Asset Transfers

- Last Will And Testament
- PROBATE COURT

Beneficiaries

Notice the "Lifetime Asset Transfers" and the "After Death Asset Transfers" labels. Study the arrows between the boxes.

The will probably doesn't address the transfer of all your assets. Almost all the people I've served in their plan design for asset transfers after death are surprised to learn that. It is true when you have assets in the other categories that are listed in the chart above.

Regarding the options in the above chart, notice there is a line going from the boxes that list your assets to the living revocable trust box and another line going from those same boxes directly to your beneficiaries. You may have it either one way or the other.

Estate Tax Issues

The assets in all of the situations in the chart above are not removed from your estate for tax purposes. They are subject to potential estate taxation by your state and/or federal governments. A few states still have an inheritance tax that is paid by the beneficiaries to your state government. The estate tax is paid out of the assets of the estate, not by the beneficiaries. Of course, distributions to the church are exempt from such taxes. This chart adds to the discussion:

> *The will probably doesn't address the transfer of all your assets. Almost all the people I've served in their plan design for asset transfers after death are surprised to learn that.*

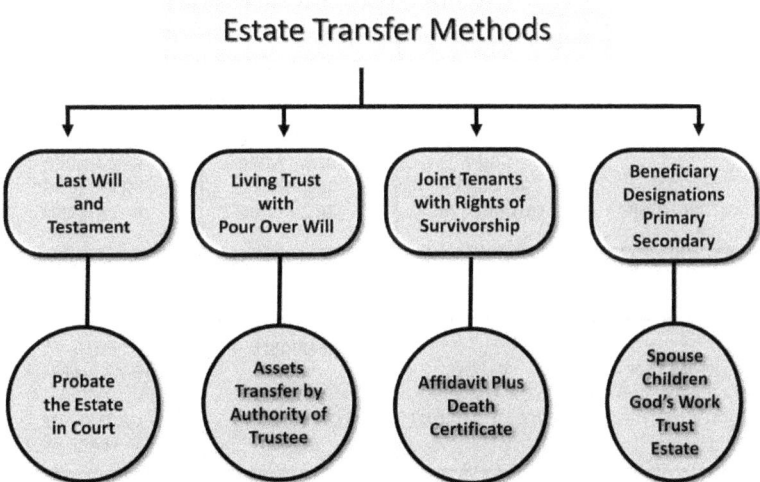

Both charts summarize the discussion of methods of transferring assets out of the estate, both before and after death.

As we said before, the will functions as a method of transferring assets after death by way of your local probate court. The trust functions by operation of law.

The joint tenants with rights of survivorship allows the title to automatically transfer to the surviving owners who are named on the title deed by operation of law. In some states, an affidavit plus a death certificate allows a new deed to be recorded, in which the deceased person is not named. In other states, it is handled in a different way.

Assets that are subject to beneficiary designations are also transferred by operation of law. The primary beneficiary is often the spouse, with the secondary beneficiary being the children. The designations may be changed to name God's work in your trust or estate. If there is no secondary beneficiary, it may default to your estate, or you may designate your estate. In either of those two options, it goes through probate court and is distributed according to your will, if the will is written in a manner to accommodate it.

Charitable (*not* revocable) trusts and annuities are life-income plans. They are listed in the next chart. The vocabulary may need some explanation. Here is a very brief set of definitions. The whole scope of their technicalities are more than space allows here.

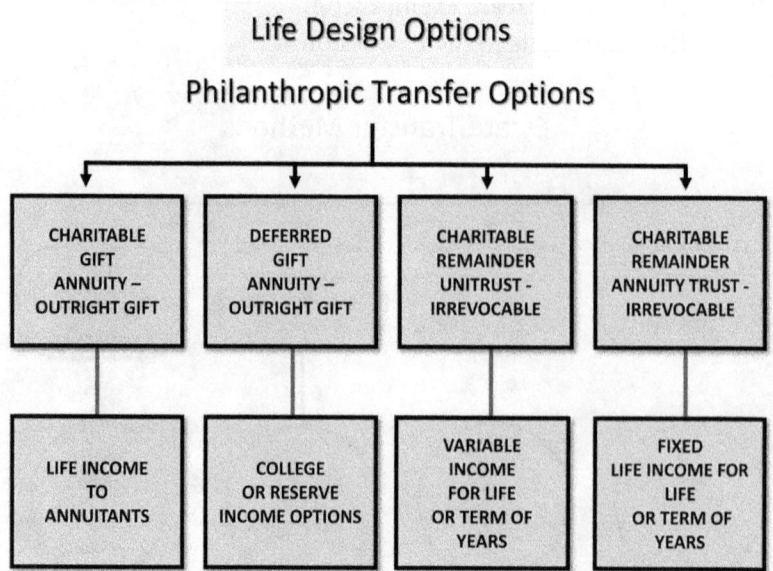

From left to right in the above chart:

Charitable Gift Annuity—involves an outright gift to a tax-exempt organization with an agreement that the organization will pay you an annuity for your lifetime. The income may be paid to one person or jointly to two people. The annuity income begins immediately, as of the date of the gift. The tax deduction amount is based on the age(s) of the donor(s) at the time of the gift.

Normally, the minimum amount of the gift to fund this plan is $10,000. And the gift becomes an owned asset of the organization to which it is given. The annuity payout becomes a permanent liability to the organization as long as the annuitant(s) live. If the gift amount is depleted by making the payouts, the organization then uses its other income to continue making the said annuity payments to the income beneficiaries.

A partial charitable income tax deduction is available to the donor, depending on the donor's life expectancy.

Deferred Gift Annuity—the same is true for this one, except the income begins at a later time. The time it is to begin may be determined at the time of the gift, or the donor may reserve the right to make that decision later.

Charitable Remainder Unitrust—involves a transfer of assets to a trust. These trusts may be funded with cash, securities, or marketable real estate. Non-cash assets are sold right away, and the money is invested to provide trust income to pay the unitrust payments to the income beneficiaries (normally, this is the donor[s]). Normally, the minimum asset value to fund these trusts is $100,000. Again, a partial charitable income tax deduction is available to the donor, depending on the donor's life expectancy.

The Unitrust Payout **rate** is negotiated between the donor and the remainder beneficiary organization at the outset and written into the trust agreement. At the end of each year, the Unitrust Payout **amount** is determined for the coming year by applying the fixed rate to the updated asset valuation. Therefore, the income from the trust to the income beneficiary will fluctuate year by year.

The Unitrust Investment plan is subject to state law. The fiduciary law of almost all states requires a diversified investment strategy for these trusts. That strategy is designed to obtain income to the trust and grow the trust corpus at the same time. Therefore, the trust asset value fluctuates. Fluctuating income from year to year is based on the market where the trust assets are invested. Fluctuations in the value of trust assets occur as a routine matter.

Unitrust agreements are tax-qualified and registered with the IRS accordingly. The trust agreement must be drafted by a lawyer who is a specialist with the appropriate expertise. These trusts are highly complex trusts to manage. They require highly skilled specialists to manage them and keep up with the trust tax returns. The trust agreement document may provide for it to terminate in a specific number of years (from one to twenty), for the lifetime of the income beneficiaries, or with the life and term certain.

Normally, the trustee is the denominational organization that will benefit from the remainder distribution after the trust terminates. Of course, the trustee may be a bank or brokerage company where they provide such services. The donor may be the trustee if an arrangement is made with an organization to handle the technical management functions of fiduciary accounting and annual tax reporting.

The donor may reserve the rights in the trust agreement to change the trustee and remainder beneficiary if that is his or her wish. Such a trust agreement cannot be revoked. It cannot be amended or changed in any way except when it is necessary to update technical provisions to comply with new laws or IRS code regulations.

<u>Charitable Remainder **Annuity** Trust</u>—is similar to the unitrust, except the payout amount is set at the outset and cannot not change up or down. Again, the trust owns the assets, which are held separately by the organization where they are managed. Therefore, it is possible for the trust assets to be depleted, which would stop the trust payouts to the income beneficiary(ies).

The chart below shows how the use of charitable trusts, charitable and commercial annuities, life insurance, IRAs, 401ks, and POD and TOD accounts fit into the overall scheme of distribution when the time comes to terminate them.

ADVANCED Estate Design Issues & Options

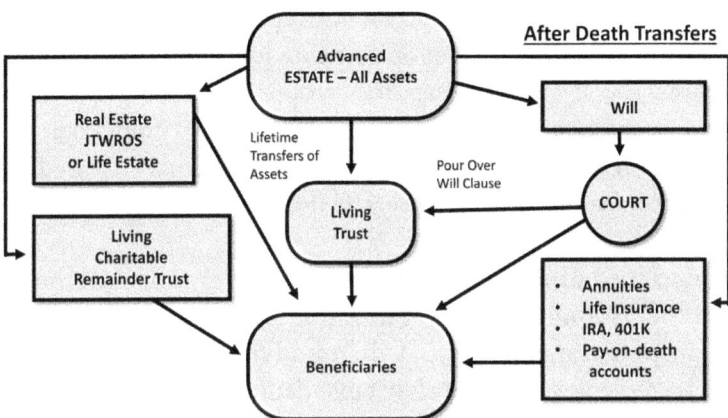

If you are interested in seeing a PowerPoint presentation of more advanced, creative planning models, such is available online in Appendix 7 at mystewardship.estate.

Life-Estate Gift of Property

The chart below reflects other transfer options. The one that is rather popular with Seventh-day Adventists is the donation of their homes or farm properties where they live and will continue to live. The arrangement is accomplished by having a new deed to the property prepared that transfers ownership to the denominational organization of the donor's choice—adding a line in the new deed to the effect of "Reserving a Life Estate Interest to the Grantor(s)."

Life Design Options - 2

Philanthropic Transfer Options - 2

LIFE ESTATE PROPERTY TRANSFER	DONOR ADVISED FUND – OUTRIGHT GIFT	CHARITABLE LEAD TRUST	PRIVATE FAMILY FOUNDATION
PROPERTY TRANSFERS BY LIFE ESTATE RESERVE	ASSETS AND INCOME USED PER AGREEMENT	INCOME TO CHURCH – ASSETS TO FAMILY	TRUST OR CORPORATE ENTITY

A life estate gift agreement is between the donor and the denominational organization that will eventually benefit from the gift. The agreement places the responsibility on the donor for repairs and maintenance of the property's improvements, such as buildings, equipment, etc. The agreement also requires the donor to keep the property taxes paid and provide appropriate insurance coverage, with evidence of payments being sent to the organization annually. A partial charitable income tax deduction is available to the donor, depending on the donor's life expectancy.

Donor advised fund agreements are increasingly popular; they may be done with the denominational organization of the donor's choice. It is an outright gift to the organization. A donor advised fund agreement allows 1) the gift to be subject to a full charitable deduction for the gift and 2) the donor to advise the organization on how the money is to be used later. The donor gives up all ownership of the gift. The use of the money is controlled by the organization and must be in harmony with its mission, as stated in the agreement.

Private Charitable Family Foundations are normally funded with tens of millions of dollars and more complex to manage than charitable remainder unitrusts are. There are super specialized legal services law firms that are available to create such Private Foundations.

In Summary

As you can see, there are a number of ways to transfer property. Each person's situation is unique. A qualified professional can evaluate your individual circumstances and goals in order to recommend the best options for you.

Chapter 17

How to Select and Work with a Lawyer

The job of a lawyer who serves as **your personal legal representative** is to draft your legal documents that will govern the distribution of your assets and pay your bills when you die, as well as other pertinent legal documents to complete your end-of-life planning.

Your attorney will study the facts of your estate's assets and liabilities and your family relationships while discussing them with you. Therefore, you will need to organize that information in a manner that allows the lawyer to review it quickly because his or her source of income is the sale of time and level of expertise. When you have selected a lawyer to be your Attorney—representing you and your interests, you should expect his/her job description to consist of the following:

1. Draw legal conclusions about the facts of your case.

2. Give you legal advice about the plan design on which you have tentatively decided. The advice will be based on the laws and customs of your state and the data of your family and holdings (estate). Most importantly, the advice will be based on your plan design wishes—what you want to do with what you have when you go to sleep for the last time. Such conversations might include your attorney describing options of methods to achieve your plan design goals.

3. Draft the legal documents for you—at a minimum, this will include a last will and testament, a general durable power of attorney*, a health care power of attorney (referred to by different titles from state to state, like health care proxy, advance directive, or power of attorney for health care), and a living will.

4. If your plan design includes a Revocable Living Trust Agreement, the transfer of real estate [such as your home property] to the trust requires a new deed to be done.

5. Your attorney will give you a draft of the new documents for your study and critique, "for discussion purposes."

6. He/she will then create the final draft of your new documents and review those with you in a meeting where you may get answers to all of your questions about the documents.

7. She/he will supervise your signing of the documents—usually in the attorney's office where other people will be present to serve you as witnesses—in a manner that meets the local requirements of laws and customs in your state. Your attorney may act as the Notary Public when needed.

*If vacant land is an asset of the estate or trust, your designated agent in a durable general power of attorney is then responsible to provide liability insurance and weed abatement on the property—as may be required by local laws—to be paid out of your bank account.

If improved property is an asset in this case, then your designated agent in a durable general power of attorney is responsible for homeowner's insurance and maintenance of the roof and heating and cooling systems, as well as other maintenance and repairs—as may be required by local laws.

My History of Working with Lawyers

I worked with a lawyer as the corporate legal counsel to the organization that employed me to serve in the planned giving ministry (where we assist supporters with their estate plan design and creation of their attorney packet) and trust management services where we carry out the fiduciary* duties that are required of the department, which has formally accepted the responsibility to manage estates and trusts for a specific donor's documents.

Praying every step of the journey, the Lord has led me to work with lawyers on behalf of donors and denominational organizations in Tennessee, Massachusetts, Connecticut, Rhode Island, New York, Maine, New Hampshire, Vermont, Michigan, Ohio, Florida, California, Hawaii, Oregon, Washington, Nevada, and Arizona. And there have been a few disappointments with the quality and character of the work product.

Note: A fiduciary is a person or corporation to whom property or power is entrusted for the benefit of another; of or pertaining to the relation between a fiduciary and his or her principal (a fiduciary capacity; a fiduciary duty); of, based on, or in the nature of trust and confidence, as in public affairs, like the case of an individual serving another individual as either their power of attorney for finance or health care decisions, an executor of a will, a guardian of a person and/or the person's estate, or as trustee of a trust (This also applies to **corporate** entities when serving as trustee or successor trustee of a trust).

Here are a few of my observations, for whatever value you might find in them: There is an amazing difference in the level of expertise in the specialized areas that have to do with the legal business of estates and trusts. For example, when I learn of a lawyer who drafts a will that consists of only one page, I say, "Don't go there."

Finding a lawyer with sufficient depth of expertise to guide estate planning for estates of a taxable size can be challenging. Occasionally, I've been disappointed in the quality of the lawyer's work product.

When I learn of a lawyer who drafts a will that consists of only one page, I say, "Don't go there."

I always try to find those who know way more than I do, whether they are to represent the denominational organization, the donor, or me personally. I know enough about drafting wills and trusts to do it myself for my family. However, I know better. Again, I go to one who knows more than I do; one who is transparent about his or her limits of knowledge; one with good skills in oral and written communication.

The legal services component of our operating program where I've served involved the approach of dual representation with disclosure and waiver of independent counsel until 2001.

In the Missouri Supreme Court Decision of 1996, a large living trust company (a high-production, highly polished trust mill with non-lawyer field sales reps) was shut down. The court's description of their practices by non-lawyer field estate planning consultants was rather a reflection of what we were doing. I saw that as a wonderful gift of God that might offer a pathway out of my distress (see Appendix 1 for a copy of the Missouri decision), online at mystewardship.estate.

In my work since 2000, I have strenuously avoided the dual-representation approach to the legal services component of our operating program at denominational organizations where I've been employed. God has led and blessed big time, with a consistent flow of new gift plans by heart-activated, mission-driven donors for the three different organizations I've represented—most thrilling to me! I can only say, "Praise the Lord for His bountiful blessings." The size of the gift is of secondary importance to me. Much more important is the heart of the donor being right with God.

The role of prayer in my journey as a certified planned giving consultant and trust officer:

➢ Prayer over the process of selecting a lawyer in each situation, either for a donor or a denominational organization's corporate counsel.

➢ Prayer over the selection of a list of candidates to be considered by the donor to serve as legal counsel—a list I may provide to donors in their local areas.

➢ Prayer over my ongoing preparation for the daily work.

➢ Prayer over individuals, couples, and families, as directed by the Holy Spirit.

➢ Prayer for the right questions to ask in each visit with donors. When visiting with people, I find the most valuable resource is to ask for and receive distinct instructions as to the questions I should ask and how to frame the questions.

➢ Prayer for God to send donors of His selection who have a heart that is tender toward Him and assets they might willingly dedicate to a finished work, as led by the Holy Spirit.

➢ Prayer over when and how to share the spiritual dimension of Adventist legacy planning with people I'm serving.

Gift Planning for the Ministry of God's Word—a Finished Work

We're here to assist you as you design your plan to magnify its potential impact on Christ's mission to seek and save lost people for His kingdom and still meet the needs of your family, with gifts to God being acts of worship in the spirit of loving trust and thanksgiving to Him.

Steps for Planning

If I were to meet with you, I would typically say something like, "I'm glad to walk you through the twenty-eight-page estate design form. It usually takes three-to-eight unhurried visits of two hours each; it may take from three-to-sixty months, depending on your readiness to make the personal and business decisions that are called for in the form. As we go through the form, we may review issues and options in planning methods as needed to equip you to make your own decisions—it must be your will!! I'll give you a list of lawyers to consider, if you wish. I'll tell you how to interview them, if you wish: Do they answer the phone? Do they return your calls? Turnaround time? Cost? Charge by the hour or by the job? I'll go with you to see the lawyer if you prefer. The goals when you select a lawyer to serve as your representative are to get high-quality service and documents at an affordable cost to you and protect the integrity of your plan documents against lawsuit."

God's Influence on Plan Design

The design of your will-plan as a Christian is a sacred matter between you and God. I may share spiritual principles and ask you to consider a gift to God's work as you pray over the principles, but you must then turn to the Lord in prayer, asking for His guidance in how to apply the principles to your own personal and family situation. This is the only way to attain peace in knowing your plan is approved in the eyes of heaven.

What does our expectation of Christ's second coming have to do with the design we make for our last will and testament? It is at the heart of it. We need to be sure our missionary witness for Christ will continue on until He comes if we don't live to see that glorious event.

Please notice the pertinent counsel below:

> *The design of your will-plan as a Christian is a sacred matter between you and God. I may share spiritual principles and ask you to consider a gift to God's work as you pray over the principles, but you must then turn to the Lord in prayer, asking for His guidance in how to apply the principles to your own personal and family situation. This is the only way to attain peace in knowing your plan is approved in the eyes of heaven.*

> The sins of some men are conspicuous (openly evident to all eyes), going before them to the judgment [seat] *and* proclaiming their sentence in advance; but the sins of others appear later [following the offender to the bar of judgment and coming into view there]. So also, good deeds are evident *and* conspicuous, and even when they are not, they cannot remain hidden [indefinitely]. (1 Timothy 5:24, 25, AMPC)

> Satan leads many to believe that God will overlook their unfaithfulness in the minor affairs of life; but the Lord shows in His dealings with Jacob that He will in no wise sanction or tolerate evil. All who endeavor to excuse or conceal their sins, and permit them to remain upon the books of heaven, unconfessed and unforgiven, will be overcome by Satan. The more exalted their profession and the more honorable the position which they hold, the more grievous is their course in the sight of God and the more sure the triumph of their great adversary. Those who delay a preparation for the day of God cannot obtain it in the time of trouble or at any subsequent time. (White, *The Great Controversy*, p. 620)

The apostle Paul offered instruction to Timothy (in his role as a young church leader and minister) for the wealthy and those who want to be wealthy among God's people ("wealthy" describes almost all of us in America and other similarly developed nations):

> **But those who crave to be rich** fall into temptation and a snare and into many foolish (useless, godless) and hurtful desires that plunge men into ruin *and* destruction and miserable perishing. For the love of money is a root of all evils; it is through this craving that some have been led astray *and* have wandered from the faith and pierced themselves through with many acute [mental] pangs … **As for the rich in this world,** charge them not to be proud *and* arrogant *and* contemptuous of others, nor to set their hopes on uncertain riches, but on God, Who richly *and* ceaselessly provides us with everything for [our] enjoyment. [Charge them] to do good, to be rich in good works, to be liberal *and* generous of heart, ready to share [with others], In this way laying up for themselves [the riches that endure forever as] a good foundation for the future, so that they may grasp that which is life indeed. (1 Timothy 6:9, 10, 17–19, AMPC, bold emphasis added)

The Spirit of Prophecy's commentary on the above passage offers very practical and revealing insights:

The Bible condemns no man for being rich, if he has acquired his riches honestly. Not money, but the love of money, is the root of all evil [see 1 Timothy 6:10]. It is God who gives men power to get wealth; and in the hands of him who acts as God's steward, using his means unselfishly, wealth is a blessing, both to its possessor and to the world. But many, absorbed in their interest in worldly treasures, become insensible to the claims of God and the needs of their fellow men. They regard their wealth as a means of glorifying themselves. They add house to house, and land to land; they fill their homes with luxuries, while all about them are human beings in misery and crime, in disease and death. Those who thus give their lives to self-serving are developing in themselves, not the attributes of God, but the attributes of the wicked one.

These men are in need of the gospel. They need to have their eyes turned from the vanity of material things to behold the preciousness of the enduring riches. They need to learn the joy of giving, the blessedness of being co-workers with God. (White, *The Ministry of Healing*, pp. 212, 213, emphasis added)

Legal Representation

If you decide to create your own will-plan, you can decide if you want to engage the services of a competent lawyer who is truly independent of the church to serve as your representative. Your selection process would normally include calling a few of them to interview them by phone. Obviously, the best attorney is the one who is the *most* qualified specialist in estate inheritance planning, the *least* costly, and the *quickest and most responsive* in turnaround time.

Issues to consider when pondering the concept of finding the lawyer who is best suited for you and your personal and family situation:

1. Have you talked it over with the Lord in a surrendered spirit of "Thy will be done"?
2. Have you made a list of questions to ask in your interviews of candidates?
3. Have you made a list of services you will need from the lawyer?
4. Some trial lawyers are focused on churches and other non-profits for their growth industry. Apparently, they are always on the lookout for an opportunity to represent a plaintiff who has a reason to sue an organization or family with deep pockets.

5. Your choice of a lawyer to represent you in getting your will-plan done is a most important matter for prayer.

Step 1 of How to Find a List of Lawyers in Each Area of Need

If you have a lawyer who has served as a representative for you, is that lawyer a specialist in estates and trusts? Are you comfortable working with him or her? If your answer is "No" to either one of these two questions, then you might network by calling friends who have had such planning done in your area.

You might call your local conference office, favorite church ministry, or educational institution and ask the Planned Giving & Trust Services Department for a list of names of independent lawyers in your area—lawyers who specialize in trusts and estates—who don't ever get paid by the conference or any other Adventist organization for legal services. It is important for you to know the denominational organization must not endorse the work or guarantee the results of an attorney on its list. It is necessary for you to exercise your own judgment in making a selection of an attorney who will best work with you and the needs of your family. It became part of my job to make such a search and present a list to the donors of specialized lawyers in their area.

If no list develops from these three steps, then do online searches, as follows:

1. Go to Google or another online search engine and type in "Estate planning lawyer in [your town and state]"
2. The American College of Trust & Estate Counsel (www.actec.org) can also be a very good source.
3. The local estate planning council, which may be found in most metropolitan areas, may be helpful.

Step 2 of How to Find a List of Lawyers in Your Area

1. Study several internet sites; look at the biographical information of the lawyers there.
2. Remember, you are looking for a specialist in estates and trusts. That way, you don't have to pay for that lawyer to learn on your time.
3. Select a few candidates to interview. This process may take an hour or more, so plan your time accordingly.

4. Call to interview the candidates. Ask the same questions of each one and record the answers so you may compare.
5. Call references provided to you by the candidates when you interviewed them.

What about legal fees? None of the numerous lawyers I've interviewed across the USA are willing to allow the church to pay them for their services to our donors. You, as our donor, become their client, and they look to you for their fee. In some cases, one of your favorite denominational organizations might reimburse you for a portion of the fees, depending on your plan. They should never tell you what your plan has to look like to get them to help with the costs because that would automatically be undue influence.

With all that said, how do I select a lawyer to represent me if I pursue the matter as suggested above? My suggestions are that you select lawyers and interview them as potential candidates to be your representative. It doesn't cost to look online for lawyers who are estate planning specialists and read about the area of their specialty. It doesn't cost to call them for an interview. When you have a small list of candidates you believe are qualified to do your work, then you should make an appointment to meet with them at their office. It doesn't cost to have such meetings—then you make a subjective decision and select the one with whom you are most comfortable working.

The professional you select to represent you in the matter of making your will-plan and related legal documents will become your attorney, who will represent you and your interests, not those of other people or organizations.

1. Your attorney must have "legal standing" in the jurisdiction (state) where you are considered to be a resident in order to represent you and defend your will-plan in a court of law, if that is ever needed.
2. It is necessary, therefore, for your attorney to have the proper authority to practice law in your state by being a member of the state bar.
3. An "Independent lawyer" is defined in the 1999 letter from Attorney Fred Marcus to me, which is summarized in Chapter 10 of this book.

In order to maximize the legal security and minimize the potential legal weakness, it may become necessary for your attorney to defend your plan and documents in a court of law. That would only be needed if a legal action has been filed against your estate distribution plan, whether it involves a will or a trust. The following advice is very important:

4. When you interview a lawyer, you might consider these topics and suggested questions:

   a. Please describe the type and scope of your legal services practice.
   b. What is the number of years you have been in the practice of law?
   c. For what types and sizes of estates you have planned and drafted documents?
   d. What types and sizes of estates and trusts you have settled after death?
   e. Are you comfortable with charitable bequests being included in a plan?
   f. What is your educational background?
   g. Please rate your people skills
   h. Please rate your technical skills with legal advice and drafting estate and trust documents
   i. What types of plan documents have you done most commonly?
   j. For example, have you done revocable living trusts, charitable remainder unitrusts, charitable remainder annuity trusts, irrevocable life insurance trusts, general durable power of attorney, health care advance directive, or proxy?
   k. Funding issues for revocable living trusts—when and how is that done?
   l. Do you do a joint or separate revocable living trust for a husband and wife?
   m. What is your fee plan? Blue collar or professional executive? Hourly or by the job?
   n. Do you do asset protection planning for Medicaid?
   o. How is your response to phone calls—how long will it take you to call me back?
   p. What is your turnaround time for plan documents?

q. Do you send out a draft of the documents to us marked "Draft for discussion purposes"?

r. What is a typical fee for a comprehensive set of plan docs—will, trust, power of attorney, power of attorney for health care, or living will?

s. Are you sympathetic to charitable gifts to your client's church?

t. Will you provide references?

5. Here are recommended qualifications for lawyers on your list of candidates:

    a. Competent in required areas of law

    b. Independent of the church—does not serve as corporate legal counsel to any Seventh-day Adventist entity in any area of the law.

6. Definition of competent legal counsel for estate planning work:

    a. Basic and advanced knowledge of wills and trusts

    b. Good people skills

    c. Good technical planning knowledge

    d. Significant experience in estate planning—various sizes and types of estates

7. Attorney Lynda Moerschbaecher Sands, of San Diego, California, wrote the following description of competent legal counsel for me when she served as corporate legal counsel for the Pacific Union Conference of Seventh-day Adventists: "'Competent legal counsel' and desirable legal counsel may be recognized by one or more of the following characteristics:

    a. Is a certified specialist in law, taxes, and/or estate planning (i.e., endorsed or licensed by the local State Bar or other state or federal agency).

    b. Holds advanced legal or tax degrees (e.g., LLM or MS in Taxation or Estate Planning; JD)

    c. Has significant experience in estate planning

    d. Has handled many types/sizes of estates

    e. Is sympathetic to philanthropy

f. Listens well

g. Considers people first over tax rules or numbers

h. Provides references from satisfied clients

i. Receives accolades from peers

j. Possesses, at minimum, a basic knowledge of charitable instruments, especially charitable remainder trusts and charitable gift annuities

k. Maintains membership with the Estate Planning Council, Probate and Trust sections, or the National Committee on Planned Giving."

> *Saturate the whole process in prayer at each step of the pathway to getting it done because the devil never sleeps and will do all he can to prevent you from providing a benefit for God's work in your estate plan documents.*

Further comments by attorney Lynda Moerschbaecher: "It is unlikely that all of the preceding indicators will be found in one person being referenced. However, the more factors that are present, the greater the likelihood that the individual in question can provide 'competent legal counsel.'"

Again, the most important thing is to know and do the Lord's will for your plan while doing what you can to minimize the potential of a legal action against it after your death. Saturate the whole process in prayer at each step of the pathway to getting it done because the devil never sleeps and will do all he can to prevent you from providing a benefit for God's work in your estate plan documents.

Keep in mind the following advice from Jesus: "But seek you first the kingdom of God, and His righteousness; and all these things shall be added to you. Take therefore no thought for the morrow: for the morrow shall take thought for the things of itself. Sufficient to the day is the evil thereof." (Matt. 6:33–34, AKJV).

The advantages of this approach of using lawyers for donor counsel who are truly independent of the Seventh-day Adventist Church and all its entities are:

1. We are not functioning as an extension of the organization's corporate legal counsel in the role of a "paralegal." When we did that, we were *not* allowed to suggest a gift to our organization because it would be a serious conflict of interest on our part, and undue influence would be assumed. Now, we are *free* to function in the role of planned giving minister rather than as an extension of a lawyer—the organization's corporate legal counsel. When the organization's lawyer simultaneously serves as its legal representative and the legal representative for our donor, there is a serious weakness in the legal security of the donor's will-plan documents.

2. The sense of freedom is most exhilarating. We are free to present comprehensive estate design proposals to our prospective donors that include gift plan options that would benefit our employing organization.

3. Freedom to be a spiritual minister—we are free to teach the spiritual estate stewardship **principles** of Adventist legacy planning as part of our consulting process, without being guilty of a conflict of interest or undue influence.

4. The donors may freely establish a plan that truly represents their wills because our proposal is evaluated for the donor by a truly **independent** lawyer without the unwarranted psychological pressure on the lawyer or the donor of being obligated to establish a gift plan to benefit the organization we represent.

5. The donors have the advantage of greater assurance of the legal security of their will-plans.

6. The donors are most satisfied with our valuable service of educating them on the pertinent issues and options—spiritual issues, business issues, legal and other technical issues, asset issues, relational issues—and assisting them in organizing their estate design materials with their personal, family, financial, and goals information—all in one place for their lawyer and for their future reference.

7. The donors often become enthusiastic about our services because of the truly objective nature of the process and the resulting high-quality plan, designed to "stand the test of law," not because they paid nothing for an estate plan (they do pay the legal fees, part of which might be reimbursed to them).

Please read Appendix 1—Missouri Supreme Court Action on Unauthorized Practice of Law. You may find it on this book's website at mystewardship.estate. Listed as Appendix 1.

Postscript: In my thirty-six years of doing this work, I've always let donors know I'm available to do their bidding as long as their requests are legal, ethical, and not in violation of our denominational policies and mission. Each and every case is different because people are different, and that fact creates a strong interest in this work for me. In every case, the goal has been to create an attorney packet and follow the best practice of getting the documents done for the donor. Therefore, the two issues for this postscript are:

1. The confidential data form. For an example, you might wish to see Appendix 8 for my 28-page Estate Design Data Organizer at this book's website, mystewardship.estate.

2. The donor's relation with a lawyer who will serve as his or her attorney.

Normally, my job is to assist God's people when they wish to create a new or updated will-plan with completed legal documents and any pertinent asset transfers. I've only had **one case** where I talked with a man in the Boston area. He worked for a Fortune 500 company. I sent him the twenty-eight-page EDIO (Estate Design Information Organizer) via email. We talked a few times by phone. My understanding was that he filled it out and took it to a lawyer to get wills made. Only one out of hundreds!

I've left the form with some people in a "first visit" who never came back to me. Whenever I have an inquiry, I visit them in their homes, at their convenience and according to their wishes. My first visit is for the purpose of getting acquainted. I explain the process and how the program works. I leave them with my twenty-eight-page confidential data form and tell them they are welcome to fill it out and get back to me; *or* I say, "If you prefer, we can set another appointment when I can go through the form with you. I would explain the planning issues and options for your prayerful consideration so that you have enough knowledge to make the necessary decisions and have a meaningful conversation with your lawyer when you take the attorney packet to him or her."

In almost all cases, the people had me assist them in filling out the form. I've always told them, "We will need to visit for a couple of hours each time to get it done. And we might get it done in three months or three years, depending on your readiness to make the decisions and discover the related documents to go with the form to make up the attorney packet."

One case took four years. A case on which I worked most recently was in process for six-plus years. It is the largest, most complex estate I've ever engaged—a thrillingly delightful one in every way! There were a couple of cases in which we could not complete the form, and we quit trying after several visits because they were not able to make the required decisions. And those never resumed to completion. It became too late several years ago. Those are heartbreakers for me.

I listen most of the time in the first visit—listening to their stories about their personal and family situations—by asking questions along the lines of, "What is your occupation?" "Tell me about your family." "Do you have any financial stresses?" "How is your walk with Jesus?" "What is your connection to the church?" "Are you engaged with your church by your influence and financial support?"

When we have the attorney packet ready, then I send them a letter about their selection of an independent, qualified lawyer with a list of at least three lawyers for their prayerful consideration. I tell them these are lawyers I've found in my online search and that I've interviewed them personally by phone. I tell them, "Any of the lawyers on the list can do the job for you. You decide which one to work with by calling each one for a meet-and-greet appointment to get acquainted. Then you make a subjective decision in selecting one of them. Of course, if you already have a lawyer, you should consider starting with that one. And if that lawyer is not a specialist in estates and trusts, then he or she can refer you to one."

In all cases, they asked me to make the lawyer appointments for them *and* go with them to each lawyer visit, which I did. After introducing them, I'd listen to their conversation until they began to talk about what they want to do with their accumulated assets. Then I would excuse myself and wait in the office lobby because I wanted the donor to be able to speak freely to the lawyer without the possible influence of my presence for that part of the visit. The lawyers appreciated that.

Chapter 18

Conclusion
Final Thoughts

Whatever your background prior to reading this book, I hope you now understand how closely linked estate planning is to committed Christian living.

If you have never prepared even a basic will, I trust you are motivated to do so now, and have found tools to help you proceed both prayerfully and confidently. Perhaps you do have an estate plan in place, but realize that you need to prayerfully consider whether it is merely *your* plan, or whether it is God's plan. Or you may have a plan that includes giving back to the Giver of all things, but you found here some methods that will enhance your stewardship, enabling you to increase your giving while benefiting your own financial future.

In short, I hope you are several steps closer to answering the question, *Whatcha gonna do with whatcha got?*

If you are convicted to make your estate plans prayerfully, consider your family's needs carefully, choose your advisors and attorneys wisely, and make the mission of God primary, my goals in writing this book have been achieved abundantly.

May God bless you as you continue to place all you are, and all you have, on the altar of God.

Appendices

Appendices can be found online at mystewardship.estate (use the QR code here, or go to 1ref.us/rdwgd2).

- Appendix 1—Missouri Supreme Court Decision on Unauthorized Practice of Law
- Appendix 2—The Making of Ellen G. White's Will of 1912—Issues and Considerations
- Appendix 3—Ellen G. White's Final Will of 1912
- Appendix 4—Valuable Gems of Counsel from the Pen of Ellen G. White on Wills
- Appendix 5—Life Insurance and Seventh-day Adventists
- Appendix 6—Vocabulary
- Appendix 7—Advanced and Creative Plan Models with Crescendo's PowerPoint Slides
- Appendix 8—Estate Design Information Organizer (EDIO)

TEACH Services, Inc.
P U B L I S H I N G

We invite you to view the complete
selection of titles we publish at:
www.TEACHServices.com

We encourage you to write us
with your thoughts about this,
or any other book we publish at:
info@TEACHServices.com

TEACH Services' titles may be purchased in
bulk quantities for educational, fund-raising,
business, or promotional use.
bulksales@TEACHServices.com

Finally, if you are interested in seeing
your own book in print, please contact us at:
publishing@TEACHServices.com

We are happy to review your manuscript at no charge.

www.ingramcontent.com/pod-product-compliance
Lightning Source LLC
Chambersburg PA
CBHW071146160426
43196CB00011B/2020